"*Off Headset* is a powerful collection of stories—a gift to fellow stage managers and the job we all love. The volume showcases a welcome range of voices to reflect on professional highlights and career arcs, to pose important questions about the industry in today's world, and to consider our role as people and artists at the same time. It will be on my 'highly recommended' list as soon as it hits the shelves."

Laurie Kincman, *University of Wisconsin-La Crosse,*
author of The Stage Manager's Toolkit

Off Headset

Off Headset is a collection of chapters containing essays by a richly diverse group of stage management professionals and educators covering the challenges stage managers face on the job, in their lives, and in their careers.

The book starts with the intersectional history of stage managers and the actors' union. In "Part 1: Work," the contributors share a wide range of experiences, from regional theatre and Broadway to operas and cruises—and even running with the circus. The essays in "Part 2: Life" explore the relevance of stage managers claiming their identity, their resilience, and practicing self-care. Finally, in "Part 3: Career," readers receive aspirational and business advice for life in the real world: leadership, networking, unemployment, managing demanding calendars, and career planning. The book ends with a moment of pause during tech—a direct response to the absence we have been enduring throughout the COVID-19 pandemic and a tribute to a world we used to take for granted.

Intertwining practical advice with personal anecdotes, *Off Headset: Essays on Stage Management Work, Life, and Career* is the perfect accompaniment to students studying stage management in a university setting and professionals working in the field.

Rafael Jaen (sounds HA-EN), Associate Professor of Theatre and Performing Arts Chair, UMass Boston. Jaen is an award-winning costume designer, educator, and author. He is a USITT Fellow, the USITT VP for Communications (2019–2022), and a past National KCACTF DTM Chair. He is the author of *SHOWCASE* (2011) and *Digital Costume Design and Collaboration* (2017) by Focal Press/Routledge, and the Series Editor for the USITT/Focal Press *Backstage* series.

Christopher Sadler, Associate Professor, University of Oklahoma's (OU) Helmerich School of Drama. Sadler heads the stage management emphasis and teaches multiple courses in stage and theatre management and dramatic literature at OU. He has degrees from Ithaca College and UC San Diego and is a proud member of Actors' Equity Association. Sadler has a successful freelancing career having been on stage management teams for over 100 productions at theatres nationwide.

BACKSTAGE

Series Editor: Rafael Jaen

Backstage is the result of a publishing partnership between USITT and Routledge. The series consists of books that focus on the various aspects of the technical theatre industry. It celebrates the professionals that make theatre happen in the shops, backstage, and every other corner of this field.

Theatre Artisans and Their Craft
The Allied Arts Fields
Edited by Rafael Jaen, Holly Poe Durbin, and Christin Essin

Off Headset
Essays on Stage Management Work, Life, and Career
Edited by Rafael Jaen and Christopher Sadler

For more information about this series, please visit: www.routledge.com/ Backstage/book-series/USITT

Off Headset

Essays on Stage Management Work, Life, and Career

Edited by

Rafael Jaen and Christopher Sadler

ChrisSadler

*Hope you enjoy —
your friendship and
support all those
years has meant
all the world
xxoo*

Routledge
Taylor & Francis Group

NEW YORK AND LONDON

Cover image: Photo courtesy of Christopher Sadler, Cover design by Rafael Jaen.

First published 2022
by Routledge
605 Third Avenue, New York, NY 10158

and by Routledge
2 Park Square, Milton Park, Abingdon, Oxon, OX14 4RN

Routledge is an imprint of the Taylor & Francis Group, an informa business

© 2022 Taylor & Francis

Library of Congress Cataloging-in-Publication Data
Names: Jaen, Rafael, editor. | Sadler, Christopher, editor.
Title: Off headset : essays on stage management work, life, and career / edited by Rafael Jaen and Christopher Sadler.
Description: New York : Routledge, 2022. | Series: Backstage | Includes index.
Identifiers: LCCN 2021011827 (print) | LCCN 2021011828 (ebook) |
    ISBN 9780367337513 (hardback) | ISBN 9780367337520 (paperback) |
    ISBN 9780429321672 (ebook)
Subjects: LCSH: Stage management—Vocational guidance.
Classification: LCC PN2085 .O34 2022 (print) | LCC PN2085 (ebook) |
    DDC 792.02/32—dc23
LC record available at https://lccn.loc.gov/2021011827
LC ebook record available at https://lccn.loc.gov/2021011828

ISBN: 978-0-367-33751-3 (hbk)
ISBN: 978-0-367-33752-0 (pbk)
ISBN: 978-0-429-32167-2 (ebk)

DOI: 10.4324/9780429321672

Typeset in Bembo
by Apex CoVantage, LLC

We dedicate this book to all the stage managers working tirelessly as part of creative and artistic teams to fulfill collaborative visions and dreams.

Contents

Preface

Off *Headset* is the second installment of the *Backstage Series*, a publishing partnership between USITT and Routledge. The series consists of books that focus on the theatre industry's technical and management aspects, celebrating the professionals that make theatre happen in the shops, backstage, and every other corner of the live performance and production field. The idea's gestalt took shape at the Kennedy Center American College Theatre Festival (KCACTF) in 2013, after chats with students and practicing professionals. Once the research process began, a group of like-minded individuals from the United States Institute for Theatre Technology (USITT) Publications Committee joined in support. We pitched it to Routledge, and the partnership with USITT was born.

Off Headset started with a process similar to the first book of the series: *Theatre Artisans and Their Craft: The Allied Arts Fields.* During a conference, serendipity brought Rafael to Chris, who carefully described an idea he had for a book of stage management essays. We brainstormed together, and discovered this idea could join the *Backstage Series.* Chris completed a robust proposal, anchored by his observation that most stage management texts available were procedurals—how to stage manage. We wanted to create a collection of essays that explored facets of stage management not normally found elsewhere and to use stage managers' personal stories to that end—a book for students and professionals, one that could be read in the classroom or on the subway. Routledge accepted it, and soon after, we were collecting essays written by remarkable artists.

Throughout the process, we juggled demanding schedules with competing engagements, staying inspired by the writers' topics, and learning about their experiences. Every chapter elevates live performance production to new dimensions, introducing practical ideas about management skills, resilience, and human wellbeing. Additionally, while we started to compile stories before the COVID-19 outbreak, we finished in the midst of the pandemic—and discovered the essays held up even after the disease had upended our lives and altered our professions. Some authors asked to revise their work in light of the events of 2020; these revisions resulted in even stronger pieces.

This collection presents several ways to create impactful entertainment from "behind the scenes" as a stage manager. The authors come from all over; they've made lives around the country while juggling family, community, and job. We start with the intersectionality history of stage managers and the actors' union and end with a moment of pause during tech—a direct response to the absence we've been made to endure, a paean to a world we took for granted pre-pandemic. We learn from their real "true and tried" sharing in "Work": regional theatre, Broadway, touring, operas, at sea, and even running with the circus! We explore the relevance of claiming our identity, parenthood, and promoting self-care with grace and balance in "Life." In "Career," we get business advice for life in the real world: leadership, networking, unemployment, managing demanding calendars, doing preemptive planning.

We hope that you will find this collective offering as thoughtful and inspiring as we do, enjoying each idea, experience, and retrospective, taking from it all the lessons that continue to hold true.

Rafael Jaen and Christopher Sadler, Editors

Acknowledgments

The Editors thank the USITT Publications Committee, USITT Executive Director David Grindle, and Routledge's Publisher Stacey Walker and the technical editors for their ongoing support.

We would also like to thank all the book contributors for their expertise and heart and the many stage managers we've worked with, whose stories inspire and guide us.

Introduction

Intersectional History
Stage Managers in the Actors' Union
Jennifer Leigh Sears Scheier

We hereby constitute ourselves a voluntary Association to advance, promote, foster, and benefit **all those connected with the art of the theatre** and particularly the profession of acting and the conditions of persons engaged therein…[1]

When Boston chorus girl Kathleen Carroll walked out of Colonel Savage's *See Saw* at the Tremont Theatre, the stage manager used underhanded means to subvert the walkout. Despite this, she led the Boston faction to victory during the 1919 strike. The stage manager, a man named Gardner, acted as the Equity Deputy for the production, and was rumored to be the producer's spy. Gardner informed Colonel Savage of any *See Saw* company members who intended to strike. These members of Actors' Equity Association (AEA or Equity), immediately found themselves being lectured at about the sacredness of contracts by a local judge who also happened to be a member of the producer's legal staff.

In spite of these threats, Carroll arrived at the Tremont the morning of the planned strike, reassuring AEA of her intention to walkout. In the meantime, Gardner lied to Fred Dempsey[2] that the full company had reported for duty, to which a nearby chorus girl responded that Carroll had not yet arrived. Gardner sent for Colonel Savage for assistance in foiling the strike and upon arrival, Savage informed Dempsey

DOI: 10.4324/9780429321672-1

that another Equity member had arrived to play Carroll's part. Dempsey announced, "That other Equity member we'd call a scab, and we do not work with scabs."

In that moment, Carroll arrived at the stage door, announced her intention to strike, and upon seeing the producer, turned and hightailed it out of the theatre. The rest of the cast and a disappointed audience headed home, and one by one the other Boston theatrical companies walked out, shutting down Boston theatre until the 1919 contract between Actors' Equity Association and the Producing Managers' Association (PMA) was signed.

As a stage management historian and an AEA stage manager, this story is both incredibly disappointing and intriguing to me. Gardner's title as "Equity Deputy" insinuates his membership to Actors' Equity Association and complicates his role as stage manager, spy, and union member. His adversarial role as stage manager is most disappointing, wherein, he attempted to prevent a historic strike which ultimately led to a growth in membership, power, and voice for AEA. It begs the question, what did he gain from siding with the producer? And why would he join a union that he wanted to undermine?

This story, as told by Alfred Harding, is not the first of its kind. In fact, *The Revolt of the Actors* by Alfred Harding[3] and *Weavers of Dreams, Unite!* by Sean P. Holmes[4] have a smattering of stories wherein the stage manager often played the antagonist in the early years of the union. This collection of stories seems at odds with the proclamation that stage managers have always been members of Actors' Equity Association. Why would AEA want stage managers to be members of their union if the stage managers were undermining their work? Even today, stage managers head to online discussion boards to pose the question, "Do you agree with Equity representing stage managers?"[5] Participants argue that by being members of the actors' union, stage managers are often put in a difficult position when they are held responsible for ensuring that contractual agreements are being followed. In addition, the contractual needs of the stage manager are different from the contractual needs of the actor, so should each entity have its own contract to cover their distinct role in contemporary theatre? To better comprehend stage managers' present-day relationship with AEA, we first need to recognize and understand stage managers' role in the founding of Actors' Equity.

There are several monographs on the history of Actors' Equity Association, including the two already mentioned, as well as: *Actors Organize* by Kerry Segrave[6]; *The Actor's Right to Act* by Joseph MacLeod[7]; and *The Business of the Theatre* by Alfred L. Bernheim.[8] However, many of these texts were commissioned by, or in partnership with, AEA, possibly biasing the information contained within. In addition, there are a handful of theses, dissertations, and scholarly journals that explore specific aspects of the formation or cultural importance of AEA, none of which grappled with the intersection of stage managers and the union.

SETTING THE STAGE

Stage managers have long been an integral part of the theatrical production. The term "stage manager" dates back to Shakespeare's time; however, their role in American theatre drastically changed in the early 1900s. Prior to the inception of the director in the late nineteenth century, the stage manager was often described as a lead actor choosing the piece(s) for production, reading the play to the company, and correcting the actors' reading or movement in rehearsals. After several rehearsals and a dress rehearsal, the stage manager's duties were essentially terminated,[9] and instead they focused on their leading role in the production. The prompter then performed many of the duties that we associate with the contemporary stage manager. If any of the actors forgot their lines, it was the prompter's duty to softly remind them, without being heard by the audience. The prompter used bells and whistles to "call the cues," which mainly involved raising and lowering the curtain, scene transitions, and special effects. The prompter was responsible for notating everything in the promptbook. This person often filled in for smaller bit parts, when all other cast members were engaged either onstage or preparing offstage for their next entrance.

As the "director" emerged between 1870–1900, the stage manager transitioned to technical oversight. By 1900, the role of the director had become a mainstream position, and left the stage manager to become the head of the production staff and physically undertake the organization and construction of the technical elements.[10] Between 1900–1940, the stage manager gradually took over the prompter's duties, while the prompter transitioned to a new title: the assistant stage manager.

The historical stage manager continued to perform as one of the actors in the theatre company until the mid-twentieth century. However, as the technical complexity of the production grew, many stage managers began taking smaller and smaller roles. When not otherwise contracted as a stage manager, they were often engaged as an actor, thus providing the motivation for joining Actors' Equity Association.

While the field of stage management transitioned to its contemporary version, the theatre structure adapted from a stock driven system[11] to the combination system.[12] Transformative practices marked the early twentieth century for American theatre as the field caught up with the developments from the Second Industrial Revolution. Elevator stages, electric lights, and other new technology brought spectacle and complexity to the stage. The effects of these changes coupled with unfair working conditions bred instability and discontent among theatrical workers.[13] There were stories of actors stranded in cities hundreds or thousands of miles from their home, who were required to pay their own way with no guarantee of payment or stable income. Rehearsals were unpaid, yet required, and the rehearsal period was growing longer and longer. If an actor was hired to play a role and fired before opening, he or she received no payment for any work performed. With few labor laws and very little protection, who could these actors turn to for support?

Theatrical workers united with their colleagues, forming theatrical unions in the late nineteenth century. These institutions fought for consistent pay and better working conditions. When the Theatrical Protective Union of New York (for stagehands) went on strike, New York actors joined them in the streets. This act of solidarity initiated a discussion with producers, wherein the stagehands attained most of their requests. This demonstrated the importance of solidarity when negotiating and fighting for contractual demands. In 1893, the local stagehand unions around the country united to form the National Alliance of Theatrical Stage Employees. By 1896, the United Scenic Artists, American Federation of Musicians, and the Actors' Society (the predecessor for Actors' Equity Association) were founded.

While the Actors' Society formed with hopes of staging a revolt, they ultimately failed because the organization had little power. On December 23, 1912, the remaining members dissolved the society and reformed as Actors' Equity Association. They held their first organizational meeting on May 26, 1913.[14] Equity, eager to join the American Federation of Labor (AFL), had to wait until the White Rats Union (representing male vaudeville performers) dissolved. The White Rats Union, having chartered with the AFL first, had right of first refusal and mandated that if AEA members wanted the protection of the AFL, that they should terminate their relationship with AEA and be absorbed into its own organization. The White Rats disbanded in 1916 after a failed strike. The AFL, having learned its lesson from the White Rats ordeal, agreed in 1919 to charter AEA under the Associated Actors and Artistes of America (AAAA or 4As) which would allow other performing unions to join the AFL, under the AAAA's umbrella.

In 1917, the United Managers' Protective Association (UMPA) signed an initial contract with AEA, but largely ignored its contractual obligations. With the support of the American Federation of Labor, Actors' Equity Association organized the 1919 strike in New York City against the Producing Managers' Association (PMA)[15] theatres after fruitless negotiations and an investigation that disclosed that only 20% of its producing members used the agreed upon contract.[16] Equity sent dispatches to other major theatre cities, and with help from local performers, like Kathleen Carroll in Boston, the strike spread within weeks. In the wake of this strike, the Chorus Equity Union was founded, AEA began fundraising and created the Actors Benefit Fund to assist actors who were out of work, and the PMA struck back at AEA in the form of a $6 million lawsuit.[17] The strike lasted 30 days (and the membership for Actors' Equity doubled) before the PMA formally recognized the union and agreed to negotiations.

THE STAGE MANAGER AND ACTORS' EQUITY

As previously noted, stage managers often joined Actors' Equity Association as a result of their acting contracts. Given the proclivity of stage managers acting, it is of no surprise that stage managers were members of the actors' union. However, it leads to a number of other questions and speculations including: were stage managers covered by this agreement even when not on an acting contract?

To answer this question, I turned to the AEA constitution, by-laws, agreements, and contracts to examine what the founders of AEA wrote about membership and to determine when the term "stage manager" was added into the language of these documents. The earliest records are fairly ambiguous, including Article II on Membership, which demonstrated who was allowed to join the union, as printed in Equity's 1913 Constitution:

ARTICLE II: MEMBERS

Sec. 1. The membership shall comprise two classes, to wit: regular members and lay members.

Sec. 2. Persons who have been actors for at least three years are eligible to election as regular members.

*Sec. 3. **Persons in sympathy with the objects of the association**, and having no business associations antagonistic thereto, are eligible to lay membership.*[18]

While most of the books on AEA's history argue that stage managers joined the unions as actors, Article II, Section 3 offers an alternative way for stage managers to join the union. This clause allowed anyone to join the union, provided they were sympathetic to the Equity cause and had no conflict of interest. AEA needed as many allies as they could find, opening their doors to any theatrical professionals who buoyed their membership and supported their goals. Strength was in numbers, and the AEA needed numbers.

In the PMA–AEA agreement from 1919, the contract refers to the "actor" rather than using the broader term "member," which allows some skeptics to take pause. Afterall, the term stage manager does not appear in the contract and provides reasonable doubt to the stage manager's use of such a contract.

Agreement made this _____ day of _____ 19___, between _____ _____(hereinafter called "manager"), and _____ (hereinafter called "actor").

The actor and the manager agree that this contract is entered into independently of any other contract between any Equity Member and any producer and of any other contract or contracts, affiliation, or understanding of any character whatever other than the agreement dated September 6, 1919, between Producing Managers' Association and Actors' Equity Association.

The manager engages the actor to render services in ★ _____ upon the terms herein set forth…[19]

The ★ is a footnote that appears on the bottom of the contract. It reads: "Here state the name of the part and of the play in which the actor is to appear; also, if he is to be required to understudy."[20] This request is not consistent with the idea that some of the members using this contract would be engaged for a role outside of acting, such as stage managing. To these naysayers, I argue that today, 100 years later, this clarification is not always made. On the Standard Resident Theatre Contract for Dramatic Productions, the previous statement now looks like this:

> Agreement made this _____ day of_____, _____, between
> the undersigned Theatre and   (hereinafter "Actor").
>
> 1. Duties: The Theatre engages the Actor to render services as _____
>   (specify Actor, Stage Manager or ASM.)
>   The Actor shall play:
>   Part: _____ Production: _____[21]

Although there is now a line which requests the specificity of what services will be performed, the member is still referred to as an "Actor" within the contents of the contract and the role executed still refers to an actor's "part." Considering that this ambiguity is still used today,[22] it bolsters the allegation that stage managers could have used the 1919 contract, despite its references to the "Actor."

While stage managers were allowed to join Actors' Equity Association and could have signed Equity contracts, these original sources do not answer the original question—were stage managers covered by this agreement even when not on an acting contract? The answer is debatable. I have no doubt that AEA believed any person who signed on an Equity contract was deserving of the union's protection. However, a producer named Romberg certainly disagreed when he laid off his assistant stage manager, Van Ness, without two-weeks' notice, directly conflicting with the agreed upon terms of the standard AEA contract. In response, the Executive Council carried a motion that endorsed the explicit inclusion of stage managers in the collective bargaining process. This motion and information stems from the Executive Council Meeting Minutes dated February 20, 1920.

> Re – Ass't. stage manager, Van Ness, Equity Member vs. Romberg –
> Mr. Mills moved, seconded by Mr. Westley, that the council rules that if a man is engaged as stage manager, or assistant stage manager, he becomes a regular member of the company and in the absence of any agreement to the contrary he must be given his two weeks' notice of dismissal. CARRIED.[23]

The notion that stage managers and assistant stage managers were included in Equity's membership is evidenced by this record, as the Assistant Stage Manager Van Ness was an Equity member. Romberg's name comes up several times in the AEA archives as an opposing party in several arbitration cases. Judging from the text provided, the reader can assert that this motion was caused as direct result of an arbitration or court case between Van Ness and Romberg. While evidence from this arbitration or court case has not been found in AEA's archives, the direct result from this comparatively short paragraph is demonstrated through changes in the constitution, contracts, and rulebooks.

The short-term effect included modifications to the 1924 Basic Agreement Between the Managers' Protective Association and Actors' Equity Association:

> Whereas the Protective Association is composed of a number of producers
> and theatre owners having substantial private interests and engaged in

presenting dramatic and musical compositions to the public; and **whereas the Equity Association represents actors and performers engaged in part by producers** herein...

Second. Subject to the exemptions herein contained, **wherever the term "actor" is used herein shall apply to any and all males and/or females portraying** any parts or characters, and/or any persons performing in any theatrical troupe or company of performers, and also understudies and permanent company **stage managers**...

Members of the chorus are not hereafter, in any computation, to be considered or counted as a member of any cast, **said computation to be based upon the number of principals, understudies and permanent company stage managers as aforesaid only**. Extras are not to be counted.[24]

As noted here, the stage manager and assistant stage manager are officially inducted and written into the agreement and contract. Not only is there little doubt of their membership and rights, but it is expressly written that unlike members of the Chorus Equity (a sister union to AEA), stage management contracts will be counted towards the minimum number of Equity hires.[25] In the Regulations portion of the agreement/contract, the first rule specifically mentioning the role of the stage manager in the agreement/contract is printed.

REGULATIONS: G. Notices – All communications which refer to the company in general shall be posted upon the call board. Notice to the manager must be given to him personally or to his company or stage manager.[26]

The only earlier rule that pertained to the stage manager (as of this writing) was found in the original Actors' Equity booklet that included the constitution, by-laws, and rules during performance. Rule seven states, "The stage manager has full control behind the curtain. Any and all exceptions of his rulings must be referred to the manager."[27] While neither of these rules pertain to why the stage manager would have been included in the union, they represent the precedence that would eventually formalize into the "STAGE MANAGER" sections in many of the rulebooks in the 1940s–1950s.[28]

CONCLUSION

Early records indicate that playwrights, directors, and choreographers were also early members in Actors' Equity Association, although they never appear in official paperwork. "In February, 1928, the Actors' Equity Association issued a contract for optional use by its members who direct."[29] The Tamiment Library & Robert F. Wagner Labor Archives also hold examples of the contracts used by playwrights and directors. These agreements were written by Actors' Equity counsel for its members to use when operating as the production's playwright or director. In contrast, stage managers were quickly added as members onto the official paperwork and eventually, after several petitions and rebuttals, were granted rules specific to the role of stage managing[30] and a committee to represent stage managers at the governing level.

In 1959, the directors and choreographers, formerly members of AEA, broke off and formed their own union. In some aspects, it is surprising to consider that the stage managers choose not to transfer their union membership over to the Society of Stage Directors and Choreographers, the predecessor to today's Stage Directors and Choreographers Society. Afterall, stage managers worked and continue to work closely with directors and choreographers to maintain their vision after opening. However, when one considers the extent in which the stage manager had built roots within the actors' union, the solidarity with AEA is understandable. By 1959, the regulations pertaining to the stage manager's role had been embedded into the rulebooks, agreements, and contracts that followed.

Stage managers were originally included in the union primarily because of their acting roots; however, they gained a foothold in stage management-specific negotiations between 1940 and 1950. Largely this was because of how strongly the union's government felt about the commonalities between actors' and stage managers' plights and didn't want to lose part of its membership to a new stage management union. The Executive Council felt so strongly that in response to a memo on contractual negotiations from the 1942 Committee on Special Working Conditions for Stage Managers, the council responded against creating a special contract for stage managers, stating:

> We do not believe that stage managing is a separate craft or art that has little to do with acting. Equity in its early days had to fight to have only Equity members as stage managers and rightly so because they belong in Equity since their interest lies with the actors and the actors' interest would be jeopardized if the stage managers were not with them.[31]

Over 75 years have passed since that was written, and while some things have certainly changed, stage managers continue to play an important role in Actors' Equity Association. With a firmer understanding of the intersection between stage managers and the actors' union, perhaps a new generation of stage managers can confidently join union leadership ranks knowing that stage managers and actors have long been intertwined from AEA's early days.

NOTES

1. *The Actors' Equity Association: A Voluntary Association Organized in New York City, May 26, 1913* (New York: Actors' Equity Association, 1914), 16. Bold for emphasis.

2. Vice-president of the International Alliance of Theatrical Stage Employees, who was on the premise to corroborate the strike and promote solidarity amongst the stagehands and musicians if the actors walked out.

3. A. Harding, *The Revolt of the Actors* (W. Morrow & Company, 1929).

4. S.P. Holmes, *Weavers of Dreams, Unite!* (University of Illinois Press, 2013).

5. This dissention is discussed on a few discussion boards, such as: http://smnet work.org/forum/the-hardline/do-you-agree-with-equity-representing-stage-managers/

6. K. Segrave, *Actors Organize: A History of Union Formation Efforts in America, 1880–1919* (London: McFarland & Co., 2008).

7. J. MacLeod, *The Actor's Right to Act* (London: Lawrence and Wishart, 1981).

8. A.L. Bernheim, Actors' Equity Association, *The Business of the Theatre: An Economic History of the American Theatre, 1750–1932* (New York: B. Blom, 1964).

9. F.C. Burnand, *How We Manage Our Private Theatricals* (New York: Happy Hours Company, 1872), 30.

10. John Dolman, *The Art of Play Production* (New York: Harper, 1928), 338.

11. These stock companies were centrally located, constantly producing work, and were attached to a community, often performing a different show every night.

12. The combination company moved from town to town with a specific start and end date, often producing the same play(s) in each area, allowing the actor to rely less and less on the prompter during the performance.

13. In contrast, Sean P. Holmes, author of *Weavers of Dreams, Unite!*, argues that AEA formed not because of the poor conditions of employment but because the perception of these poor conditions was hyped-up by a small, but influential group of actors. Sean P. Holmes, *Weavers of Dreams, Unite!* (Urbana: University of Illinois Press, 2013).

14. *All For One and One For All* (New York: Actors' Equity Association, 1924), 17–18.

15. UMPA and PMA are arguably the same organizations: UMPA dissolved so that the producers could create a new organization and restart negotiations with AEA. See Kerry Segrave, *Actors Organize: A History of Union Formation Efforts in America, 1880–1919* (Jefferson: McFarland & Company, Inc., 2008), 152.

16. Segrave, 154.

17. Segrave, 161.

18. *Actors' Equity Association* (1914), 17–18. Bold for emphasis.

19. *Producing Managers' Association–Actors' Equity Association Minimum Contract* (New York, 1919), 1.

20. *PMA–AEA*, 1.

21. *Standard Resident Theatre Contract for Dramatic Productions* (New York, 2012), 1.

22. This ambiguity is not present in all of today's contracts; it is determined by the agreement between AEA and the theatre, and the contracts used by the company.

23. *AEA Council Meeting Minutes* (New York: 1920). Microform, Reel 4.

24. *Agreement Between Managers' Protective Association–Actors' Equity Association* (New York, 1924). Bold for emphasis.

25. At this time there was an 80–20 rule, where 80% of the cast needed to be members of AEA. Chorus Equity had a similar rule, however, at this point the calculations were separate to ensure even 80–20 membership across both parts of the cast (Principal and Chorus).

26. *Agreement MPA–AEA*, 2.

27. *Actors' Equity Association* (1914), 33.

28. Correspondence from Rebecca Brownstein to the Printing Department, September 18, 1940, WAG.011, Box 6, Folder 42, Actors' Equity Association Records, The Tamiment Library & Robert F. Wagner Labor Archives, New York.

29. Alfred L. Bernheim, *The Business of the Theatre* (New York: Actors' Equity Association, 1932), 111.

30. *Equity Rules Governing Employment* (New York: Actors' Equity Association, 1948).

31. Correspondence from Executive Council to Council, March 2, 1942, WAG.011, Box 6, Folder 32, Actors' Equity Association Records, The Tamiment Library & Robert F. Wagner Labor Archives, New York.

Part 1

Work

1

The Big Picture

Joseph Drummond

As a stage manager I embraced several "mantras" during my 42 years at the Goodman Theatre in Chicago. One that served me well was "Always carry a fork; you never know when you might encounter a chocolate cake!" Weeks and sometimes months passed between cake encounters, and co-workers were always impressed when I pulled out my trusty fork at the sight of an unexpected treat. What they didn't realize was that, as a stage manager, I encountered the unexpected on a regular basis. Being prepared was simply part of my DNA.

PREPARE FOR THE UNEXPECTED. IT WILL HAPPEN

As a young, inexperienced assistant stage manager, I observed unexpected situations handled well and many that were not. One stage manager I worked with requested a backup gun in case the onstage gun that shot a main character did not fire. On opening night, the onstage gun did *not* fire, but the stage manager didn't fire the backup gun either! Later he said he assumed the onstage gun would eventually fire, because it had gone off for all the previews. The next day, the review headline read "Benito Cereno Misfires at the Goodman."

DOI: 10.4324/9780429321672-3

This was a major learning experience for me. I realized that being prepared was more than just having the gun in your hand. Preparing for the unexpected is key in many professions and life situations. Pilots go through a pre-flight checklist before every flight. I have read that people who focus on the flight attendant speech before takeoff go into auto response during real emergencies. The same holds true for people who check the route from their hotel room to the nearest emergency exit. Something as simple as counting the number of doors between their room and the exit means getting out of an unexpected situation safely. Once the brain has processed the info, that file pops open with the escape plan, and you execute it without thinking.

In the same vein, stage managers rely on completing pre-show checklists prior to each performance to ensure that everything required during the performance has been accounted for before the curtain goes up. Defending yourself when a prop is missing because you skipped using your pre-set checklist is impossible when it comes to being honest with yourself. No one's safety has been compromised, but you have lost the trust of your cast. Additionally, I always assumed that every understudy will go on. During pre-production week for every show, stage management compiled a document for each performing actor that covered everything that needed to happen if said actor was not able to perform. The unexpected I was prepared for was learning at half-hour that an actor would not go on. When it happened, I consulted my "If X is out..." document and checked off all the necessary items, even though it meant opening the house late.

Although the document provided a blueprint of what had to happen during a performance, much of the preparation took place during regular weekly understudy rehearsals run by the stage management team. Understudies need to know more than the lines they must say; they need to physically experience the stage set. For example, expecting an understudy to get offstage safely in a blackout without rehearsal is totally irresponsible of a stage manager.

For technical issues, I drew on my past experiences to prepare for possible issues. I let my brain do the work in advance, so I was ready with a plan if needed. To be clear, I wasn't thinking about how to tell someone how to fix something in an emergency; it was about asking the right questions in the moment.

Absorbing and organizing the different elements in advance is the plan that has served me well. Nothing beats a detailed checklist for pre-production, pre-tech, and pre-closing. When I started at the Goodman there was no generic checklist for any of the production stages. Each stage management team did its own thing. Eventually fellow production stage manager Chuck Henry and I decided to create shared checklists. We started with two pages; when I left the Goodman the pre-production checklist had grown to 13 pages. It was edited every time a stage manager encountered a new situation that warranted documentation or there were changes in policy or technology (making sure there was enough carbon paper for paperwork was deleted within months of creating the original checklist). There were sections for working with different kinds of animals (dogs, birds, chickens, and fish); another section for working with young performers; and several pages for musicals.

While it sounds tedious to maintain this working document, we knew that once each item on the pre-production list was completed, we were ready to enjoy first rehearsal. Beyond that, the checklist serves as the communal brain of the stage management department. Over the years as the Goodman grew from a local institution to a national theatrical force, the lowly checklist provided consistency in stage management performance, so that each production team could maintain the high production values and rehearsal process that the Goodman is known for.

GROW WHERE YOU ARE PLANTED

What honed my attention to detail and affinity for documentation that led to a 46-year career in stage management? Two words: summer stock. I trained to be an actor and transitioned into stage management under the guidance of producer/director William (Bill) Putch at Totem Pole Playhouse located near Gettysburg, PA. I worked for Bill—a former stage manager himself—for 12 summers. When I started in 1970, we did one-week stock, rehearsing one show during the day and performing a different show at night.

Bill taught me not to lose sight of the Big Picture. One-week stock taught me to be fast, efficient, and accurate. This meant cutting windows in stacks of blank paper to paste in the pages of a Samuel French script. This allowed me to see both sides of the published script and provided room for taking blocking and writing cues. My first stage manager (SM) kit was a small cigar box filled with pencils and pens, as all paperwork was handwritten (in the 1970s, summer stock theatres in the woods had no computers, no copy machines, and no air conditioning; yes, there was indoor plumbing).

In 1974, I started my long career at the Goodman. However, at the time I didn't know it was going to be a long career. Since I was basically a self-taught stage manager, I was in for an education of making a lot of mistakes. Regional theatre is a whole different ball game than summer stock. Like any young person who makes a big leap professionally, I felt out of my depth for a while. I kept a log of items I felt were requirements of the position and stole ideas, procedures, and paperwork from the other Goodman stage managers. When I felt uncertain or insecure at any given moment, I would do what I did as an actor: I pretended. It worked! Just giving the impression of confidence made others think I was and in turn made me more confident.

I was an assistant stage manager for several years, working with three different stage managers. The Goodman mainstage season consisted of six productions with two teams of stage managers working on every other production. Each team also had to be on hand for the other team's tech weeks. Observing the other stage management team during this time allowed me to take in the nuances of the job—those things that weren't in Bert Gruver's *Stage Manager's Handbook*.[1] For example, developing people skills was always a challenge. On one show, a crew member was consistently late on a deck cue. The issue, I finally discovered, was the location of the cue light. He had to be a contortionist to see it but didn't feel he had the power to tell me. Solution: move the cue light.

As I moved up from assistant stage manager to production stage manager, I kept hearing Bill Putch's admonition, "Look at the Big Picture." In doing so, I realized what an ideal situation I had at the Goodman. My arrival there coincided with Chicago's great growth as a theatre mecca. During this time the Goodman grew in stature as other theatres came on the scene: St. Nicolas, Wisdom Bridge, Steppenwolf, Victory Gardens. This creative synergy attracted a multitude of talented directors, designers, choreographers, and actors. I worked with many established names: Tennessee Williams, Edward Albee, Hal Prince, Gregory Mosher, Robert Falls, Michael Maggio, Frank Galati, Chita Rivera, David Mamet, and hundreds of other professionals. I was fortunate to have the stability of an established yet forward-thinking theatre as my home base.

I worked on 133 productions at the Goodman, including 12 musicals and 12 seasons of *A Christmas Carol*. Early in my career I took the Goodman production of David Mamet's *Glengarry Glen Ross* to Broadway. Another career highlight was opening the Goodman's production of *Death of a Salesman* on Broadway. I was turning the show over to another stage manager after the opening. Previews were not going smoothly as we approached opening night in New York. The production stage manager replacing me commented that "It's unnatural that you keep so levelheaded in moments of stress." I answered: "Twelve years of doing *Christmas Carol* trained me to remain calm."

It's another way of saying that every production is a rehearsal for the next production. My cumulative stage management knowledge kicks in automatically in times of crisis. Whether Tiny Tim is throwing up in the wings or a major star is throwing a fit on a Broadway stage, I remain focused on running the production.

EVERYONE IS PART OF THE TEAM

The Goodman stage management staff often felt we were working in a vacuum. Working at a major regional theatre, we weren't looking to move to Broadway. We were putting down roots in Chicago. When the Stage Managers' Association (SMA) formed in the early 1980s in New York, production stage manager Chuck Henry and I joined and waited for snail mail to bring us news of what was happening with stage managers elsewhere. The SMA was hosting events, roundtables, forums, and workshops in New York, difficult for any of us to attend. So, Chuck Henry, Marsha Gitkind, Malcolm Ewen, Alden Vasquez, and I started our own mini SMA by getting together and re-creating those events in Chicago. We built a stage management community that worked to improve some of the issues stage managers were facing in Chicago. That community has thrived: the Chicago Kick-Ass Stage Management Facebook group now stands at 1,061 members, many of whom are SMA members.

Bill Putch's Big Picture guidance reminded me to look beyond my own world and acknowledge the help of others. For example, I learned the value of working under great leadership from Goodman's executive director Roche Schulfer. My fellow Goodman staff members also taught me respect: when you give it, it's returned.

As the Goodman grew in stature, it also grew in staff size. I was responsible for maintaining communication with this growing and ever-changing staff. Stage management issued daily reports on rehearsals and performances and I needed to keep staff updated on what was happening onstage and in the rehearsal room. FYI (For Your Information) was my solution. By giving staff FYIs in the reports—for example, if script pages that involved design elements were being cut—I allowed them to decide if the info was important to their department. I also tried not to overreach in my information. For example, prop master Jimmy Swank told me to give notes without the suggested solutions. I wasn't respecting his talents with my suggestions. I understood his point of view, and it illustrates how difficult it is to determine what or how much information is needed.

The stage management team is the hub of the wheel of a production; we had to determine where the information needed to flow, how much and what kind. I preferred to err on the side of too much than to be in the position of seeming to withhold valuable information.

Tech week was always a time of intense stress and little sleep—often self-inflicted—as the clock kept ticking towards first preview. In the 1970s, Goodman management started providing beer to the crew and stage management after the first preview. It was a way of say thanks for getting us through yet another tough tech week. Years later pizza was added to the thank you. As one who latches onto mantras, I embraced "You can't stop beer night." No matter how stressful tech week is, there is *always* a first preview and then beer night. Just focus on what you need to do to keep tech moving forward.

Acknowledging your own team members is also important. While working as an assistant stage manager, I wasn't always included in production discussions and it made me feel less valuable to the team. I decided to address this issue when I worked with assistant stage managers. The Equity rule book defines the stage management staff as stage manager and assistant stage manager, not assistant to the stage manager. I introduced assistant stage managers as team members; included them in discussions and decisions; trusted them to take care of our agreed responsibilities; and laughed with them whenever appropriate, often after everyone left for the day. While dealing with some stressful issues after opening, Assistant Stage Manager Marsha Gitkind and I found that throwing the leftover break-a-way china from the previous show was extremely therapeutic. As the production stage manager, I sat in the hot seat, but creating a strong cohesive team meant a better working relationship.

MAKE THE CAREER WORK FOR YOU

Many young stage managers burn out at an early point in their careers because they allow the position to control them. I made a conscious decision to manage my time effectively. I worked with my team members Malcolm Ewen and Lois Griffing to set up daily habits that worked for all of us. Since we could not control the number of hours we had to be in rehearsals, tech, or performances, we could require ourselves to complete as much of the day's work during those hours as possible. I wanted us to complete the day's tasks during the rehearsal hours, focusing on the reports and schedules at the end of the day. Once those were completed, we could leave the job at the theatre. It took time to make it work, but our mental health rewards were well worth the investment in making the change. I also made some healthy choices for myself. I upped my trust level, delegated responsibilities to my team members, and made sure our interns felt valued and respected as team members, even providing them with networking connections to the Chicago stage management community.

In 1999, as the Goodman was preparing to move into a newly built theatre, we had to throw out items that did not need to be moved. I started going through boxes and file drawers and instead of finding things to purge, I found the history of Goodman stage management department. There were handwritten forms, memos, reports, cards, thank you notes to stage managers, a telegram from Tennessee Williams, drawings, mementos, photos, and sheets of carbon paper. These items could not be tossed out; they were historical artifacts. I kept everything. I compiled an Excel document of shows starting in 1969 when the Goodman became a professional company, adding the names of stage managers, assistant stage managers, and interns who worked on each show. Pages included lists of published scripts where Goodman stage managers were credited. This info went into binders along with the artifacts from boxes and file drawers. I also documented the present stage management staffing and asked every team member to provide a personal page that included their resume, the show(s) they worked on, and their own special experience. Nine large binders now hold the Goodman Theatre's stage management history.

Will anyone ever look at this stuff? Who knows. But theatres are more than the plays they produce; they are living organisms that produce art. If nothing else, these binders contain fine examples of how humans can work together!

THE TRUSTY FORK

I have had a rewarding career beyond my wildest dreams. I stumbled many times and was stressed to the point of tears. During one production, for example, I called the intermission times while an artistic director stood next to me screaming about something that I had no control over. Fortunately, such moments are outweighed by the delightful experiences and the pure joy of calling a perfect show.

The final show of my Goodman career was a 5½-hour production of *2666*, a challenge I felt I had been preparing for my entire career. I had to be the one to production stage manage (PSM) it. After the final performance, there was chocolate cake and I took out my trusty fork one last time!

NOTE

1. B. Gruver, *Stage Manager's Handbook* (New York: Drama Book Publishers, 1972).

2

Maximum Flexibility
Tom Humes

I'm always fascinated when I'm reading job descriptions to discover the ever shifting and expanding definition to what a stage manager (SM) will be expected to do for an organization. Sometimes it depends on the art form; for example, a company SM for a ballet organization may spend more time as an administrator than actively working in a rehearsal space. They may have duties that are more akin to production or company management from a theatrical lens but are standard amongst other SMs in the ballet world. Other times, it may be a classification of a type of producing organization, most likely Equity vs. Non-Equity or Union vs. Non-Union, where a third party may have, arguably, "strict" definitions as to what a stage manager may be required to do/work.

While I am certainly just one of many out there, I have my own set of criteria that I've found to be universal to most of the organizations I've come to know as my "home." Stage managers are central to the production's interdepartmental communications. Almost every piece of information related to that production will be obtained or passed on by them. SMs should have knowledge in all aspects of production in order to facilitate this communication. Something that I often talk about in my management classes is the importance of clear communication and how that's facilitated by having a shared jargon with each of your departments. It's no small feat to obtain this common language, but being open to new experiences and learning—even when you think you know everything—makes a better

DOI: 10.4324/9780429321672-4

leader. My own path towards my current position has been full of twists and turns. It is my hope you will find it entertaining, informative, and impactful to you, my future colleagues and friends.

A REAL JOB

Beginning your journey as a person who is flexible to the max will incorporate your patience with your biggest supporters. I'm sure many stage managers have had friends, or more likely family members, that have told them that they needed to have a real job. It was my intention entering college to teach middle/high school math and perhaps run a drama club after school. It turned out that math was not for me, and I would have to switch my major to theatre so I could graduate on time…ish.

While working on my degree during the academic year, I would spend my summers working for Cain Park,[1] an outdoor concert/theatre venue in my hometown of Cleveland Heights where I worked in various departments each year. I knew then that I wanted to be a professional stage manager, with grandiose hopes of working on Broadway, so I knew that experience in a bit of everything would make me truly versatile in theatre. I spent one summer in the box office, where I learned the various types of reporting that you have to do for the venue and city while also creating percentage reports for the concerts and productions that would be negotiated based on a split of the proceeds from ticket sales. The next summer I worked as a house manager, coordinating volunteer usher staff and making determinations whether to hold the house for concessions/box office congestion. This is also where I first started directly interacting with patrons inside of the theatres and discovered the trial and error of working with the various groups of patrons, based on the art form, and the privileges to which they believe they were entitled. These interactions gave me a healthy perspective about the impact of my words, the filters I should utilize, and the accountability that I need to have when I react without thinking. I rely on this experience today when I have a house manager that needs to hold, embracing the delay with empathy rather than frustration.

I spent my final two summers (while still in college) as an assistant production manager. On my graduating summer, I was finally able to be a non-Actors' Equity Association assistant stage manager on an AEA[2] production and join the Equity Membership Candidate program to earn weeks towards membership. This position was one of those "all other duties as assigned" opportunities, which I was happy to oblige. After my primary assistant stage management duties for the first part of the season ended, I continued my regular responsibilities for the concert side of productions at Cain Park. This included advancing the events, working as the deck chief throughout the concert, coordinating hospitality/catering for the larger events, and working with all departments to build risers, lay out marley, focus lights, etc. After this particular summer, I was going to graduate and was not going to be able to support myself. Cain Park's days were numbered at the end of the season. While I was frantically applying for theatre jobs in state, out of state, even internationally, a co-worker (Jill) asked me if I was able to read music. Having been a mediocre trombone player for most of my secondary education, I responded with "Yes, but not the greatest at playing" assuming she wanted me for some sort of orchestra pit gig. That answer got my foot in the door with the world of opera stage management.

DIFFERENT THAN THEATRE

Embracing the vast differences in the way art forms utilize stage managers differently than theatre is another aspect of your maximum flexibility goal as a stage manager. "Opera production is different than theatre," was my biggest takeaway from that first production. Not only did I have the expected duties, but there are so many extra things that I felt, at the time, kept getting added to my plate. I couldn't believe that in addition to making run sheets, rail sheets, and supervising the organization of everything prop-wise, I now had to cue entrances for all singers on my side of the stage and I would be responsible if I didn't have the singers in the correct costumes and with the correct props. I had to help create and maintain the monstrous document known as the Who/What/Where, which has almost every detail about each singer's entrance or exit, their costume, and props known to stage management embedded within.

I was grateful for the experience and once I got over the first opera, it became easier when I worked as an assistant stage manager for the subsequent four. Once I finished the opera, more freelance work came about in Cleveland. After working several theatre stage management gigs (sprinkled with a few more operas), I was feeling a bit taken advantage of in terms of compensation, time, and more strange/abnormal "additional duties" clauses in my contracts. I was yearning to get my AEA card, not only to have collective bargaining in my corner, but also because I found it emblematic for being a professional stage manager. I had my opportunity to join the union during another summer at Cain Park while also working as the assistant to the general manager. I was thrilled during this time to finally get something I worked so hard for, but then the theatres that had been contracting me as a stage manager were not interested in hiring an AEA stage manager in addition to contracting the AEA actors. So, I spent some time working as a part-time run crew member at Cleveland Play House (CPH),[3] while taking on the odd opera every once in a while. Then I found another opportunity to get some steadier work (while waiting for more AEA opportunities) as an electrician/lightboard operator for Cleveland Play House. Since the electricians and carpenters at this venue were represented by the International Alliance of Theatrical Stage Employees (IATSE),[4] I was able to not only work a fairly steady 40-hour work week, but I could be called for more evening work/weekend work as an extra stagehand.

TOOLBOX OF COMPASSION, EMPATHY, AND CAMARADERIE

As much as I advocate how much flexibility the stage manager will need to practice, sometimes we are met with folks that are not able to be flexible or simply won't. While it is certainly worth exploring negotiations to move that line a bit more towards flexible, an important lesson to be learned is when it's not worth the energy expenditure. My knowledge of the union was fairly limited because my only experience with the stagehands was as an assistant stage manager for the operas I worked on. Becoming an IATSE member[5] helped me gain more knowledge about the structure and reasoning behind departmentalization backstage and exactly what can and cannot be expected from the folks you work with. I also gained a perspective as to how grueling a stagehand work schedule can be, especially in a busy local. This knowledge added to my toolbox of compassion, empathy, and ultimately camaraderie when I later obtained more AEA work at CPH. While I was doing a stagehand work call before the next tech, I would see the folks loading out the previous night's concert until 3:00 a.m. the next day. Sometimes misery loves company.

I always find it useful to work stagehand calls because I get exposed to so many new and interesting bits of stagecraft. These experiences help inform me during any troubleshooting or short-term fixes during the performance run of a show. It's also nice to have a bit of a break from leadership and just go with the flow of load-ins and load-outs for concerts, where the most hectic part of the day is finding available truss tools or where to park for your call.

OPPORTUNITY CALLS: EQUIVALENT PROFESSIONAL EXPERIENCE

I worked this flexible duality as an AEA stage manager and IATSE stagehand for six years when another opportunity presented itself; Kent State University created a new position for a 12-month NTT (non-tenure track) Assistant Professor. I had always thought that teaching in higher education was off-limits for me because of conversations I had with two stage management mentors who are and have been essential to my success. Jen Collins was a stage management professor at Northwestern University and long-time resident stage manager at Chicago Shakespeare Theatre before moving to live in Ohio. While she was searching for employment at some local universities before joining the CPH staff, she kept running into the same problem during her inquiries, the lack of a terminal degree.

She loved mentoring and taught me more than I could even quantify now. Hence, it always perplexed me why universities required a Masters of Fine Arts (MFA) or higher when real-world experience in professional theatre seemed the equivalent and much more valuable to me. In my case the search committee also saw that "equivalent professional experience" was just as valid as a terminal degree. John Godbout, another stage management mentor and friend, helped me get over my self-doubt and encouraged me to apply. Now that I have been in this position a couple of academic years, I can honestly say I'm happy I applied. I will say that the adjustment from the professional life to higher education is still a work in progress. While I was stage managing, I truly thought that was the busiest time of my life, but working with a 12-month producing organization, while teaching, mentoring, and working on my own knowledge and self-improvement, is phenomenally complicated. I do enjoy the challenge though, even on the days that I fail, because there is always something to learn/improve upon and more importantly, finding forgiveness in those mistakes.

My colleagues, staff, and students at Kent State University have been very supportive, helpful, and patient while I find my path in this environment. My own experience both as a professional stage manager and a former undergrad student really helps to navigate my investigations into subject matter within my classes. I tend to speak frequently about the unions that stage managers, production managers, and theatre managers will often interact with. Being a member of both AEA and IATSE, I feel it's important for any successful manager to have some sort of knowledge on how they differ and what can be expected when work needs to be done with folks represented by them (though I will admit that I am a bit more pro-union when I get wrapped up in these topics). I also find that my experience with automation and what can go wrong on a tech-heavy production propels my need to talk about safety, the importance of pre-show checks, and more importantly, instances of when scenery goes awry.

FROM PREP WEEK TO FINAL PERFORMANCE, OR BEYOND

I draw from my past to anticipate the differences in the structure of productions and how I might incorporate my flexible approach to things differently, given the situation. For example, I have different processes for plays/musicals that are in development and for established shows. I know that I will be spending a lot of my time keeping up with script changes with new pages being printed on a daily or even hourly basis when a show is in development (or perhaps delegating to an assistant or apprentice). Within this structure if we're doing a staged reading, inside of the four days we have to rehearse this play, we need to be up on our feet at music stands by midway through day 3, or else the production is going to be in peril—something I have yet to be successful imparting on the director.

I know that a smaller cast show or a remount is always a bit more of a casual atmosphere than the chaos that can ensue in a larger cast show. If the production involves a larger cast, we will need more structure and strategy in the SM team as to how we utilize time wisely. Personally, I know that I feel more at ease and able to be more myself when I'm working on a show that has more diverse representation of not only folks onstage, but designers and production staff as well (part of my continuing work is to pinpoint and articulate why this is so). In this regard, the venue where I'm working can also play a huge role. I know that when working with Karamu House[6] there is much more community engagement through connections with actors and audience members after the show in talk backs and greeting lines than I find at other theatres or venues in town.

As we see a slow return back to in-person production, I'm hopeful that folks will appreciate how different we were pre-pandemic to now. I'm hoping that the engine that drives production forward will be slowed down a bit to accommodate mental health, family, and our needs. No matter how big or how small a production will be, it will need a great stage manager who will rely on their intuition, experiences, and adaptability to help steer the production on its journey.

In short, all of this is to say that each entertainment experience is unique and requires maximum flexibility in the stage management team engaged in seeing the process through from prep week to final performance, or beyond.

NOTES

1. City of Cleveland Heights, "Cain Park Home Page," CivicPlus, 2021, www.cainpark.com/

2. Actors' Equity Association, "AEA Home Page," 2021, www.actorsequity.org/

3. Cleveland Play House, "Cleveland Play House Home Page," The Form Group, 2021, www.clevelandplayhouse.com/

4. International Alliance of Theatrical Stage Employees, Moving Picture Technicians, Artists and Allied Crafts of the United States, Its Territories and Canada, "IATSE Home Page," 2021, www.iatse.net/

5. There are three ways to join. "To get on the Organizational List requires that you must earn at least $35,000 per year for three consecutive years in employment with employers who **have** collective bargaining agreements with **Local One**. While it can seem daunting, the vast majority of our current members **have** gained membership in this manner." "Three Ways to Join," LocalOne IATSE – Three Ways to Join, accessed July 6, 2021, https://iatselocalone.org/public/Become-a-Member/Three-Ways-to-Join.

6. Karamu House, "Karamu House Home Page," 2021, http://karamuhouse.org/

understanding IATSE and your music director or music contractor can help with AFM. Knowing where your resources are, so you are following the union rules and being fiscally responsible, is important, but no more important that creating an atmosphere of community, a team, where everyone feels valued and works towards a common goal. This is what true leadership and stage management is all about.

When on tour with *Les Misérablés*, our new PSM addressed the company holding up the AEA union book. He told them that we can strictly follow all the rules in this book, or we can just get along and that he'd rather do the latter. While he wasn't suggesting that we ignore the rules, he emphasized that if we all just work together everyone will be happy. This was a big lesson in leadership and stage management. The rules are there to protect us, but the goal is the same, to create a great working environment, where we all feel respected and appreciated, making a wonderful show together.

THE BUILDING

Another unique aspect to Broadway is that the producer of the show doesn't own the physical building the show is in. There is a unique relationship between the theatre owner and the show producer (unlike regional theatres, where the venue and the producing agent are usually, though not always, the same thing). The show producer is renting the venue from the theatre owner. The show then employs a set of stagehands to be their production heads to supervise the show. The venue (called the house) also employs a set of stagehands. They are the house heads and protect/maintain the theatre. The house heads will also provide any additional stage crew labor needed beyond the production heads and house heads. This can occasionally result in tricky situations to manage, especially when the production carpenter and house carpenter don't agree on something. Awkward, right?

The theatre owner can be, and sometimes is, a producer or investor in a show, but not the executive producer, the one leading the project. The Shubert, Nederlander, and Jujamcyn organizations own almost all the Broadway theatres (Disney owns the New Amsterdam and The Ambassador Group owns the Lyric and Hudson), so Broadway producers have to partner in some way with one of them to get a venue. You can check the credits in the playbill and see if one of these organizations is credited as a producer. It's a unique relationship for sure, theatre owners can be both landlord and investor/producer. One piece of the contract between the show and the theatre is the stop clause. This is a weekly gross income number where the theatre owner can close the show. This amount can be different than the amount the show needs to make to stay profitable (i.e., the weekly operating costs). If a show breaks even that may not be enough to keep the show open. This allows the theatre owner to essentially kick out one tenant, when they think bringing in a new show will be better for their theatre. For stage managers reporting the house numbers nightly, this knowledge can be nerve racking. To this day, I believe the original production of *Les Misérables* may still be running if the theatre owner didn't want to bring in *The Boy From Oz*, with Hugh Jackman. Granted it was a bigger money maker at the time, but it certainly didn't have the run *Les Miz* did!

CALLING THE SHOW

One other small, but important, difference with stage managing on Broadway is where we call the show from. Most regional theatres usually call from a front-of-house booth—that was how it was set up both at LJP, the Old Globe, and San Diego Rep, my old stomping grounds. However, on Broadway we usually call from the stage (*The Lion King* and *Wicked* being the two big exceptions). On many shows the calling desk is just offstage right or left. The actors literally walk right past you for their entrances, the crew sets up scenery inches from you, and you are in the thick of the action.

We have monitors to see from the front-of-house angle, color, infrared, conductor camera, and sometimes many others for safety. Most Broadway theatres don't have a booth that would work anyway; they were built a century ago and the placement of the stage manager was usually in a prompter location for feeding lines!

It takes some getting used to, but after doing 20 plus Broadway shows, I greatly prefer being near the company, accessible, and connected to the heartbeat of the show and not separated by hundreds of feet. It's a different experience, requiring focus and discipline, but also allows you to be part of the show, breathing along with the cast and crew, in each and every moment. When you can make that connection with a moment that is happening onstage and call your cue in sync with the drama unfolding, that is a magical moment that I am so thankful my career has led me to many times over.

THE ART AND CRAFT OF STAGE MANAGEMENT

But despite this and the other differences of unions, charities, financial pressures, commercial producers, and theatre owners, the art and craft of stage management is essentially the same on any show. We all create schedules, write reports, give notes, call cues, and most importantly and hardest to qualify, lead a company. We are there from pre-production and the first day of rehearsal, communicating with every department, ensuring all needs are met. We coordinate tech rehearsals, becoming the instrument through which the movement of the show onstage happens, calling cues to align with the vision of directors and designers. We maintain and run the show, evaluating, steering, and motivating the company to stay on

course and invested. Our people skills and the ability to create positive relationships impact our ability to grow our network and get work, as well as how effective and successful we can be in our role as stage manager.

BIG DREAMS

Broadway was my big dream and desire as a young actor performing in high
school. All I wanted was to build a life where I could work in the theatre and
hopefully, someday, if I was lucky, to work on Broadway. The dream set me on my
course, but the hard work and the relationships I made working in San Diego set
me on a path. In my early career, I learned the tools and skills that lead to making
important connections with others. I didn't just get to Broadway, but have had a
career of 20 plus years on Broadway and national tours. I've had the pleasure and
privilege to work alongside some of the industries greatest theatre artists and am
happy to share my journey with you, the reader. I wish you the best of luck on
your journey, whatever dream inspires you and whatever road you take.

NOTE

1. For more info on either of these programs, visit: www.broadwaybeyondaccess.
com and www.broadwaysymposium.com

4

The "Smusedays" of Touring a Broadway Show!
Kristi Ross-Clausen

Ah, the glamorous life of the road! There are people who work their entire theatrical career on the road, and some who only last a few days or weeks. Touring is not for everyone, but it can be one of the most fulfilling, exhausting, and simultaneously crazy jobs you'll ever have. Let's start by looking at a typical week on the road for a First National tour of a First Class Broadway show!

It's called "Smuseday" because Sunday, Monday, and Tuesday all blend into one. You wake up Sunday morning at 9 a.m., grab a quick breakfast in the hotel lobby, and finish packing except for the few things you'll need that night. You drag your "truck" suitcase to the theatre and put it where the props department head tells you to leave it. The props crew will make certain it gets on one of the dozen trucks that carry all of the scenic, rigging, lighting, sound, video, wardrobe, hair, makeup, and office equipment to the next city. With your team, you run the matinee and evening performances as usual—catching a quick dinner between shows with a local friend you met three years ago when you last played this city. After the evening performance, you pack the stage management office into the work boxes and head back to the hotel to finish the performance report[1] before a nap while the crew does the rest of the load-out.

You, your fellow stage managers, and the assistant company manager check out of the hotel at 3:30 a.m. and climb into a small bus euphemistically called the "airport shuttle." Your "plane" suitcase will be your only piece of checked baggage;

DOI: 10.4324/9780429321672-6

your roller bag carry-on and "personal item" (AKA backpack) with your computer, Kindle, chargers, and vital items stay with you.

You meet the show's crew at the airport check-in counter when it opens at 4 a.m. The crew members haven't slept at all and took taxis to the airport straight from the theatre after finishing load-out. The 15 or so of you are all well experienced travelers, so you get through the check-in, baggage drop, and security process reasonably quickly— especially since there are very few others awake at the airport at that time.

You grab some food and a bottle of OJ at the one restaurant that is open—a fast food place—and head to the gate to see if you've been upgraded to more comfortable seats. You wisely joined every frequent flyer program you could when you started touring, and it pays off occasionally. The miles you've been earning will be turned in for your vacation ticket to Hawaii, the only state you haven't been to yet.

While you eat, you check with the crew to see how load-out went. You're happy to hear there were no injuries or incidents and the theatre's pair of loading docks, coupled with an excellent local stagehand crew, helped everything get done almost an hour before the estimated finishing time. Most of the crew even had a chance to get showers before leaving the theatre. They are tired, but in good spirits.

You finish your breakfast and look up at the gate monitor at the same time your phone buzzes to see your hoped-for upgrade has come through. The gate attendant prints a new boarding pass and you resume chatting with the crew until boarding time. You board the first plane with the priority group—another perk of the upgrade earned by flying every week for the past few years—stow your luggage, fluff your convertible travel pillow, and fall asleep before the plane even leaves the gate. Your body wakes on command when you feel the plane start to descend about 90 minutes later. Once on the ground, you grab a snack to save for later and head to the gate for your connecting flight.

The performers and the rest of the company have arrived at the airport you just departed for their flight which departs at 10 a.m., so you text a friend in the cast asking how they are doing and chat a bit about plans for the next city until it's time to board your connecting flight.

On the second plane, you take another nap until arrival at the next city around noon on Monday. Once you have recombobulated, you board one of the rideshare vans that the assistant company manager ordered in advance. As soon as everyone and all their luggage is accounted for, you travel to the hotel with just enough time to check in, grab a container of soup from the mom-and-pop lunch place you discovered last time you were in town, and get to the theatre around 1:30 p.m. for the start of load-in at 2:00 p.m.

THE TOURING SHOW LOAD-IN

At the start of load-in, the tour head electrician confers with you about the placement of some lights which will be hung in a slightly different location than what's on the plot—one consequence of the fact no two theatres are exactly the same is that front-of-house lighting positions sometimes need some compromise to still be artistically useful but safely installed. You agree that the box boom locations will work in place of the plotted cove location and think how great it is to be on tour with people who have also toured in the past—he knew this would be an issue and discussed options with the venue head electrician when the show was advanced.

You introduce yourself to the building rep, then talk with the head carpenter (the leader of the touring crew) to confirm where the moving light repair area, wardrobe, wigs, and makeup crews will be located backstage.

You walk through the venue with the building rep to determine dressing room assignments for each of the performers along with locations for the resident direc-tor, music director, and physical therapist, then create a list of the room assignments to be put on the callboard.

The truck door to the loading dock opens at 2:00 p.m. on the dot, and a quartet of strong stagehands pop the ratchet straps holding the cargo in the first of a dozen semitrailers that carry the show's accouterments. A line of stagehands quickly forms to the right of the dock plate as they take turns pushing crates of various sizes to various places based on the label identifying the contents and destination of each box. A knee-high rolling toolbox labeled "Stage Management: Signage and First Aid" is one of the first boxes off, and you take it to the room which is typically used as a conference room, but will serve as the stage manage-ment office for that week.

The box contains a variety of laminated arrows and signs pointing to company management, green room, front of house, callboard, wardrobe, hair, makeup, the names and part numbers of all of the individuals who travel with the company, and the most important sign: stage door. The other stage managers place them in appropriate places while you post items on the callboard. These include the dressing room assignment sheet you just completed, the daily sign-in sheet for the entire company, information about this city and the next two, a complete itinerary of the tour, information about publicity calls, the Broadway Cares/Equity Fights Aids fundraising showcase, workers comp information, Equity harassment/safety line info, upcoming travel arrangements, and other announcements for the entire company. There are sheets with recommended local businesses who (hopefully) understand the life of someone on the road and are able to accept the insurance provided though the various performing arts unions for their members as well as businesses that provide comfort items such as coffee, late-night food, grocery, pharmacy, laundry, and gym.

While you and the stage management team work on signage, the load-in con-tinues with rigging boxes coming off the trucks first followed by power racks, lighting, scenic, and sound items. The props crew is working on provisions for break and keeping things clean. Stagehands in the wardrobe, hair and makeup departments will report tomorrow morning when those trucks are unloaded.

As you finish with the callboard, you see the road cases for the stage managers have been delivered. One waist-high box contains an industrial quality photo-copier for making program stuffers that are printed as needed to note which

performer is replacing which in the printed program. This road case also has car-
tons of paper and other office supplies.

One of the two tall armoire-like road boxes contain the show "bible"—a
collection of three-ring binders with all of the information and documentation
about the show. These production books include the blocking diagrams, choreography documentation, information about stage combat sequences, designer ren-
derings, scenic build instructions, blueprints, musical score, and a calling script
for each stage manager which is essentially the same, yet customized as each pre-
fers. Other binders contain printed copies of the show reports: a detailed report
describing what happened for each rehearsal and performance is generated and
distributed to those who need the information it contains.

There is also contact information for everyone who has ever been associated with the show, in case someone needs to be called to fill in for an injured
performer.

The other road box contains a small refrigerator, microwave, coffee pot, and an
assortment of foods and beverages that can be made with hot water. Upper shelves
are lined with a smaller printer/fax/scanner, assorted office supplies for rehearsal
and performance use, and a large first-aid kit. Each stage manager also has a drawer
for storing personal belongings and there is a place to hang coats.

The entire stage management team unpacks the road cases and creates your
office on tables set up by the local props crew. The house electrician stops by to
check that you have enough power cords and are using the right circuits—not the
orange ones reserved for audio. Once unpacked, you work on the rehearsal schedule for the following week while load-in continues for the crew, with occasional
forays to the stage to see how things are progressing. The rest of the team sorts
through a pile of packages and pulls out the ones for stage management. Ordering
for delivery saves needing to carry everything to every city; a new case of paper is
quickly emptied into the copier workbox storage compartments.

The three over-stage lighting trusses are in the air before the 15-minute
break that starts at 4:30 p.m. The props crew has made runs to the grocery
store and various vendors to provide a smorgasbord of fruit, pastries, donuts,
bagels, peanut butter, bread, an assortment of tea, and plenty of strong coffee.
Theatre is fueled by coffee, and the IATSE property master who makes it is
justifiably proud of her brew. There is also a plate of cheddar cheese curds and
a ring of apple kringle—local favorites which keep break time from becoming
boring and provide a topic of conversation for those who are making their
first visit to that venue and are introduced to the local gustatory delights. At
4:45 p.m., the steward loudly proclaims "We're back!" And everyone quickly
returns to work.

The props crew cleans up the break food, saving most of the leftovers for
tomorrow's morning break. You proofread the rehearsal schedule and ask the other
SMs to double check that the schedule ensures all roles are covered and no one is
earning unapproved overtime.

At 7:00 p.m. the crew takes an hour-long dinner break. You head to a bar and
grill across from the stage door for a burger and fries while you go over your

checklist of tasks, noting what still needs to be done and assigning them to the assistants, so everything can be finished promptly.

At 8:00 p.m., work resumes again. All of the lighting trusses and dance towers and most of the scenic drops have been installed, so the work of laying down the show deck begins in earnest. Two teams of carpenters alternate laying the deck down starting at down stage center and swapping between sides, one 4' x 8' panel at a time to create the 40' wide by 28' deep show deck. The crew here is quite good, so the work that was scheduled to go until midnight on Monday is finished by 10:30 p.m. and everyone is sent home to enjoy an extra hour of well-deserved sleep while the rest of the trucks from the previous city are still en route.

You quickly walk back to the hotel, shower, unpack, and go straight to bed because you have to be back at the theatre by 7:30 a.m. which means being up at 6:30 a.m. to catch breakfast in the hotel lobby. It's not eight hours of sleep, but seven hours is far better than no sleep, which is what most of the crew has been working on.

SMUSEDAY TUESDAY

Tuesday morning call time is 8:00 a.m., so by 7:45 a.m. the entire touring crew is present. The industry phrase is "on time is late," so the local crew members will have checked in with the union steward, donned their tools, and finished their coffee before the next set of truck doors open at 8:00 a.m. sharp. Again, lines quickly form and contents are pushed to their respective destinations.

Once the majority of the set is in place, the electrical crew has all of the lights hung, and the head electrician has confirmed everything is operational, you go onstage to call the light focus, giving instructions to local crew members of the angle and shutter cuts for each conventional lighting fixture in the rig. This works best with two local crew members, one on each side of the balcony, so you can give instructions to one while checking the work of the other. Knowing the names of the parts of the lights and understanding how they work is key to making focus call go smoothly. The lighting designer created a focus book—part of the show "bible"—back when the production was in tech and the target, hot spot, shutter cuts, and color/diffusion for every conventional fixture in the rig are each checked one at a time. A local electrician selected by one of your touring electricians fills in as board op, running the lighting console on stage. You call channel numbers to her over the radio but are also able to converse without the radio if the board op encounters a problem.

You pull up the documentation for the first page and walk to the indicated position on the deck—aided by the number lines stretched across the x- and y-axes to make the deck into a life-sized version of the Cartesian plane you learned about in high school algebra. You then speak, "Board, channel 1 at full, please. House right, please pull the frost and shutters from that lamp then put the hot spot on me."

For each fixture, you have the electrician adjust the focus so the "hot spot" of the fixture is in your eyes—checking the angle by holding a piece of welding glass up to protect your vision as you stare down the barrel of the luminaire. Once the aim is correct, you turn around and indicate the positions of each shutter cut—off the walls, off the curtains, and parallel to the edge of the deck plus whatever other items you want included or excluded for that particular fixture. While that electrician is working to perfect those cuts, you do the same procedure with another electrician on the other side of the balcony, alternating until each position is complete. One assistant stage manager works with a third local electrician who's in a lift focusing the conventional fixtures onstage. The tour head electrician goes through the focus of the moving lights—again consulting with each fixture's instructions from the focus book. She's got another light board sitting on one of the hampers that normally stores soft goods; this setup enables her to move about the stage seeing the lights from all angles while attached via a DMX/Power umbilical to the lighting rack in the wings.

You get most of focus done before lunch starts at 12:30 p.m.—the sound crew remains in the building to tune the room, taking advantage of the quiet while everyone else is gone. After lunch, you return and complete the remainder of the focus before 3:00 p.m. The local crew is released for a long dinner break before the show that evening while you work on vacation scheduling and plans for rehearsals next week.

THE HOURS BEFORE HALF-HOUR

A reporter and cameraperson from a local TV station come by to take a brief backstage tour and get some B-Roll for tonight's feature on the local news. You guide them around the set and the wardrobe quick change area laid out just upstage of the set, careful to only let them film what is approved. The press rep for the company has provided you with facts about the show—how many trucks, how many people are in the company, how many lights are used, the number of costumes, miles of cable, and other interesting bits of trivia. There is no one from the area on the tour, so you act as show ambassador inviting the TV/internet audience to see the show in person.

At 5:00 p.m., you go back to your favorite diner in this town to grab a bite. In the middle of dinner, one of the featured performers calls to say she's not able to perform that night. You call her understudy and let them know they will be going on in that role, then call the understudy's swing to let them know they are on. Once those three dominoes have fallen into place, you call the wardrobe head to give them a heads-up and finish dinner without further interruption.

At an hour before half-hour, you walk the ins and out sheet to the various crew members. The ushers stuff programs with two small pieces of paper which say "At this performance, the role of (Featured Role) will be played by (Understudy)," and another that says "the roles played by (Understudy) will be played by

(Understudy of Understudy)." Wardrobe crew members swap out the costume pieces and prep them for the show. The sound A2 ensures the mic packs are correct and the props crew makes any changes needed to their presets. As much as we try to make every performance exactly like every other, actors always bring their own flair to the role and slight adjustments are made to accommodate those peculiarities. In tonight's situation, everyone has performed the role several times before, so there should be no "shove with love" that sometimes happens when an under-rehearsed person has to go on and the rest of the company helps guide them to the right positions onstage.

Once the onstage presets are completed, the head carpenter lets you know everything is ready for fight call. Your fight captain is a seasoned vet who has taken classes to become Society of American Fight Directors (SAFD) certified which means you can relax and focus on keeping others out of the way while he leads the actors through the sequence twice, insuring everything is done safely.

The dance captain, a performer responsible for ensuring the chorus does their dance moves correctly, takes tonight's swing onstage to double check placements. The downstage edge has a number line with 0 at the center and markings every two feet to each wing, which helps performers know they are in the exact place they need to be. At 30 minutes to curtain time, you let the house manager know the stage is all set and they can begin seating the audience. You also make an announcement over the backstage intercom:

> Good evening everyone! Welcome to NewTown. Featured Performer is out, Understudy is on. Understudy of Understudy will fill in her roles. Our opening night is sold out. There is a reception in the rehearsal hall next door after the show. The call is half-hour, half-hour please, half-hour.

A chorus of "Thank you half!" comes from the dressing rooms. You make the same announcement on the radios used by the crew and receive the same acknowledgements.

At 15-minutes, and five-minutes, you make similar announcements, helping the cast and crew to be ready on time. At 7:27 p.m. you call "Places please, places for the top of the show, places." And the performers arrive for their initial entrances in the wings.

As calling stage manager for this performance, you go to the calling desk in the downstage left wing, a location which affords a good direct view of the action onstage as well as via cameras which provide views of the stage from the audience, each wing, and overhead. You run through a list checking that all the needed crew members are on the show intercom. This is different than the radios the touring crew wear, so there are two ways to get a hold of each crew member during the show—a backup that has come in handy on several occasions. In addition to the touring crew, the house lights operator and two spot light ops who are local crew members are also on coms. It may seem silly to have one person whose only job is to turn on and dim the house lights, but if there is an emergency and they need to be brought up mid-show, that's an important safety factor. The two spot light operators are on a separate channel with the road spot light caller. She listens to you calling the show, but gives instruction to the local spot ops over a different channel at the same time. The spot caller has a good view of the audience from her position in the booth high in the back of the auditorium, and lets you know that the audience is mostly seated.

Once the audience is in, the house manager gives the house to you and you signal the sound board op to play the pre-show announcement reminding the audience to look for the two closest exits and that recording or photography are strictly prohibited. You then flip the light to signal the conductor to begin the overture and start the timer that records the length of each act.

For the next 75 minutes, you focus intently on calling the show. Lights, sound, video, and special effects all have numbers for their cues; the conductor, fly rail, deck carpenters, and automation have colored lights. When the light turns on, that signals "stand by"; when it turns off, that's the visual "GO!" Each cue is only executed when you say "Go" or flip the light off, so the pacing of the show is entirely on you. As these are professionals, you don't need to give a warning for every upcoming cue, you just provide a standby and then the Go. When there's not enough time to do that for each cue, you group them together. Others on the intercom are careful to not say anything that can be confused with the word Go, and chit-chat is kept at a minimum.

A small note pad enables you to quickly jot down any issues as they come up. Even with the understudies on, tonight has no big mistakes and the small errors are not noticeable by the audience.

At intermission, you hand the house back to the house manager and once the ladies bathroom line has cleared, she gives it back to you. You note the time for your show report. Second act runs much like the first with the addition of a short curtain speech asking for donations to Broadway Cares/Equity Fights AIDS, a non-profit initially started to help those with AIDS but which now helps provide health care in a variety of ways as well as funding domestic violence shelters and helping those in need due to natural disasters. After the show, cast members take red buckets into the lobby to collect the donations and the money gathered in that location is used nearby when possible.

The house manager brings a group of VIP donors to the stage door and you give them a tour similar to what you did with the news crew that afternoon. The VIPs take selfies onstage and express their thanks. It's a mutually beneficial arrangement—we provide once-in-a-lifetime experiences and they help fund our art.

A GOOD WAY TO END SMUSEDAY

You change into a festive outfit for the opening night party and head out intending to have one drink before leaving for the hotel. It's been a long couple of days, but making an appearance is important and the chance to see local friends in an informal setting is worth the time. Plus, free food and beverages are always a good way to end Smuseday. The local promoter offers a toast to a successful run. You make a point to introduce yourself to him and thank him for making this all possible at this venue.

Though you try to stick to your one-and-done promise, you are having such a good time, you stay for a second and nosh on more food while you work the room. These opportunities where everyone is in one place offer a great chance to see people interact and know where friction may lie. Though you are not the boss, keeping an eye on the interpersonal dynamics and knowing how to subtly influence things for the benefit of all are good skills to have.

STARTING AGAIN

A hot shower and not setting an alarm for the morning are the post-opening night rewards. On Wednesday, you get to the theatre around 3:00 p.m., confirm rehearsal arrangements for Thursday afternoon, and run the show. Thursday often has an understudy rehearsal starting at noon. Other than shoes, no costumes are used, and the atmosphere is more relaxed.

On alternate Thursdays, the crew comes in for a work call to repair and maintain the equipment. Because this city has a particularly good local electrics crew, this week's main task is to replace all of the lamps in each lighting fixture. Though the crew is careful, it may affect the focus, so you quickly check each one before that night's show. Simultaneously, the props crew is doing some touch-up painting and the carpentry crew is making minor repairs.

Friday daytime permits some sightseeing of local museums, historical attractions, or other points of interest. After the show, you do laundry at a local laundromat/bar combination—the perfect pair for folks on the road—then re-pack your luggage in preparation for the double-double of Saturday/Sunday with two shows each day and not much time for anything else.

Sunday morning begins Smuseday all over and the weeks continue on much the same. A new city, new faces—some you've worked with before, and new challenges. It's hard work with long hours but you love it.

Many of us dream of running away to join a show on tour. It's both one of the most challenging and enjoyable positions in the entertainment world. You are paid to travel and see the world while bringing a bespoke experience to people who are excited to see you and eager for your return. It's both exhausting and addictive.

CONTRACT LEVELS

The Broadway touring world is divided into various contract levels. As of this writing, the top level is the "production" contract with salaries that start around

$2,000 a week and go upwards from there. Lower-level contracts pay significantly less. "Bus-and-Truck" shows that play one-nighters where the load-in, show, and load-out all happen on one day are the lowest level of the touring Broadway world. The relentless toll of working with little sleep makes one-nighters the marathon of touring. Each contract has slightly different provisions, but the goal is that you are safe and reasonably compensated for your work.

There are approximately 250 cities in the USA and Canada which host touring Broadway shows, and many more that host Theatre for Young Audiences, regional LORT tours, concerts, dance companies, variety shows, comics, bands, operas, and other entertainments. All of them tour with some version of a stage manager. The duties of a stage manager on tour vary slightly depending on the needs of the show. If you are doing a children's show, you may also be asked to drive a van or occasionally run the sound and light boards.

Stage managers on tours tend to progress from assistant stage manager to stage manager to production stage manager. It is important that each be able to cover for the others, so although it seems that there is a hierarchy, there is really interdependence. Often the PSM on a tour has toured extensively before and may even have the ability to request who will be hired for the other positions. Because all of the stage managers work so closely together, it's important for the team to get along and complement each other's skill sets.

SHOW BUSINESS AND URBAN DEVELOPMENT

I live in Appleton, WI, a town of about 75,000 in northeast Wisconsin, about 30 miles south of Green Bay. Twenty years ago, downtown Appleton was dying, a victim of the regional mall that had just opened a few miles out of town and a mayor who refused to run a bus service to it. But a local employer made a sizable donation to the city, and the Fox Cities Performing Arts Center opened in the Fall of 2002. Subsequently, more bars and restaurants opened on College Ave, and then, more coffee shops, boutiques, and additional businesses moved in. Today, downtown Appleton is a thriving vibrant place to live, eat, and play: development was instigated by having a theatre that hosts Broadway tours and other events in the heart of it!

The Broadway League estimates that for every dollar spent on a ticket for a touring Broadway show, another $3.50 is spent in the community on things like hotel rooms, restaurants, travel expenses, and shopping.[2] That infusion of cash helped keep the hotel open, which inspired new restaurants and bars, which led to pedestrian traffic returning to downtown and then new boutiques and offices. Appleton is not unique with this experience. Cleveland's renaissance also centers around Playhouse Square and other towns have had similar fortunes. Across the USA and Canada, touring Broadway has about the same effect as Broadway in NYC does: a multi-billion-dollar industry employing thousands of people and bringing joy to millions every year. It provides an intergenerational opportunity to make a lifetime memory.

As a stage manager, you represent the tour you are on and the understanding that you are in show *business* is vital to being successful. If the show stops making money, it will close and your job will end. The fact the job happens in a different city each week does not negate that it is a job with significant responsibilities. To the local crew, you are a guest in their "home." You've brought your "toys" to their house so ask for input on where to put things and how challenges have been addressed in that location in the past. The local crew wants you to feel welcome and have a great run, so they are eager to share the interesting things about their city. If you need something, ask; they'll help you find it. Do not get involved in local politics, but do not lower your standards, either. I'd love to say we're past the days of racial and sexual harassment, but it still occurs sometimes. Document and pass the information to the appropriate person. Neither you nor anyone in your company deserves to be mistreated.

PREPAREDNESS AND TOURING JOBS

If you do take a job on tour, you'll want to be well prepared. You will be away from home for months (or years) at a time, so you'll need to ensure your financial affairs are in order. Get Powers of Attorney for both your financial and heath affairs. Have the difficult conversations with your family about what you want to have happen if you die. Make a will. Yes, the odds are very slim, but it does happen and you don't want your family a thousand miles away trying to figure it out when they are mourning. Also, having a trusted someone who has the legal authority to handle your affairs back home will give you peace of mind. A subletter or house sitter can add income and keep your home secure.

Talk with your credit card holders to let them know when and where you will be traveling. Nothing is worse than being told a fraud hold has been put on your card because a charge was attempted in a city you haven't been in before. Sending an itinerary or letting them know where an online version of it can be found is helpful. Have two credit cards: one used primarily for your touring expenses, and one as a backup or for personal expenses. If your travels will be mostly flights, an airline branded credit card that earns points or frequent flyer miles can quickly pay for itself. It also helps with tracking expenses for taxes. Also, have a debit card for accessing cash on the road. I strongly recommend using the Actors Federal Credit Union as they understand the touring lifestyle and there are free ATMs for credit unions all over; most banks still want to charge a fee.

There are several firms that specialize in tax returns for touring folks. I declined to use one when they insisted they would put down the "industry averages, to lessen the chance of you being audited" as I wasn't willing to submit a return with numbers I know to be fraudulent. Instead, save all your receipts with detailed notes of what they are for and hire a competent tax pro to compile an accurate return which won't land you in trouble with the IRS. A single page scanning wand which then saves a digital receipt that you can annotate is a good investment. It can also be used to scan, fax, and email documents. Cloud storage and backup will save you if something happens to your computer.

YOU ARE THE ONLY PERSON IN THE WORLD WITH THIS JOB!

When I started touring, I was told, "You are the only person in the world with this job. You can't get sick and you can't get hurt." Of course, it's true that another person can be trained to do the job eventually, but you are a unique performer and others are relying on you to be there and do your job as close to perfect as you possibly can eight shows a week, so do all you can to keep yourself physically and mentally healthy. Before you go on tour, get a complete, thorough physical. Make certain your inoculations are current and you are in good health. There are people with diabetes and other chronic conditions who tour, but they have their condition very well managed. See your dentist for a thorough cleaning and get a full set of x-rays. Have your optometrist check your vision and update your prescription. See your chiropractor, gynecologist, etc. as well. As soon as you have your itinerary, make appointments with each of your health care providers for the next time you are home. Continuity of care helps you maintain your health when regular visits with the same providers aren't possible. Urgent care facilities are helpful in a pinch, but having a baseline back home that can be compared with is valuable—especially for things like EKGs and blood work. For minor things like an ear infection or pink eye, the online doc can save both time and money, though they are not yet available in all states. Have all of your medical records sent back home, so documentation of what has happened is kept in a central location.

Check with your health, dental, and vision insurance to make certain they will cover you outside of your local area. If you are going into another country, a short-term plan for that area may be a good investment, but even if you do have to pay cash, out-of-pocket costs are typically a lot lower than in the USA. If you are hurt while at work, it will be covered under workers' compensation, but you still need personal health insurance. If you see a therapist, see if you can continue to do so via teleconference. Try to get any prescription medications in a 90-day supply with another 30 days as a reserve at home so it can be over-nighted to you if needed. The National Health Directory from the Actors Fund can help you get info on medical personnel who have worked with touring performers.

The company may travel with a physical therapist. Find out what the procedure is for booking an appointment, realizing the cast usually has priority.

Get a passport. The known traveler schemes like CLEAR and TSA PreCheck are worth it as they save valuable time on travel days plus they may be reimbursed by your credit card company. Enroll in the frequent flyer and hotel points programs. You'll quickly have enough to be able to take a "free" vacation.

If you are on a larger tour, you may spend multiple weeks in the same place, so the ability to cook can be a plus. Many folks rely on Airbnb or similar companies to find lodgings. Executive rentals and hotel suites are other popular favorites as they provide more of the comforts of home than a standard hotel room. Or travel with an instapot, small cutting board, cutlery, and bowl to be able to cook anywhere.

Have a system for everything you do. Checklists are used in life-or-death situations because they minimize the chance for error even if you are exhausted. Pack your suitcase with the same things in the same way every time, so you'll always be at the same weight when you check in for your flight. Take at least two weeks' worth of shirts and underclothes, sturdy work pants/shorts and a few business-casual pieces. You'll want one dressy outfit for opening night receptions and other special events. Try to bring pieces that can have multiple uses. A lightweight robe can double as a swimsuit coverup or even a blanket. A three-in-one jacket where the outer layer is rain-repellant and the inner one is fleece can combine to keep you warm in winter weather. If you're doing one-nighters, flip-flops are a must for the shower; you don't want to bring a nasty infection along.

If you can get by with using hotel toiletries, that leaves more room in your suitcases for other things. Bring a couple of toothbrushes and combs so you can freshen up anytime. Have a small first aid kit including an assortment of bandages, antibiotic cream, anti-diarrheal/anti-gas, ibuprofen, cough drops, muscle ointment, and anything else you commonly need.

Invest in good luggage designed for frequent travelers; Travel Pro, Tumi, or Briggs & Riley are popular brands due to their durability and warranties. Yes, they are expensive, but they are well worth it. Briggs & Riley will ship replacement parts to you. A backpack that can lock and a Kensington lock for your computer are smart security purchases. Don't worry about wearing the same thing all the time, you're not in one place long enough for anyone to notice, and theatre folks won't care. A tool belt or fanny pack comes in handy, too.

The simple fact is touring is often a very physically and mentally stressful job and not everyone is up to the challenges it presents. There is no shame in saying "It's not for me." I first went on tour in my 40s and most of the crew were a decade or more younger than me. There are folks who have been on the road well into their 60s, so age isn't the deciding factor, but most folks "retire" from the road by their 40s. The best part of touring is the people you meet and then see again the next time your tour visits that city. When you leave the road, you have a network of friends all over and priceless memories.

NOTES

1. The performance report is the lifeline to those who are not on tour with you as well as insuring those who are on tour are all getting the same information. It is a simple form, designed to be read on a cell phone, that consists of a listing of any performers who

substituted, running time, attendance, and information about that performance. Fortunately, both of this Sunday's shows were uneventful, so the report is brief and quickly completed.

2. "Touring Broadway Facts," The Broadway League, 2019, accessed November 8, 2020, www.broadwayleague.com. The Economic Impact of Touring Broadway 2016–2017 and The Audience for Touring Broadway 2017–2018.

5

Running Away with Cirque du Soleil[1]

Alana Clapp

As a kid, I thought about running away to join the circus a few times. My parents took my best friend, Ben, and me to see Ringling Bros. and Barnum & Bailey Circus when it came to town and I loved the spectacle of it all. I remember one time we had the opportunity to enter the center ring before the show and try on costumes, take some pictures, and meet the clowns. To be honest, the clowns were my least favorite part (some aversion to them after spying on my babysitter watching Killer Klowns from Outer Space one night after I was put to bed). Years later, I find it somewhat amusing that I'm working with clowns on a regular basis, in a town with a whole hotel dedicated to them. Never in a million years would I have thought that what started as a hobby in playing around with some lights at the local theatre would one day transform into the wild, fun, challenging, and eventful career I have had as a stage manager for Cirque du Soleil (CdS). I have learned volumes since I first started with this company in 2009—lessons on how to work cross culturally with large groups of people, the limits and resiliency of the human body, how to manage some of the world's largest and technically complicated shows, all while having the ability to develop my management style along the way. During my time here, I have been fortunate to see this company grow from the days of founder Guy Laliberté to the entertainment group giant it has become, with its many acquisitions and expansive global portfolio. I'm humbled every time I walk into one of our theatres or tents, and I hope

DOI: 10.4324/9780429321672-7

that sharing some of my own experiences will perhaps spark some curiosity about what I call the "Circus of the Sun."

INTEGRATION, MAINTENANCE, AND REINTEGRATION

Cirque du Soleil Entertainment Group is a Canadian-based company that creates diverse theatrical circus experiences. Currently, CdS employs more than 4,000 people, including 1,300 artists, who originate from nearly 50 countries. On top of producing world-renowned shows, CdS also produces a large variety of entertainment forms such as multimedia productions, immersive experiences, theme parks, concerts, and special events. The Resident Shows Division (RSD), located in Las Vegas, Nevada, is responsible for, among others, the seven currently running productions at the various casinos' properties, one of which is my current show, *Mystère*, located inside the Treasure Island Hotel and Casino. *Mystère* was the first permanent CdS show in Las Vegas and is the company's longest running production since its premier in 1993. It has a cast of 78 artists, representing 18 different countries, 62 technicians, and a number of others on the artistic and operational staff. The stage management team is comprised of one general stage manager, two stage managers, one assistant stage manager, and one to two on-call assistant stage managers at any given time. The general stage manager, technical manager, and associate company manager make up the show operations trio, and are responsible for the daily operations of the production. We are managed by the senior trio—the senior company manager, senior artistic director, and senior operations production manager, who are responsible for the oversight and management of multiple shows in Las Vegas. This structure places the general stage manager in a unique position that could be most closely compared to a production stage manager. Responsibilities fluctuate mostly between artistic maintenance, artist management, and show operations daily, and often hourly. In addition to the operations teams, we work alongside a coaching staff responsible for the acrobatic elements of the show, as well as performance medicine team, which manages the health and rehabilitation requirements of our artists. Together we implement fully custom and specifically designed integration, maintenance, and reintegration processes and plans for each performer you see onstage. To help us do this, we use a computer program designed specifically for the company, called Aurora. This software helps us manage everything from the training programs of each artist, to the way we cast the show lineup, to sending out show reports nightly. It's essentially a one-stop shop for our show needs, and was designed by a former stage manager, who continues to look after its maintenance to this day. We release software updates to Aurora as our needs change, and it aids us in communicating with the various other departments at RSD and in Montréal.

The stage management operations of a show can be divided into two main parts, the preparation that takes place during the first half of the day, followed by running the two shows at night. We perform ten shows a week, which breaks down to two shows a day for five days. Each year we perform between 470 and 480 shows, and our year calendar has dark weeks built in to allow for larger technical projects and maintenance. It takes three stage managers to run a performance of *Mystère*—one calling stage manager, one backstage right, and one rover. During the days, our daily tasks are rotated weekly between the assistant stage manager and stage managers who move between running the daily trainings (rehearsals), casting the show with the creation of the nightly talent lineup, and scheduling/projects. Part of the way we keep things fresh for the team is by constantly rotating duties and show tracks. It can be challenging to keep teams engaged on long running shows, so weekly and daily rotations help prevent things from becoming stale while keeping task lists fresh. PR and press events are also a frequent part of our reality, which provides stage managers with their own set of perspective change and challenges.

POSITIVE RESOURCES AND OUTLETS

Cirque du Soleil productions are known for many things, not the least of which is their sheer scale. When I first started as an intern at O, this is what I found to be most intimidating initially. How did I end up here? I had never worked on anything remotely close to this size before. What made me qualified to work with this company? A million questions came, along with the self-doubt and fear of failure, classic imposter syndrome that I seemed to feel creep in with each new role I took on. When I called O for the first time, it was not lost on me that the last time I had called anything was *Grapes of Wrath* in college. All of a sudden, I was calling one of the company's biggest shows. Years later, once I became the general stage manager, I was the one managing and mentoring interns and now calling stage managers who were expressing the same insecurities I had felt at the beginning, and it forced me to see my own path of where I had started and how far I had come.

This was an important lesson for me: how perception can influence you at the beginning, and how you can work to manage your perception to be a positive resource and outlet for you. The same can be said for how perspective plays a role in your management style. When working on shows like ours, where the risk factor is of great prevalence, you learn quickly what is of immediate importance. Safety is always first and foremost, and is where your energy and effort must be placed from the beginning. When you must prioritize your tasks with safety at the forefront, you can sooner spot what really is "small stuff" and how not to sweat it. Stage managers, especially early into their careers, can be harshly self-critical after having made a mistake. "I didn't set the prop table right," "I forgot to do this report," etc. Although attention to detail and continuous improvement are always important, don't let it cloud your judgment in areas where something more serious, like an injury, can occur. The perspective of self-deprecation in minor moments rarely reflects the reality of the impact. I continue to work on letting things go, reserving my energy for issues that will require attention. The more practice you get with shows that challenge your perception and force you to re-evaluate your priorities, the more confidence you will build, and the kinder you will be to yourself and others when small, unintended mistakes happen that ultimately result in little consequence. I have learned not to focus too much on these happenings. Grow from your mistake, do your best not to make it again, and then let it go and focus your energy where it really matters.

A MATTER OF RESPECT

Perception and perspective come into play often when things don't go as planned. Running a perfect Cirque du Soleil show is not a challenge—the challenge comes in the contingency moments, and in the constant state of mental preparedness you must be in to deal with potential issues. When put into one of these situations, we must simultaneously work to get back on track while doing an assessment to make sure we are addressing the priorities in order. Although the perception might be that something is wrong, and we must get it fixed ASAP, we must first look at the bigger questions before immediately getting the show to move forward: Is anyone hurt? Is anyone in danger? Am I going to endanger someone if I move forward in this way? Once we sift through these points, we can continue to move down the priority list to ultimately resume on track. It's in these moments you are reminded about the amount of respect that is required for these types of shows—respect for the human body, respect for the technology, and respect for the specialists, both artistic and technical, who know their craft. As stage managers, we should know a little bit about a lot of things, but in a time of crisis or contingency, it becomes necessary that you rely on the ones who know more about the "broken thing" than you do. We prepare as best we can for what to do when things break. Sometimes it's little notes on the side of the call, other times it's full scripts that are on standby. It's important to think through as many scenarios as possible, come up with a plan for the ones that warrant them, and understand that you cannot possibly prepare for every random event. As an exercise, my team and I often discuss potential "what ifs" to keep the thought process fresh. On several occasions those plans we later used in a show situation.

I'm often asked what my favorite part of working for Cirque du Soleil is, and each time my answer is always the same: the people. When you work with this many cultures in one location, you learn more about the human condition then you thought possible. My favorite time of year is when the Olympics or World Cup comes on the TV. Sitting in a room full of people rooting for their own countries during an event or match is quite magical. I'm convinced that if world leaders came to spend a week with us and saw how our tiny community can function, global conflicts could be easily solved. As wonderful as they can be, managing people is also challenging, if for no other reason than that we are naturally emotional beings each with a different calibration for our range of emotions. When you add cultural differences into the mix, your challenges increase. Sometimes to ensure a successful conversation, it is necessary to tailor your delivery depending on the person's cultural background, however you must do this without compromising your integrity. Your integrity is key to being a successful manager, and there is a line between customizing the way you present information and treating others differently because of it. If you are working with someone who is from another country, making an effort to learn a word or phrase in their language can go a long way. You might also need to spend a period of time educating someone who is new on unexpected topics. Artists that come to CdS often come from a sports background and have very little knowledge of the entertainment world. Trying to explain what stage right/left or upstage/downstage means to someone who has never been on a stage before, who also doesn't speak the same language as you, can be an interesting process. Likewise, you might need to educate them on what your role as a stage manager is and how it relates to them. It's your responsibility to educate them if they don't know, but once that is done, they must be held to the same standard as everyone else. Managing creative people comes with its own rewards and challenges, and managing high level athletes can be the same—blending the two together is unique to CdS.

MANAGEMENT STYLE AND SERVICE

An early mentor of mine once gave me the objective to develop my "management style" during a workplace evaluation. It was the first time I had ever really thought of my management style as a definable attribute, but it instantly made perfect sense and has since become a working goal for every stage manager I hire. The sooner you are able to define your style, the clearer your motivations, and the structure you have defined for yourself will make your abilities to be a productive leader stand out to the rest of your team. For example, it is my strong belief that when managing creative and artistic individuals, you must do so from a place of empathy, while also maintaining your integrity, and so I am constantly working on ways to manage in this way. Knowing your style will also help you decide what types of people to surround yourself with to ensure the success of yourself, the team, and ultimately the show. Good leaders are self-aware, they know what their strengths and weaknesses are and are thus able to identify individuals and situations that will help them be successful and avoid the ones that won't. I've learned to pick people for your team that supplement your shortcomings and highlight your strengths. Do not be afraid to work with people who might be better at things then you. A responsible leader is open with their team. They give projects to set others up for success by identifying their interests and managing them in a way that is free of excessive overcite and micro direction. It's important to mentor when you can, and be open with those that aspire to reach the same goals as you. If I haven't taught others how to be successful at my job, then I haven't done it properly.

Ultimately, I have concluded that no matter my position, whether as an intern, ASM, SM, or GSM, to be a stage manager in any capacity is to be continually in service—in service of the show, of the individuals onstage and offstage, of your team, and so on. It therefore becomes increasingly important to set up those "giving" boundaries so you are able to replenish your reserve, and not allow others to take everything, preventing you from giving further. One of the most important tricks I have implemented for myself in the particularly draining moments is to sit in the house, amongst the audience, during my favorite moments of the show. The gasps and cheers remind me that we are so fortunate to have a job where we play a part in the entertainment of others. Yes, entertainment can sometimes be heavy, thought provoking, and sobering at times, but ultimately, we are part of an industry that provides an escape for others to explore a new reality and experience joy. It is for this reason we should also find joy in the work we do, although likely not all the time or perhaps every day, but definitely as a whole. If you are ever feeling in a rut, or are trying to inspire a disengaged artist or team member, have them swing out for the night to sit and watch the show with the audience. It immediately creates a feeling of pride in the work being done that can be sustaining for some time. Ten years later, it's that pride for the show, for the company, and for the colorful individuals that have entered my life that keeps me in the center ring still. Every job comes with its own set of challenging moments and uplifting rewards, but it is certainly a unique experience that's all its own to run away with Cirque du Soleil!

NOTE

1. For context, this essay was completed December 2019, pre-COVID closures. On June 28, 2021, *Mystère* reopened, Cirque's first Vegas production to do so.

6

Opera Stage Management 101

Erin Joy Swank

If you've stage managed plays and musical theatre, but have never stage managed an opera, many of the traditional opera practices can seem downright strange. "What do you mean, you call 'Places' for performers to get to the stage more than just the top of each act? You said the assistant stage managers cue them on for their entrances, too? Can't they pay attention and get there on their own? Why is everyone so concerned about the stage manager knowing how to read music? It all seems so high maintenance." These are just a few of the differences that pop up when comparing working in this genre to a traditional theatre setting. However, if you learn some of the reasons for the differences, it all starts to make a bit more sense.

THE MAIN STAR OF THE OPERA

First and foremost, the main star of an opera is the music itself. The genre has been around for hundreds of years; a large percentage of the works performed are the "old warhorses" with titles you've likely heard, including *La Traviata, Carmen, The Magic Flute, La bohème,* and *The Barber of Seville.* Even if you think you don't know opera music, it underscores some of your favorite commercials and cartoons, and inspired *Rent, Miss Saigon,* and Elton John and Tim Rice's *Aida,* among others.

DOI: 10.4324/9780429321672-8

An opera is just another version of a story set to music, performed in front of an audience, but in opera the music gets the most attention.

Opera also tends to have some of the biggest production requirements compared to some of the other genres. To fill out the music, you need orchestra musicians in addition to the singer. Unlike modern musicals that are often stripped to a piano and a handful of other instruments—or a synthesizer made to sound like multiple instruments—operas tend to use a full lush orchestra of dozens of musicians. When there's a group village scene, you want it to sound like the entire town has come out to check out the activity, too. Now you've added more than a handful of chorus members. Those chorus members all need at least one set of costumes, and they're probably carrying a few props throughout to make the scene more realistic. Likely, all of this isn't happening on a unit set in one location, so we've now added in a whole bunch of technical staff to make it all happen. That's a lot of extra personnel. You don't want all those extra people sitting around being paid but not utilized, so the rehearsals are divided up for max efficiency. As a result, the creative process for an opera can often be quite piecemeal; the stage managers are the ones who help pull all the puzzle pieces together.

Back to the music—it is the highest priority in opera, so the singers start preparing on their own as early as possible. While I hate the phrase "industry standard"—as there are usually multiple ways to do anything we do—it really is quite usual that singers are expected to fully know their music before rehearsals start. In the union theatre world, some Actors' Equity Association contracts state that actors are to be paid additional money if they are asked to be memorized in advance. You may spend three or more days of the musical theatre rehearsal process hashing out all of the music and teaching parts. This is not so for opera. The first day of rehearsal may be a sing-through of the **principals'** music (the lead characters' numbers, whether solos/arias, duets, or quintets), primarily to agree on what tempo (plural: *tempi*) will be used, and where breaths may or may not be taken. Many of the performers have likely already done the role several times, so it becomes more "plug and play" to fit the parts together, and see where any variations lie between the singers and the **maestro** (conductor). After that, the staging rehearsals begin. The **stage director**[1] will decide who is moving when and where, but always with an eye towards whether something is physically possible to do and still have the music produced by the performer. There is a perception (not always accurate) that opera singers stand and face straight downstage and perform while standing perfectly straight up and down. Some of this is due to logistics—for the most part, opera singers do not wear microphones. They're also singing over an orchestra of perhaps 30 musicians. If you want the audience to hear them, depending on a theatre's acoustics, they're going to have to face front, or at least angled that way, a majority of the time. Opera is also an older art form, perhaps more stylized as the theatre of earlier days was also quite stylized. There's been a trend towards more realistic acting, but ultimately, opera still has some vocal production logistics that require more front-facing action.

I've found that when I'm rehearsing a musical, the director has the final say quite a bit. After a rehearsal run-through, the cast sits around and is given notes. As a stage manager, sometimes I need to make sure the music director is not forgotten and is given a chance to give their handful of notes. In opera, however, the maestro is highly included in an opera rehearsal…most of the time. There are a few companies who don't have the maestro come in until closer to tech, but the process goes much better if he or she is involved from the very beginning. It's already a short process, and if we don't have to re-stage due to differences in the music, it's better for everyone.

ANOTHER DIFFERENCE: THE SCHEDULE

This brings us to the other main difference in opera—the schedule. As mentioned earlier, there are a lot of personnel involved. Producers don't want to call in all of those people (and pay for their time) any more than is required. Also, the singers can only be called upon to sing for so long—without using microphones—before their voices are strained. Schedules are arranged to maximize the best use of vocal production, bodies for staging, and logistics of paying for all of it. Chorus members are often only called for two or three days a week, usually on weeknights or weekends, scheduling around other jobs. (Wednesday nights are often out, too, as many have paid "church gigs" that occur those evenings.)

The principal performers' hours are a bit more open, but need to be limited due to vocal strain. A frequent standard—yes, I hate to call out any kind of standard—is to have rehearsal "chunks" that are three hours long, which could be a morning, afternoon, or evening session. A principal may be called for two of those chunks, totaling six hours, and the chorus could take another one. This means stage managers, the stage director, and the maestro may work nine hours of rehearsal, utilizing the time as much as possible. (Much of this schedule is also determined long before the stage manager is ever on contract, at least as to who can be called each day.) All of the performers may be called at different times, so stage management is also filling in for anyone else missing onstage, keeping track of who comes in when, and any crucial prop or scenic moves.

One of my favorite examples involves a stereotypical drinking scene in an opera. A **supernumerary** (non-singing extra, also referred to as **super**) may enter the scene with a tray of champagne glasses. A chorus member (the group term is often shortened to **coro**) will take two glasses from that tray, keeping one for him or herself, and presenting the other to the **principal** (lead) of the scene. The principal then gives a toast for all. At any given rehearsal two of those people may be missing, due to scheduling limitations. An assistant stage manager will be ready during the rehearsal to fill in wherever needed so that rehearsal can go on, as well as cue every move if needed. (The supers are rarely given any music, for example.) Other than this kind of blocking—involving the use of props, costumes, or critical staging between groups of people—stage management is generally *less* involved in recording the **blocking** (stage movement) in opera.

Larger opera companies will utilize an assistant director, who records all blocking and helps advise the chorus and supers. Stage management may not need to record any of the blocking, but since I started in the other genres, it's still in my nature to take things down. I focus more on entrances, exits, and big group moves, as my lighting cues and paperwork are most affected by these, but I worry less about getting every hand move and gesture, or the directing. It can actually be a bit freeing if you give in to this opera standard, while you're concentrating on all of the technical aspects and tracking people on and offstage.

THE FINAL ROOM RUN

All of the performers may not make it into the room together until the **final room run**, the very last rehearsal before moving to the stage. By this point, a chorus member hopefully remembers that they exit stage right for the first scene, and need to re-enter stage left for the second…but they don't have a clear perception of how much time elapses in between. They probably were not given the music to the scenes they're not in either, and, as mentioned, the supers likely weren't given any music at all. Stage management, once again, are the ones who help keep everyone understanding what is happening next and pulling it all together. Putting all of these puzzle pieces together requires paperwork—a lot of it. Opera paperwork is some of the most detailed that I have seen in our industry, and can be truly awesome. It also means you have to start working on it as early in the process as possible. Since the music is so integral to everything, that's where I usually start. During pre-production, I find out which recording (assuming there is one) is most preferred by the maestro, which edition/translation of the score we are using (obtaining a reduced piano/vocal score), and if there are any known cuts we are taking in the music. I then sit with my stopwatch and the recording, taking timings every 15 seconds and recording the location in the music.[2] The major piece of opera paperwork is the **Who/What/Where**—a document in table form listing everything that happens during a performance, particularly every performer's entrance or exit, and what they're wearing or carrying. If you can start this during pre-production, you'll be so much better off, but there's only so much you can do until rehearsals start. Every rehearsal, you'll want to take notes of the exact beat that an entrance happens, usually cued by an assistant stage manager. In the paperwork, it is recorded with one column of the rough timing into that act (taken from your timings with the recording), as well as the **placement**. An example of placement might be 20/2/3/4, which would translate as page 20, the second **system** (line) of music, in the third measure, on the fourth beat. An assistant stage manager would place a marking in their script (often using a small Post-it® or sticker) notating exactly which beat they should use to cue the entrance. Having them adjustable is quite important in the squished time frame you're going to have later for tech. You know how having the masking curtains in a theatre will suddenly change all entrance times for a play or musical, taking longer for the performers to make it to their onstage marks? The same thing can happen in opera, but there's no time to go back and learn the timing. An assistant stage manager will simply be told, "Move the super/coro entrance back two measures." The sticker is moved, and that's how it's cued the next time around. No one needs to know exactly what that earlier music sounds like (which they may or may not have been given anyway), and the performers keep their same speed of walking, it's just moved earlier. It can take a village of stage management team members to create this paperwork, so it's helpful to put it on a cloud-based server so that each can input their side of the stage or department.

THE TEAM AND THE PROCESS

As for the stage management team, opera is one time where you often get to work with multiple stage managers on the same project and not feel quite so alone. It is typical to have at least three running an opera—the production stage manager (PSM) calling the show typically from the side of the stage, plus one assistant stage manager (ASM) on each side of the stage. It is also standard to have one ASM be the costume liaison and for the other to focus on props. The scenic elements may fall to the PSM, or to an ASM, depending on the show's needs. This breakdown of duties is similar in theory to a play or musical, but is often much more involved in an opera. The costume ASM may be asked to attend all costume fittings to take notes, and prepares additional paperwork of first entrances for each performer (the first time they are seen for each act, so that call times can be adjusted appropriately), and the wardrobe presets and running documents. The props ASM focuses on the tracking for the props, creating those running sheets. Both need to know what happens on their own side of the stage, but one of them is each the primary liaison for their department, helping fill the other in on any details. Each run sheet is then often more detailed than the crew paperwork for other genres. Many more preset diagrams and photos are usually included, to save time explaining during the crunched tech process, as well as those ever-present timings and placements. Keep in mind, though, that while there is a lot of paperwork to create, many times you do not have to start from scratch. Because of the nature of the genre, productions are frequently remounted and have paperwork attached from previous incarnations. Additionally, while not every production of *Traviata* is staged exactly the same, there is a strong chance that the group entrances will take place at roughly the same place in the show—certainly for the same scene order to occur—so you can start from some pre-written base paperwork if you obtain it.

Rehearsals are held with piano as the only instrument as much possible. Orchestra time is so expensive that musicians are not called to join in until everything else is nearly ready, and then those are run so as to not incur overtime. One dedicated rehearsal is set aside for putting the singers together with the orchestra for the first time. It is usually a **sitzprobe** (German for "sitting rehearsal"), with everyone seated with instrument stands—or perhaps the singers standing for their individual sections. This rehearsal may even take place off-site from the regular performance or rehearsal locations due to the space needed. On occasion, a **wandelprobe** is scheduled instead, with the singers onstage and the musicians in the orchestra pit. Stage management may have the crew set up for a single set look onstage, so that a rough idea of acoustic placement can be perceived, but this performance is focused on the music and acoustic needs, rather than any other technical or performance aspect. This rehearsal is great for stage management, as no one is moving around using props and costume pieces—and it's even less work if they're all just sitting and not wandering around, and you don't have to prep the next group. The time can be used for you to familiarize yourself with the music, too, including making notes of which instrument is really playing versus the piano you've heard for all of rehearsal. Because it's so important to protect the voice, much of tech you may not actually hear the singing any more. The performers will likely **mark** the singing— which has probably occurred during staging rehearsals too, but even more is about to occur. High notes may be sung down an octave, or they may only mouth the words. This is why it is even more important for an opera stage manager to be able to read music.[3] You can also call on your fellow stage managers and ask over headset, "Can I get a placement, please?" if you've been pulled away.[4]

For tech, there is no time to create the lighting looks while the performers are standing there, so additional light cueing sessions are held, usually in the morning or daytime. Rehearsals now lean towards the evening, in chunks when everyone including chorus can be present. **Lightwalkers** will be placed onstage, whether they are stage management staff or volunteers, with the assistant director or production stage manager telling them where to stand while the lights are adjusted. The PSM then starts putting together the call script; you'll only get a few chances to call the cues before opening—and there won't be any finessing it in real time with the performers. After the sitzprobe/wandelprobe, you'll probably have one or two evening piano dress rehearsals to pull all of the technical elements together. You'll then get just one or two orchestra rehearsals—in full costume—before opening. This is also when your Places calls become crucial. Remember that the performers are off between scenes in the dressing room or makeup room, changing for the next look and discussing pieces with the dressers. The singers onstage are likely marking and can't be heard, and opera is often repetitive and in a foreign language. The chorus and supers probably haven't heard that music before anyway, to know where we are in the show. Over the paging system, roughly five minutes before their entrance (depending on the venue), they hear a clear voice saying, "This is a Places call for Mr. Smith & Ms. Jones, please. Places for Mr. Smith & Ms. Jones,[5]" to know when they should start heading to the stage. The assistant stage managers will have an additional script marking for two minutes prior to each entrance, and may ask for a re-page if they don't have the person in sight yet.

A BEAUTIFUL FINISHED PUZZLE

With the compressed timeline, it may seem suddenly strange to get more free time the closer you get to opening, and throughout performances. It is typical to have days off between performances to rest the voice…including before opening. One of your longest nights in theatre may be the night before opening, trying to get everything just right; in an opera, you may actually get the day off! You might have Thursday off for a Friday opening, and then Saturday off again before a Sunday performance. After all that work organizing it, this can be an awesome perk of working in opera, using the time to rest or reorganize your book and paperwork. Another really odd thing? In smaller companies, that Sunday performance may also be your closing night. All of that work is done for just two performances, and then you're on to the next job.

If you have the stage management skills to be adaptable at a quick pace on a large technical show, and have a strong musical background, you can transition into opera (I recommend trying it when you're younger, before you're pigeon-holed into a genre, however). With the short nature of the contract, you might also be able to fit in quite a few opera gigs in a year, including in the gaps between longer productions. It can be hectic being an opera stage manager, but you definitely end up with a sense of accomplishment when you pull it all off, creating a beautiful finished puzzle.

NOTES

1. In opera, the title used is stage director, rather than simply director.

2. I love using colored erasable pens for the timings, to pop off the page a little bit. Some stage managers time only every 30 seconds. I attempt to get them every 15 seconds, so if I miss one, it's easier to go back and fill in the ones missed. If I'm using a video, I'll also list what timing in the video each piece starts, for my own reference, should I get really off or need to take a break. Additionally, these timings may often remain quite true throughout the run, as musical timings rarely change. Think about a tap dance number in a musical—you want the timing to remain consistent so that the steps remain the same. The daily running time may vary depending upon dialogue scenes and audience reaction (laughing, clapping, etc.), but music remains pretty consistent. I try to get additional timings during the first sing-through, individual scene runs, and final runs if possible, but often those preliminary timings remain fairly accurate.

3. It's highly likely an opera is written and performed in another language besides English. You don't need to know the language if you call from the music. It can be quite handy to get a translation, however. Even if the words are printed as optional lyrics in your score, know that it's likely a singable translation and not word for word. If you learn the word "*Andiam!*", you'll realize your principal may be about to head for the exit, and you probably have a light cue to match his or her movement.

4. My blog at www.erinjoyswank.com includes several tips of how to highlight your score to help you keep track, too, if you are pulled away. I highly recommend color-coding between characters.

5. In the past, opera has been very formal, using last names and a gender salutation, or "The Chorus." Character names or group names may be substituted, but many stage managers are adjusting their language to be more gender-inclusive. Depending on your needs, a location of stage left or right may also be useful. Wardrobe changes or scene shifts may also be paged in advance.

7

Off Headset at Sea

Charlotte Sachetti

"Miss Char-LOT?"

My DECT phone, a small brick-like piece of technology you must carry as a reminder you're always at work, wakes me at 7 a.m. on a Saturday morning.

"Yes?"

I clear my throat, pretending I've been awake for minutes rather than seconds.

"Miss Char-LOT, this is Arnel from the deck department. Miss Char-LOT, the pool is overflo... ." He breaks up. " ... you come to the theatre?"

"The pool is what? Never mind. I'll be right there."

Outside the porthole, my 18-inch, washing-machine-like window on the world, I see the sun shining with not a cloud in the blue, southern Florida sky. I'm eye-level with growling forklifts moving to and from, banging hundreds of heavy luggage carts and a mind-boggling parade of pallets: 2,200 bottles of wine, 86,000 eggs, countless crates of pineapple, 8,000 gallons of ice cream, all bound for the ship's kitchens. And somewhere amid all those consumables may be a piece of an

DOI: 10.4324/9780429321672-9

engine or an air conditioning unit, or maybe that Mac 2000 we sent off for repair three months ago. The pier is a stage for a mechanized ballet; to the untrained eye, chaos, but to those who know the planning and preparation that goes into it, a thing of organizational beauty.

I wash my face in my cabin's tiny bathroom, just large enough to "take care of business, shower, and shave" all at the same time (which, after three years at sea, has left me with a quirk: I pace the room while brushing my teeth because standing still in a space that small makes even this non-claustrophobic nervous).

I put on my uniform—black board shorts, a black polo, and slip-resistant sneakers—and begin my 12-minute commute from deck 2 starboard side forward to deck 6 aft: my workplace, the Aqua Theatre, the first of its kind, an outdoor aquatic amphitheater at sea. Located at the stern of the ship, the Aqua Theatre is a huge open space, the back of the house starting on deck 6 with raked seating plunging to the stage surface on deck 4.5 and the dressing rooms and pump rooms on deck 3. With control booths towering above two rock climbing walls on deck 12, the theatre is ginormous and the open-air views off the back of the ship are beyond compare.

I crest the back of the house and look down to Arnel, standing in the second row of seats looking perplexed at the pool, which is closed to guests. A porous, rubber stage surface allows three giant lifts below to travel seamlessly through the water without displacing any, creating pools of varying depths from a few inches for splashing to 15 feet for high diving. When not in show or rehearsal, the pool looks like a flat, blue bean stage surface spanning the width of the ship. Hidden diving boards, trampolines, fountains, and aerial equipment are tucked away from view; below the stage floor, the pool rests tranquilly until showtime. Except for this morning. Our normally peaceful giant gurgles and spills into the front row of seats (don't worry, they're made to get wet). It looks like someone left the bathtub water running for hours! With a pool this size, we're looking at a lot of water. Arnel waves me into the splash zone.

"What's happening?" I ask.

"Something's wrong with the pumps," He shrugs.

I studied stage management in college. I know my stage lefts from my stage rights; have a speedy code for blocking books that would be the envy of a court reporter, and I can say GO with such confidence you'd never know I'm wondering: "Did I land that on the AND of 7 or was that more on the 8?" But I don't know squat about pools or pumps, nor did I study the physics of how 135,000 gallons of water sloshing around in a tank affects the distribution of weight and list of a ship that's nearly a quarter-mile long. So, I'm at a loss as to what must be done to make this giant pool stop spilling hundreds of those gallons into the front row drains.

"Have you called the chief engineer or staff captain yet?" I ask, running through my mental marine Rolodex (a rotating file device used to store business contact information).

At this point in my career at sea, I've been a stage manager on five different ships in a fleet ranging in sizes from an 800-seat to a 1,300-seat proscenium-style Broadway house. Our show features two performances nightly; our cast of 26 singers, dancers, and acrobats and our crew of 16 technicians rarely need to interact with anyone outside of the Entertainment department. We are the department that puts the glitz and fun in these floating cities. We don't affect the propulsion or whether the ship will dock on time in Cozumel tomorrow. In fact, apart from a technician forgetting to call in the hazers, I could go whole contracts without calling the bridge at all.

But the Aqua Theatre is a venue like no other I've ever worked in; it gives new meaning to "all hands on deck." The pool is maintained by the deck department; the operation of the hydraulic lifts is the responsibility of the engine department; fountains and lighting are a joint project involving our own lighting technicians and the electrical department; and the safety and success of the show is a collaboration between myself and the navigation team on the bridge. Before each show, phone calls are made between the cruise director, who's the head of all entertainment, the stage manager (me), and the officers on the bridge as we work to position the ship in the smoothest waters while still continuing towards our next port; the goal is to keep the water in the pool stable for our divers and acrobats to safely do what they do while delivering the best show possible for our guests. It is no small feat.

"Let me just give Staff Captain a heads-up."

He's going to want to know that an excessive amount of gray water is being dumped into the drains while we aren't in show and we're sitting alongside the dock. A brief phone call later, I report back to Arnel.

"Staff Captain is on his way up. He says they are monitoring water levels in the ECR [engine control room]. I'm going to check out what's been happening backstage."

I slip past the blue curtains and down the metal staircase that runs back to the theatrical electrical lockers, SCUBA tank rooms, costume storage, and dressing rooms. Half-expecting to see a cascading waterfall into the backstage area, I'm relieved to find only two synchro-girls dancing to their music in their dressing room as they wait for laundry to finish. The humidity and thick scent of chlorine blankets the backstage, giving it a locker-room feel with a bunch of funny-looking buoyant props strewn about.

"Any extra water back here this morning?" I ask the ladies.

We giggle. The backstage is never dry; wet costumes, wet props, wet scuba gear, wet bodies are a constant.

"Just the yoozh!" they smile.

I continue on my way, popping my head into the trap room, which contains the automated trampoline and controls for the rest of the automation. I find only humidity and no puddles. Thank goodness. My mind starts rolling ahead to this evening. It's coming up on 8:30 a.m. Within the hour, the ship will be clear of last week's guests, giving the crew two hours to prep and reset for embarkation at 11 a.m. with a new ship full of excited guests. If any unsightly repairs need to be made in guest view, this is our window. Thinking even further ahead, having TOO much water in the pool isn't necessarily a problem for the show. Some modifications to some tumbling tracks or hand balancing may be necessary, but we can determine that in warm-ups. I make a mental note to call the acrobatic captain this afternoon; he's probably ashore now anyway hunting for things you land-dwellers take for granted, like Wi-Fi and a Target.

With the right partners working on a solution, no immediate damage visible, and a plan in place for contingencies, I make my way to my control booth/office to make my next phone call ... the boss, our cruise director.

"Morning, Richard. So here's the scoop ... "

I brief him on this morning's discoveries and promise to keep him updated if anything more dramatic happens that would affect embarkation or tonight's shows.

"You got it! Ciao! Ciao!"

Neither Richard nor I are from Italy, but when you join a ship's crew you join a global community, picking up slang and sayings dropped into everyday life. Hello is Hola. Friends are mates. Bathrooms are washrooms. Trash is rubbish. And good-bye is Ciao or Tchuss. We become a rich mix of backgrounds and cultures, all learning to collaborate and thrive in whatever situations the day serves up.

Headset conversations are a fun learning experience as we navigate the vagaries of planetary communication. "No" and "Go" sound quite similar, depending on the accent. Twice I've had to declare a "no Afrikaans on headset rule"; it's a beautiful language, but not helpful to a multinational team in the heat of a trouble-shooting moment. I've also acquired a colorful vocabulary of, shall we say, "words of frustration" with which to vent when things go haywire. We are sailors after all; we speak the part.

Working in the Aqua Theatre adds yet another level of challenge to communication. Two technicians are on underwater com and all of the headset chatter and show tracks are broadcast into underwater speakers for the performers. Neither underwater communication device turns off during the show, and I will forever hear the pattern of those techs inhaling and exhaling in my ear. When they would stop breathing to sneeze or swallow, my heart would skip a beat until I heard them resume their cadence.

Talking to an underwater international team forced me to become efficient and clear in my communication. Calls need to be short, succinct, and repeatable. Every call is repeated three times into the underwater speakers, a code enforced by the venue's safety experts who taught us that your brain hears someone is talking during the first call, listens on the second call, and confirms the message on the third call. It's an interesting communication fact that I've carried with me throughout my stage management career, and is applicable in hard-to-hear environments or when interrupting performers on in ear monitors (IEMs).

Having brought my cruise director into the sloshing loop, my focus turns to the daily battle with my email inbox: show reports, training schedules, cruise details, and recaps pour in faster than the water is pouring out of our pool. I sail through them and turn my attention to setting up the next week for success. With the future unknown, I always try to do as much work up front as possible, clearing the decks, so to speak, to cope with any changes or incoming chaos. As the venue owner of the Aqua Theatre, I'm responsible not only for the care and keep of the shows, cast and crew, but for all of the maintenance reports that auto-populate with pre-determined regularity in our maintenance system. I print, highlight, and organize the reports into each head-of-department's folder and mailbox. I have every stage manager's lust for office supplies; stranded on a floating island for months, I obsessively hoard pads of sticky notes and label maker tape (ten years later and now mostly on land, I still haven't shaken that quirk).

Wrapping up my weekly paperwork prep, I log onto my personal email. No matter where in the world, no matter the venue, always remember to write home. I'm pretty sure my grandmother thinks I'm still tap dancing on stage, but sharing glimpses of this strange at-sea reality with my family makes this fantastical life of travel much more real.

Gazing out at the panoramic views from my office (remember, I'm 12 decks up in the office/control booth looking off the back of the ship), I daydream of a life on land, of coming home to my own kitchen, my own couch, my own spacious bathroom. But then again, I get to wake up in a different country every morning; I get to call amazing shows nightly with amazingly talented artists; and I get to travel the world with some of my closest friends and colleagues. Sure, every once in a while a storm hits (literally), the grilled chicken and pasta in the mess can get monotonous, or, you know, a ginormous pool starts slopping out water for no apparent reason. Still, in that moment, I wouldn't trade this life for anything.

Speaking of, I turn my gaze down to our stage and see there's a gathering of white shirts with stripes congregating in the splash zone. I grab my DECT phone and sunglasses and head back down six decks to join them. Arnel smiles as I approach.

"Morning, gentlemen!"

I greet the staff captain, chief engineer, second engineer, and a collection of other assistants.

"What's the update?"

The chief engineer briefs us on the problem with the pumps and the correlating effects: depletion of the fresh-water holding tank and excess in the gray-water holding tank (which can't be dumped until we're 12 nautical miles out at sea.

Don't worry, it's filtered prior to dumping.) The engineers have the part to fix the one that failed. The right people are on it. We just have less spare water for the next day. "Shower with a friend," Chief chuckles in his thick Nordic accent.

I text the boss, "Good for shows tonight. Getting off the ship," as I head back to my cabin to change into civilian clothes and go hunting on land for luxuries: a bagel and Wi-Fi. In a few hours, I'll be back on board, refreshed and restarted for the cruise ahead. Another wave of guests will have embarked with expectations of spectacular. We will deliver.

As we back out of port that afternoon, I wave at the people along the shoreline from the balcony outside my booth before slipping inside to start that evening's presets and cast warm-ups. Two of the high-divers are working on perfecting a new dive from the ten-meter platform. When one of them lands wonky, the Aqua captain jokes:

"Hey! Try to keep the water IN the pool!"

We all laugh, myself just a little bit harder.

With everyone and everything, including the ship herself, in "Places," we stand by for the top of show. As the cruise director hypes the audience with his pre-show announcements, I complete headset roll call (including a final check-in with the bridge navigational officer), I take a few seconds to gaze beyond the theatre to the deep blue ocean behind us and reflect. No matter the venue, no matter where in the world, and no matter the problem, it's the relationships we build and the care we take to nurture them that enables us to cope with any challenge. I am no expert on pool pumps or physics, but I've learned whom to call, and when and how to ask for help.

The cruise director wraps up his opening with a warning to those sitting in the splash zone, then tosses the show back to me. Tracks roll, lights and video fade as we all stand by:

"Lifts are moving…Lifts are moving…Lifts are moving."

8

A Mutualistic Symbiotic Model

Stage Manager and Designers' Strong Ties and Participative Intentions

Rafael Jaen

Early in my career, a mentor advised me that designers and stage managers thrive in symbiotic professional relations. Hence, the best thing I could do is consider them my best friend in each production.

Fresh out of NYU's Tisch School of the Arts, while completing my first professional experiences, I realized the meaning of the specific reciprocity implicit in such a suggestion. Successful collaborations between theatre designers and stage managers consist of interactions with both parties benefitting throughout the production process. Such is the definition of a mutualistic symbiotic relationship; two "organisms of different species working together; each benefiting from the relationship."[1]

One of the stage manager's critical jobs is to help realize the full design for a show on the stage; they are the filter that all the knowledge of the production passes through, in one way or another. They take that knowledge and synthesize it into easily communicated ideas. During rehearsals, tech, and run of shows, the process demands will vary. At times benefits may seem one-sided yet leaving the other unaffected to reap gains at a different moment. By acknowledging each other, appreciating each job's work scope, and asking timely (design) questions, the gains spread around. This fact still holds today 30-plus years later, when meeting and working with new stage managers that are a lot younger than me!

DOI: 10.4324/9780429321672-10

ACKNOWLEDGING: SEEING, LISTENING, AND RESPECTING ALL PARTIES

As a designer splitting my time working in Regional Equity houses and academic theatre, I have always been mindful of each situation's particulars when collaborating with stage managers. Through the years, sometimes I have been the mentor in those situations, and other times the mentee learning new ways to approach the process.

In 2019, I had the privilege of working with Stage Manager Madeline Hartrich[2] at UMass Boston's Performing Arts; the department hired her for the season. While handling costume rehearsal pieces—tracking shoes, quick-change garments, and real show accessories nightly, she reminded me that stage managers support every person on the production team without taking sides and listen to every story and opinion without judgment. "One of our main jobs," Hartrich says:

> is trying to see problems before they occur and warn the appropriate people ahead of time. Many times, we can see these possible issues because we are privy to what all of the design aspects are, so if a dress has too large of a hoop skirt to fit through a standard size door frame, we can call it and nip the problem in the bud before it becomes any real issue.

In the designer/stage manager/actor triangle, a thriving theater collaboration also means that all parties feel seen, heard, and respected. Hartrich achieves this goal by making a point to verbally thank the people she works with in front of others, the design-tech folks, and the assistant stage manager (ASM) crew, in particular, which helps foster an environment of recognition. One of her proudest moments, while working at UMass Boston, she said:

> was hearing the actors complement their wardrobe crew on a speedy costume quick-change that had been giving us issues and seeing the crew's faces light up. They had all worked so hard together, drilling the change to make sure they would be able to complete it in the time prescribed by the music and set change.

Recognizing that collaboration is the foundation that good theatre is built upon is imperative to creating good art—especially when design, technology, and management crafts blend together (e.g., are canes a costume, a prop, or a choreographic piece?). The final product is an immutable melding of all facets working together.

"Tech is my personal favorite time in production of a show," says Hartrich; collaborations heighten, and "while it is a high-stress time for everyone involved, I get to see all of the different pieces and designs coming together." During college, while working on one of the largest productions, she was worried about calling the song "Going Up," from *Man of No Importance*. The lighting cues during that number were the heaviest she had ever called, and most were back-to-back, meaning there was no time to say "LX 358 GO" let alone "LX GO." She had to devise with the lighting designer how to make some cues "auto-follow." Basically, a cue set to auto-follow will trigger the next cue after it (the initial cue) has completed. For example, let's say there are two cues, cue "X" and cue "Y," and "X" has a duration of three seconds. If it is set to auto-follow, when cue "X" is a GO, cue "Y" will start automatically after the three seconds. During tech, Hartrich worked the number multiple times until she was able to call all 200+ cues properly. Everyone in the room was patient and supportive throughout the process, and the far more seasoned lighting designer did not shame her inexperience. "This experience," she says, "greatly built my confidence, and has been integral to how I approach working with others." The mantra in her program was "Don't hate, educate," meaning not shaming someone for their lack of knowledge, but instead doing one's best to show them how something works while assessing the needs of a situation.

We all agree that maintaining a clear head in this industry's high-stress environment is imperative to avoid burnout. Hartrich's teaching point is that successful collaboration requires emotional self-regulation; "controlling one's behavior, emotions, and thoughts in the pursuit of long-term goals."[3] Thus, she became my mentor during times of high stress. Keeping a positive attitude while finding solutions to problems is essential to facilitate communication. No matter a folk's capacity in a production, emotional calmness, breathing, and listening allows all parties to feel seen, heard, and respected. Taking a moment to breathe and listen before reacting and responding to any situation driving up your feelings is always beneficial.

MENTORING: THE "HUB" OF THE PRODUCTION WHEEL

In 1991, I became acquainted with *The Back Stage Guide to Stage Management: Traditional and New Methods for Running a Show from First Rehearsal to Last Performance* by Thomas A. Kelly.[4] Considered the godfather of modern stage management, his teaching reminds us that a successful stage manager can weather the ensuing stress and tension around them during the production process by never partaking too directly in any chaos. They need to keep their heads above water, never whipping others into a frenzy. Every individual in a company can feel the tremors of a high-strung or out-of-control stage manager. The reverberations such an issue can cause always translate into lasting trouble for a production.

While I have used Kelly's textbook to learn myself and mentor students, I have never worked in a professional setting where a collaborator has directly acknowledged its influence. This fact changed in 2014 when I met multi-hyphenate (designer–stage manager–production manager), John Traub.[5] He had the distinct pleasure of working with Tom Kelly and has modeled his approach after him. The latter "was calm, collected, friendly, knowledgeable, and completely unflappable, even during the moments when the show was crashing down around everyone," according to Traub. "Tom kept the communication lines open and ensured that every team member had the tools they needed to succeed." As a result, designers felt full support, and the stage management (SM) team felt full connection to every other department, including the performers.

Kelly's teachings and Traub's approach are psychological-minded and propose that streamlined communication ensures that everyone can present their best work possible, including the design-technology team. They promote emotional intelligence[6] (something I subscribe to), facilitating process awareness, emotional self-control, and informed and empathetic interpersonal relationships. Above all, designers must implicitly trust and have confidence that the stage manager will be faithful to their work long after they have moved on. Equally, the stage manager must have the conviction that the designers have created the best framework possible that allows the occupants to inhabit their world in every performance fully.

Traub also believes that "Stage Managers are the 'hub' of the wheel on every production. Everything flows into and through them, including (and especially) the critical work of the design team." Just like the literal hub makes a wheel turn, a good stage manager ensures the production runs smoothly and in the right direction. "The mark of a great manager – stage, production or otherwise," he says, "is to try to get as much 'Art' on the stage, as safely and efficiently as possible!" I have seen this happen in small and large shows. A detailed rehearsal report can aid the placement of furniture and props. A timely question about available rehearsal pieces during a meeting will help the show's blocking. Scheduling the essential rehearsals (costume quick-changes, scenery changes, fight choreography with props rehearsals, etc.) ensures all concerned parties are present and keeps tech-rehearsal surprises to a minimum.

He firmly believes that to get the tools they need to succeed, it is in the stage manager's best interest to work in at least one of the design fields (and vice versa!) before fully committing to their craft. That's why we get along so well! Theatre artists who have worked in related disciplines bring an understanding and empathy for the work of those fields, and at the very least, know the lingo when interacting with experts in those areas. "This translates to immeasurable benefits for the work behind the scenes and onstage," Traub says, adding that while he often heard the refrain: "Stage managers and designers exist in two different worlds, and never the twain shall meet," early in his career, he quickly learned that such sentences couldn't be further from the truth. As each area is vital to, and couldn't exist without, the other, he concluded that "the term 'collaboration' commonly used (and sometimes abused) to describe a hypothetical ideal, is an archetype that cuts to the point of an exceptional production process."

Finally, Traub reminds us that we must learn from watching experts at work throughout our careers. We need to get the guidance and "the occasional swift kick" of many superlative theatre practitioners over the years. "The incredible thing," he says, "is that virtually everyone in this industry probably has a similar story of a mentor who has provided guidance, advice, support, clarity, or at the very least, bail money." Such mentorship allowed him to learn how to become that "literal hub that makes a wheel turn," ensuring that a production runs smoothly and in the right direction from beginning to end.

SORTING: ASKING THE DESIGN QUESTION

According to Production Manager Joshua Kohler, navigating rehearsals in the modern theatre presents several challenges, especially for prolific designers who are often unable to have a significant presence during the rehearsal process due to juggling other projects' timelines. By carefully reporting on the work taking place during rehearsals, stage managers serve a function essential to designers. They rely on the information articulated in the reports to respond to the demands of the process appropriately and prepare for technical rehearsals. A skilled stage manager can help them sort the needs of the process "through clear communication, which will help raise questions a designer can answer."

To illustrate this point, Kohler describes one fun but challenging production of *A Winter's Tale*, the classic Shakespeare play that begins in an icy winter palace and changes to a lush pastoral world. While working on it as production manager, he observed how the stage manager, a veteran of the industry and a long-time collaborator with the director and the scenic designer, provided incredibly detailed reports about the rehearsals. The show had a stark white design with moving walls and a trap door, and it was a lot to wrangle. Fortunately, the incredibly detailed rehearsal reports included descriptions with small-scale graphics, photos, ground plans, etc., of the show's many tricks and effects. While:

> it was a lot of e-mail communication, phone meetings, and constant discussion with the scenic designer. Their efforts fostered an incredibly smooth technical process which made a large, unwieldy late Shakespearian comedy land on stage with the ease of a one-person monologue.

A more specific example of how the right question can trigger effective solutions was using the trap door (in the same play). The famous stage direction "exit pursued by a bear" stems from this play, and Act I culminates in a grand chase of Antigonus offstage by a bear that emerges from the floor below. "Determining the landing place of the trap door was an expensive design element requiring multiple levels of production support." The stage manager worked directly with the designer, the scene shop, and the production manager to select the final spot. By studying the ground plan, blocking from rehearsals, and scenic construction drawings, the stage manager (SM) helped find the bear's perfect place to enter for all parties. In doing so, almost entirely via telecommunication, the SM and designer worked together sorting out a crucial technical element before going into tech.

At work, Kohler spends most of his time troubleshooting problems, trying to be the best ally of the design, technologies, and management folks. As a production manager, he realizes that sometimes the pressure can lead to taking for granted how the SM team wants to help by figuring things out by themselves. Skilled stage managers can help sort the rehearsal process's needs through clear communication and insightful questions; less experienced ones may need help from time to time to avoid assumptions. They may feel pressured to tackle what seems a simple note in good faith, not differentiating it from what may be an off-hand comment. This matter can become an issue, primarily when a designer (or his assignee) aren't readily available. Such is the experience that he calls "a glass bottle of Mountain Dew." Kohler keeps one in view on his shelf every day as a reminder of the effect that a single rehearsal report, not listening to your instinct, and not asking timely questions can have. "When you are working on a play involving period furniture," he says, "you anticipate a lot of odd requests," and that was the case during the last week of rehearsals of a small, two-character, off-Broadway play set at the Tenement Museum in New York.

"The play required a lot of period or facsimile props," Kohler says, "but an interesting note came up about a modern soda drink." The report asked for a "glass bottle of Mountain Dew." Kohler observes that typically, such requests come from the director, and he doesn't question them, but it felt odd in this instance. "The initial thought was: what place would a vintage version of a modern soda bottle have in a theatre piece that straddles present day and the Victorian era, and why Mountain Dew?" Instead of asking the question, he sourced and purchased a glass bottle of Mountain Dew off Etsy within minutes. The next day, when he mentioned he had ordered the bottle, the director laughed, saying he had no idea why the report focused on that. He explained that it could be any present-day soda container with an opaque straw to conceal sipping water, "probably a Big Gulp." While it was a small mistake and a laughable moment, it was also a clear sign of a miscommunication that led to a choice. Had Kohler trusted his instinct, asking the "why" question and initiating a conversation with the stage manager, director, and designer, there would have been a different outcome. Taking the extra time would have also allowed the stage manager to make the experience part of their bag of tricks. Thus, the bottle sits to this day (on Kohler's shelf) as a reminder that to be an ally, it's important to trust one's instincts asking design questions to support stage managers in doing their jobs.

IN CONCLUSION

I genuinely believe that stage managers are a designer's best friend, and this fact has not changed through the many years I have been working in the field as a designer. They serve an essential function, articulating important information at production meetings, rehearsals, and via rehearsal reports. Their constancy allows for timely responses to the production process's demands in preparation for technical rehearsals. During rehearsals, tech, and run of shows, the process's intensity will vary, and at times benefits may seem one-sided. That's when designers can join in modeling emotional self-regulation while helping sort solutions to challenges. When things feel successful and are running seamlessly, that is a sign that reliable communications are taking place. By acknowledging and appreciating the stage manager's efforts and supporting their objectives with timely questions, interactions become symbiotic in mutualistic ways, with each party benefiting from the relationship.

SUGGESTED BIBLIOGRAPHY

Daniel Goleman, *Emotional Intelligence: Why It Can Matter More Than IQ* (London: Bloomsbury, 1996).

Thomas A. Kelly, *The Back Stage Guide to Stage Management: Traditional and New Methods for Running a Show from First Rehearsal to Last Performance*, 3rd revised, expanded edition (New York: Back Stage Books, 2009).

Leah Kuypers, *The Zones of Regulation: A Curriculum Designed to Foster Self-Regulation and Emotional Control* (Santa Clara, CA: Think Social Publishing, Inc., 2011).

NOTES

1. Source: https://necsi.edu/mutualistic-relationships

2. Madeline Hartrich is a freelance theatrical artisan and manager with a specialization in Shakespeare and musicals, working with a variety of performing arts companies and venues.

3. Arlin Cuncic, "How to Develop and Use Self-Regulation in Your Life," Verywell Mind, January 20, 2020, accessed February 17, 2021, www.verywellmind.com/how-you-can-practice-self-regulation-4163536

4. Thomas A. Kelly has been a professional stage manager and production manager for over 40 years. He most recently worked as production stage manager for New York City Opera, Broadway, and major production venues in New York City and nationally. He has taught Stage Management at Rutgers, SUNY Purchase, and Columbia University and is the recipient of a Lifetime Achievement Award from USITT. He authored the most widely used manual for aspiring and veteran stage managers: *The Back Stage Guide to Stage Management: Traditional and New Methods for Running a Show from First Rehearsal to Last Performance*, 3rd revised, expanded edition (New York: Back Stage Books, 2009).

5. John Traub is a Professor of Production Design at George Washington University, as well as a Producer, Arts Manager, Designer and Technician in Theatre, Dance, Opera, and Broadcast Television.

6. Emotional intelligence (EI) "refers to the ability to perceive, control, and evaluate emotions. Some researchers suggest that emotional intelligence can be learned and strengthened, while others claim it's an inborn characteristic." Source: www.verywellmind.com/what-is-emotional-intelligence-2795423

9

The Art of Management
Joanna Obuzor

OPENING

My name is Joanna Obuzor. Obuzor. That's a Nigerian name. When translated to English, it means "Leader." What is leading if not managing groups? I come from a long line of those who were leaders. My father was born in a small village in Nigeria. Each of the villages had a chief and my grandfather was the chief of all the chiefs. The skill of leading is quite literally my heritage. While I have never considered myself an artist, it is safe to say I have always considered myself a leader. My friends and family were the first that I preyed on with my superior leading skills be it when I was three years old and I instructed my older brother to bake the wooden blocks in the toy stove, or when I convinced my one-year-old sister to let me cut her hair with my plastic safety scissors, or when I gathered a team of friends to cover another friend's car with layers of bread and cellophane. I have always been an exemplary leader. If I've learned anything in my years of leading it is that there is a true art to leading an assembled group of people.

DOI: 10.4324/9780429321672-11

EVERYDAY ART ABOUNDS

In all projects, be them work or non-work, I find beauty in organization and a succinct method paired with process; I enjoy the art that can be inherent in any profession. For instance, an accountant who tallies millions of dollars down to the penny: that's beauty. The janitor who waxes the floor to a high sheen: that's art. When I drive my car and crest a big hill at the same time the music hits a crescendo, the convergence causes me to smile. Beauty and art exist everywhere. These are things that I take pleasure in, mini moments of joy found in milliseconds of fleeting perfection. As soon as I knew what stage managing was, I knew there was opportunity for boundless moments of those small joys; instants when skill and craft meet to form a second of ephemeral perfection. The skill of running a rehearsal room and successfully working with the director, actors, and production team can have a seamless beauty that is nothing short of breathtaking. I strive to find those moments.

MANAGING A ROOM

One of the ways that I lean into the art of stage managing is through prep work and a beautifully organized prompt book. In my book, there is a right and wrong place for every piece of paper. The room could be in the deepest level of chaos, with the production team being walking balls of stress, and I am able to find a slice of ease because tangible tools that I needed to quickly reference are at my fingertip. I'm a fan of tabs, color coding, binder pockets, the "right" pencil, run times on every page, one specific spot for my stopwatch, and general organization. This is at work, please don't look in my home because that level of anal-retentive organization is not found there! After ten-plus years of working shows, a lot of prep is second nature, but all the same, I have a process for everything. The processes help create ease when things are difficult. One of my most useful personal tools during prep week is a one-page checklist that I created for myself and continually update as the years go by. It includes reminders for who to email, which documents to collect, lists of whom I ought to schedule meetings with, and other handy prep week and tech week reminders. I use the checklist for every show that I do; it is a shorthand of my quick "to dos" and "don't forgets." I lovingly titled it Joanna's Amazing Document Checklist.

Another thing that was important to me when working was to keep the levity in the room. To me, that doesn't mean overt jokes or pranks. When I say keep the levity in the room, I mean a lighthearted confidence. Theatre is serious business and I take it seriously, but I like to remember that at some point in our lives, each person in the room fell in love with the craft. There was nothing we wanted more than to be able to work in professional theatre. I like to remember that what is now the more mundane day-to-day is also living a dream that "past me" had. That adds a smile to my face and keeps my step light.

SM STYLE

There are many kinds of stage managers and a hundred ways to be effective in the job. It takes time to grow into your own and figure out what your personal stage manager style is. After years of working, I had solidly developed my style of managing a room and it was smooth as butter! I am a stage manager that works by building trust and human connection among the team. Several years ago, I started teaching at West Liberty University and later at Point Park University. The process of teaching others how I work was a nice exercise for me to better explain the traits that I think are important to bring to the table. To this day, I still use the same exercise on day one of class one to hopefully get students thinking about the traits of an effective stage manager.

The activity goes something like this: I create groups of students and give each group the same list of statements. I didn't write the statements that I give them, it's from a source that I'll explain in a bit. The challenge for the student groups is to discuss each line and determine if the statement or phrase is that of an effective stage manager. The list of statements is as follows:

1. Don't criticize, condemn, or complain.
2. Give honest, sincere appreciation.
3. Arouse in the other person an eager want.
4. Become genuinely interested in other people.
5. Smile.
6. Remember that a person's name is to that person the most important sound in any language.
7. Be a good listener. Encourage others to talk about themselves.
8. Talk in terms of the other person's interest.
9. Make the other person feel important—and do so sincerely.
10. The only way to get the best of an argument is to avoid it.
11. Show respect for the other person's opinions. Never say, "You're wrong."
12. If you are wrong, admit it quickly and emphatically.
13. Begin in a friendly way.
14. Get the other person saying, "Yes, yes" immediately.
15. Let the other person do a great deal of the talking.
16. Let the other person feel that the idea is theirs.
17. Try honestly to see things from the other person's point of view.
18. Be sympathetic with the other person's ideas and desires.
19. Appeal to the nobler motives.
20. Dramatize your ideas.
21. Throw down a challenge.
22. Begin with praise and honest appreciation.
23. Call attention to people's mistakes indirectly.
24. Talk about your own mistakes before criticizing the other person.
25. Ask questions instead of giving direct orders.

26. Let the other person save face.
27. Praise the slightest and every improvement. Be "lavish in your praise."
28. Give the other person a fine reputation to live up to.
29. Use encouragement. Make the fault seem easy to correct.
30. Make the other person happy about doing the things you suggest.

After a few minutes, we come together and collectively decide if we feel each statement represents a behavior or trait of an effective stage manager. Every time, the room overwhelming decides that yes, the vast majority of items on this list are those of an effective stage manager. After the final tally, I let them know that this list was created by Dale Carnegie and is from his book titled *How to Win Friends and Influence People.*[1] Mr. Carnegie wrote this book in 1936 and it's still a best seller today. As a group, the class just decided that an effective way to stage manage is to "win friends and influence people." That method is synonymous with my SM style; it is how I run a room. To be clear, stage managing is a job, it is a profession; it is not necessary to be everyone's friend. But, in order to be effective, you DO need the room to be with you, to trust you, and to follow your direction. I do that by influencing and inspiring trust; the same skills that I use when building a friendship.

RIGIDITY VS. FLEXIBILITY

I am a lover of rules. I like process and find beauty in well-executed plans; chaos is not my friend. With that said, I am also a fan of knowing when and how to bend the rules to best serve the show. I use the rules as a framework to assist the process.

There is mastery to knowing how to read the room and make fast choices; one of the small ways I do this is also the most frequent: Breaks. Rules around Actors' Equity Association breaks are hard and fast. A five-minute break every 55 minutes and a ten-minute break every 80 minutes. That is the rule, that is the framework. I don't bend the framework. Never. That is the rule. However, there are a dozen ways to get in and out of a break, that is where the flexibility is found. When it's time for a break, some directors like a five- or ten-minute warning before break. Some don't want to remember that breaks exist and would like them announced only at time. Some directors want you to tell them when it's time then immediately announce to the room. Sometimes people outside of the room need notification of break time so they can do things like drop off a prop. There are several ways in and a bit of nuance surrounds them all.

When coming back from a break, there is also an art to returning to the room. I find that this process varies more in regard to the actors on contract and process than it does with the director. I like tight, to-the-minute breaks, but this doesn't always best serve the process. For example, I was working on a show with a director I had worked with several times before. I knew that she also liked a tight break.

However, this particular show was an intense one-hander. Due to that, it served the actor better to have a soft return. It was common that a ten-minute break would turn into a 15, or following a ten there would be some light tablework and chatting rather than getting up on her feet. Both the director and I modified our wants because at the end of the day, we had a better room and more productive work with a loose end time on breaks.

I find the need for finesse via breaks varies less in big rooms with chorus rehearsals such as musicals or opera. These types of rehearsal generally benefit from a hard in and a hard out. But, for the smaller cast working on a play, the room is often more productive when there are layers of tact around starting and stopping.

MONDAYS, AM I RIGHT?

One rule that I have very little patience for bending is time off. Monday is the typical SM off day. Department heads tend to work Monday–Friday. After a weekend of rehearsal, it's not unusual for someone to want some follow up information on Monday. I learned over the years that it's okay to let them wait. Waiting is not my style; I don't like to keep anyone waiting for anything. But, at the end of the day, theatre is a profession where we are only granted one day off; take the day and rest up. Come back on Tuesday ready to go. If you need to read the email for your own peace of mind, do what's best for you. But, try to remember that your off day is just that; your day.

BEAUTY IN MOTION

I have always enjoyed tech week. I feel it is when the most exciting parts come together and everything starts looking like a show instead of a well-staged reading. Even more than tech, my favorite is week three or four of a six+-week run. That's the time when the cast can feel a little slump in energy. The excitement of tech and opening have passed but the nostalgia of closing night is still in the distance. The backstage energy may be a little low but everyone knows what they're doing and things move like a well-oiled machine so there is more time to play. Literally play, I like to have my ASM play a quick game of cards with me at half hour. The big reason I love everything after week three is that the show has settled. There have been enough audiences that the actors have really set their reactions and responses; even in a comedy with variables, they have settled on a few of their favorites. I like a show after it settles because I can paint with the cues so everything looks exactly how the designers want it to. That three-second light shift which must be called five seconds into a pause can be more consistent because I know exactly how long that performer is going to wait. If the audience laughs, I know how that actor will react and I can time the coming sound cue appropriately. The beauty of being able to paint the world of the show so everyone and everything looks as good as possible every night will never get old to me.

ALWAYS A STAGE MANAGER

Stage managing was a lovely and challenging profession that fed my soul. I worked primarily on new work and I adored the learnings that came with the job. I planned to stay in the profession till a ripe old age. But life is long and short, surprising and dull all at the same time. There were new adventures on the horizon.

One day, I found myself with the opportunity to take a job as a production manager with the largest presenting company in the region, The Pittsburgh Cultural Trust. It was easily the hardest decision I've ever made. Taking a full-time job outside of stage managing would mean saying goodbye to so many things I loved, including week three+ of that long run. In the end, I went for the new gig with the knowledge that stage managing is not disappearing and I can always go back. Turns out, I liked my new adventure well enough; it suited me. I stayed and moved deeper into the world of artistic administration. After several years, I'm still with the Cultural Trust but now I spend my days as the operations manager of the Benedum Center. The Benedum is the 2,800-seat home of touring Broadway as well as the Pittsburgh Opera, Pittsburgh Ballet Theater, and Pittsburgh CLO. In 2019, before the COVID-19 pandemic, there were 274 performances in one calendar year; it's a wonderfully busy place. The thrill of live art abounds; the only change is my vantage point.

The artistry of management, specifically stage management, is with me every day. When I come across people behaving in a challenging manner or situations in the workplace that require some problem solving, I still use the phrase, "I stage managed the situation." To me, that phrase will always mean, I took a problem and solved it with aplomb.

I found that stage managing cultivated a multifaceted and creative skill set; it is a singularly amazing career that forever changed me for the better.

BIBLIOGRAPHY: RECOMMENDED READING

Lawrence Stern and Jill Gold, *Stage Management* (London: Routledge, 2016).

NOTE

    1. Dale Carnegie, *How to Win Friends and Influence People* (New York: Simon & Schuster, 1936), 1–291.

10

Stage Management is Only Just Beginning[1]
David McGraw

O ver a decade ago, a colleague told me a story about a museum that was launching a new theatrical show in one of its auditoriums. The show was to be a historical narrative performed by a single actor. This show would be performed several times each day and the museum sought ways to remove the need to employ anyone but the actor. They hired a production team, who built a set with buttons and sensors for the actor to trigger lighting and sound cues at different parts of the narrative. Everything was automated. The stage manager on that production team essentially programed herself out of a job. Every few years since I heard that story, I have read incendiary posts from other artists and technicians, often in connection with the latest advances in cuing technology, claiming that it is only a matter of time before stage managers will be replaced by automation.

This story would be cause for alarm, provided you believed that all stage managers did was call cues. On the hard days, I wish I could just call cues and go home. For the majority of our productions, cueing performances is perhaps 20% of our workload. Yet we must remember that cueing is the most visible part of our work, and most producers and even many of our fellow artists see our primary job duty as calling performances. Social media videos of stage managers focus on the cue lights and headset calls, not on the personnel management and the quality control when a performance is a fraction off its mark. In the museum story, I always wonder who is training the subs and replacements, checking to make sure the actor

DOI: 10.4324/9780429321672-12

is both on script and on tempo, and confirming the light looks, sound levels, and costume maintenance. These are the parts of our work that cannot be automated.

As much as we can be confident that stage management itself will not fade into oblivion, we should be mindful of losing that most visible 20%. It will not happen on the short runs, where the expense of automating anything for just 25–50 performances cannot be justified. But what about the shows that have been running for years without major changes in cueing? It will probably start as a university project to show that a stage-manager-less performance can be done without thought to the consequences. As cue programming continues to advance well past simple auto-follows, our future in calling cues is anything but guaranteed. We understand how many finite adjustments we must make on even a stable production, but a producer's tolerance for tiny pauses, skips, and mistakes has to be balanced against weekly expenses. If, or perhaps when, we are replaced on this most visible part of our job, are we prepared to demonstrate how we are essential to the efficient and cost-effective operation of the performing arts? Otherwise, we are doomed to join the elevator operators, encyclopedia editors, and switchboard operators at the obsolete profession table at the retirement home.

COST DISEASE IN THE ARTS

The economist William J. Baumol is well known for his diagnosis of a "cost disease" in the arts: the labor costs in the performing arts will only continue to rise but only so much of our work can be reduced through technology.[2] The rehearsal process for shows has not gotten significantly shorter, nor does *A Christmas Carol* or *The Nutcracker* perform significantly faster than they did a century ago thanks to technology. Some producers may double-cast roles or cut back on musicians, but these are neither technology-based nor new cost-saving measures. The biggest technology innovation of the past decade that reduces labor in the performing arts may be the rise of projections over constructed scenery. Projections may eventually diminish the need for many carpenter and scenic artist positions, but they will actually increase the need for a stage manager in the running of shows.

One of stage management's historical weaknesses may, oddly enough, prove to be what delays the eventual automation of cue calling. As a field, we are incredibly decentralized: we lack a governing body or any form of accreditation. A college degree in stage management, let alone a graduate degree, is not required or often even listed as a desired qualification on most job applications. This decentralization has meant that there is no single accepted way to call a show, let alone manage a production. I recall some of the reactions I received when I attempted to produce the Stage Manager Simulator, a program that used a laptop and USB headset to display a video of a stage production and provide real-time feedback on the user's cue calling. Ultimately this 2010–2015 experiment (unofficial tagline: Guitar Hero for Stage Managers!) never made it to market, despite a successful demo version, because the licensing for the speech recognition components was much too high for what would likely be just hundreds of users. But I recall being taken aside by some peers at a USITT conference where I was providing demos and being cautioned that this simulator would actually hurt stage management. Cue calling would become standardized. This warning became very real when I was later approached at the same conference by a major entertainment company that was interested in using the simulator to train and assess its stage managers. I had designed the simulator to help students learn to call cues without all of the pressure of performers and technicians waiting on them. But now I see that, had the project continued, I could have reduced the artistry of cue calling—adapting calls within a fraction of a second based on the technicians on headset and the subtle changes in performance each night—to the lowest common denominator. The goal of providing guidance could have resulted in me designing myself out of a job.

Moreover, as soon as something is standardized, the drive for innovation fades away. At the beginning of any new technology or system, there are competing groups who are all trying to create the best solution to the problem. But once we agree on a solution, experimentation gives way to distribution. Many stage managers are turning towards groups in social media for guidance and asking for help. It troubles me when a question is answered so vehemently and confidently, in the first couple of responses, that no other suggestions are made. We should not rush to a final decision, there should be multitude of solutions offered. Just as our productions are never perfect, we should never be fully satisfied with how we stage manage those productions. I actually received a complaint about the Stage Manager Survey (http://smsurvey.info) that I was not recommending best practices. The SM Survey has never been about identifying the correct solution but rather celebrating our multiple approaches. Want to know what to name your video cues? Here are a range of options. Should you try to negotiate your salary? Here are your chances and potential risks and rewards. Even if 99% of stage managers choose one option, the question is still up for debate. If we don't see it as a question, we will stop innovating and that will be the day our profession begins to ossify.

ROBOT-PROOF COLLABORATION AND TRAINING

Certainly, there is a need for collaboration and training—we will not save stage management by becoming secretive with our practices. If anything, we need to become more open and adaptive and less dogmatic. Most importantly, we need to prepare for that not-too-distant future when we are calling fewer cues by focusing more on the other parts of our job. I was recently part of a strategic planning process in which we discussed Joseph E. Aoun's book *Robot-Proof*.[3] *Robot-Proof* proposes that, with the rise of artificial intelligence, we need to prepare the next generation for jobs that machines and algorithms cannot complete. Aoun defines a new Humanics discipline by which we can see just how stage management cannot be replaced by automation.

Stage management, as a profession, is robot-proof because our job requires an extremely high level of what Aoun calls human literacy. Human literacy "equips us for the social milieu, giving us the power to communicate, engage with others, and tap into our human capacity for grace and beauty."[4] If that isn't stage management in a nutshell, I don't know what is. Sure, Siri, Alexa, or any other speech recognition apps can complete requests for a transfer of data, but that isn't true communication. Think about when a design change is first envisioned in rehearsal. There are layers upon layers of interpretation, motivation analysis, prioritization, and diplomacy needed to successfully develop an idea from the rehearsal room through a design team to the production shop. A win–win negotiation with everyone moving forward together is not possible with a blunt request; it requires empathy, tactics tailored to the individual team member, and a balance of achievable goals. Can you imagine Siri delivering rehearsal room notes to the production shops?

After decades of making stage management a more technical field, we need to return to our roots to restore the balance with human literacy. It is a matter of balance: we cannot afford to ignore the technical side of our work in our push to focus on the human element. The need for data literacy and technological literacy (Aoun's terms) are completely justified: as operation teams shrink in size and experience, we need to understand more of the technology in use. As stage technology has improved, there is less manual work to be done to achieve the same effect. Decades ago, if a lighting instrument died mid-show, I could have the operator, who likely hung and focused many of the instruments, manually compensate with other nearby lights. I typically had a veteran crew because a veteran crew was necessary to run even a standard show. Such direct control, and operator training, is more rare today. Moreover, more advanced show control systems mean that the technical threats are no longer a single lighting instrument or speaker malfunctioning, but system-wide failures. While a technical problem is not our fault, it quickly becomes our responsibility.

One change that we can make, to restore the balance of human literacy and technological literacy, is to revisit how we teach stage management. At present, it seems that most college stage management courses and majors are housed in design programs. While it is important to learn design literacy, stage managers have been part of Actors' Equity Association for a century, so housing stage management with acting majors would not be a new alignment. We spend most of our time with the performers and are ultimately responsible for the precision of their work, so why not train the next generation of stage managers within the acting curriculum?

Given how much time a stage manager spends in rehearsal, whether as part of the original creative process or the understudy calls, stage management programs need to offer comprehensive courses in directing. Students need to learn how to conduct rehearsals, provide notes to the performers, and maintain the artistic vision of the production. The final exam for a stage management course in directing could model a put-in rehearsal: students observe several rehearsals and performances and then put understudies into the show.

In the 2019 edition of the Stage Manager Survey, only 72% (1,161 of 1,605 stage managers) report being comfortable reading music. Yet it is hard to think of a stage management career that would not benefit from this crucial skill. Offering a generalized music theory course or an Intro to Piano course is better than nothing, but stage managers need a specifically designed music literacy course. The same applies to fight choreography and dance choreography. While a computer program can be taught to create choreographic models, it cannot anticipate problems; only a stage manager's eye can see when the choreography is about to go awry. Moreover, as international tours, multinational casts, and global arts organizations increase, our human literacy requires training in additional languages and expanded cultural competence. Language skills can also assist in broadening career options in opera and ballet. Only a handful of programs offer even just one course in opera stage management, despite 18% of stage managers reporting in that same survey that they have managed an opera.

EMPATHY AND ETHICS

If science fiction has taught us anything, computers struggle with empathy and ethics even more than humans do. The arts will survive because we deal in emotional honesty and the hard questions. So many artists unionized as protection to create great art. We need to equip the next generation of stage managers with the tools to engage with this messy and often painful business and emerge as ethical leaders. What are the power dynamics in the creative process and how have the #metoo and #notinourhouse movements changed the collaborative process? When an abuse of power in the rehearsal room is reported, one of the first questions asked is "Where was the stage manager?" Yet how are we training stage managers to respond? With a lack of Human Resource personnel within production companies, it only makes business sense to better prepare the stage manager to at least perform triage on the problem. Our profession is stronger than others in the battle against being replaced by algorithms and artificial intelligence, but we must not just claim "human literacy" but study and practice it.

The collaborative process itself might be what ultimately saves stage management from automation. But we as artists must be vigilant that collaboration is not sacrificed or deemphasized. The push against collaboration has already taken root in the recorded art forms. Film directors are controlling every single visual choice through CGI; music producers are assembling every single audio track of a song without any musicians through sampling and editing of every note. These are not collaborations—group dynamics are lost to stripped-down components and the sum is not any greater than the parts assembled. Therefore, everything but that film director or music producer could be automated. There are playwrights who are writing more cinematic scripts that remove creativity from the rehearsal room, though we should note that G.B. Shaw's lengthy stage directions attempted to do the same thing. There are stage auteurs who conceive not only all the acting choices but also all the design choices before launching a project. What can we as stage managers do to counter these anti-collaboration trends? We can choose to not lend our talents to these projects. Just like the story of the automated performance at the museum, we can choose to not automate ourselves out of a job by accepting work that does not treat us as artists and collaborators.

There is no point to fighting advancements in technology; they are as old as theatre itself. I am sure there was some ancient Greek stagehand who complained about how the new *deus ex machina* was ruining everything and how his team used to carry Medea onstage themselves without a crane and no one complained. We must find ways of detaching our value from the purely technical. We are not the elevator operators who wrangled machinery until that machinery could run itself. We are not the encyclopedia editors who compiled all the information and thus were considered experts until information became freely shared. We are not the switchboard operators who served as the communication hub until communication could run person-to-person without a relay station. Our jobs will change. But if there is one thing that stage managers do very well, it is adapt.

NOTES

1. The basis for this chapter is rooted in my original essay, "A Robot-Proof Profession," published March 26, 2019, in the Stage Manager's Kit blog by *Stage Directions Magazine*.

2. William Jack Baumol and Ruth Towse, *Baumol's Cost Disease: The Arts and Other Victims* (Cheltenham, UK: E. Elgar, 1997).

3. Joseph Aoun, *Robot-Proof: Higher Education in the Age of Artificial Intelligence* (Cambridge, MA: The MIT Press, 2018).

4. Aoun, 58–59.

11

Hold, Please

Addressing Urgency and Other White Supremacist Standards in Stage Management

Miguel Flores, R. Christopher Maxwell, John Meredith, Alexander Murphy, Quinn O'Connor, Phyllis Y. Smith, and Chris Waters

This essay, "Hold, Please," by Miguel Flores et al, was originally published on HowlRound Theatre Commons at https://howlround.com/commons/miguel-flores on October 15, 2020.[1]

"Seven stage managers in the United States—Miguel Flores, R. Christopher Maxwell, John Meredith, Alexander Murphy, Quinn O'Connor, Phyllis Y. Smith, and Chris Waters—explore a few places white supremacist culture play out in their work—focusing on urgency, quantity over quality, perfectionism, objectivity, and power-hoarding."[2]

Regardless of your age, race, or political leanings, if you live in a culture touched by colonialism, it is inevitable that racist ideals have crept into your work—theatrical work included. As such, anyone in the field—including the seven of us working as stage managers across the United States—must actively dismantle these aspects of our beliefs and practices. For stage managers in particular—whether acting as a production stage manager, assistant, or intern—we must be mindful of the ways we facilitate our rehearsal and performance processes. Choosing not to practice continual self-reflection and adjustment perpetuates harm to ourselves, everyone around us, and particularly Black, Indigenous, and people of color (BIPOC).

DOI: 10.4324/9780429321672-13

In their book *Dismantling Racism: A Workbook for Social Change Groups*,[3] activist-scholars Kenneth Jones and Tema Okun name thirteen characteristics of white supremacy culture in the workplace. With items like urgency, perfectionism, and objectivity, the list doesn't look all too different from a stage management job description. Not only are stage managers often guilty of these characteristics, these are industry standards we have been explicitly trained to cultivate.

Narda E Alcorn and Lisa Porter recently wrote a wonderful article providing a foundational curriculum on **committing to anti-racist stage management**.[4] We believe a continuous education like the one they provide is crucial for all stage managers, and we want to continue this vital conversation. As educators, mentors, and peers, we have a responsibility to dismantle harmful precedents and share new and inclusive ways forward. While we couldn't possibly cover every aspect of white supremacy within stage management norms, we want to explore a few places we have seen white supremacist culture play out—focusing on urgency, quantity over quality, perfectionism, objectivity, and power-hoarding—that we can uproot in our workplaces.

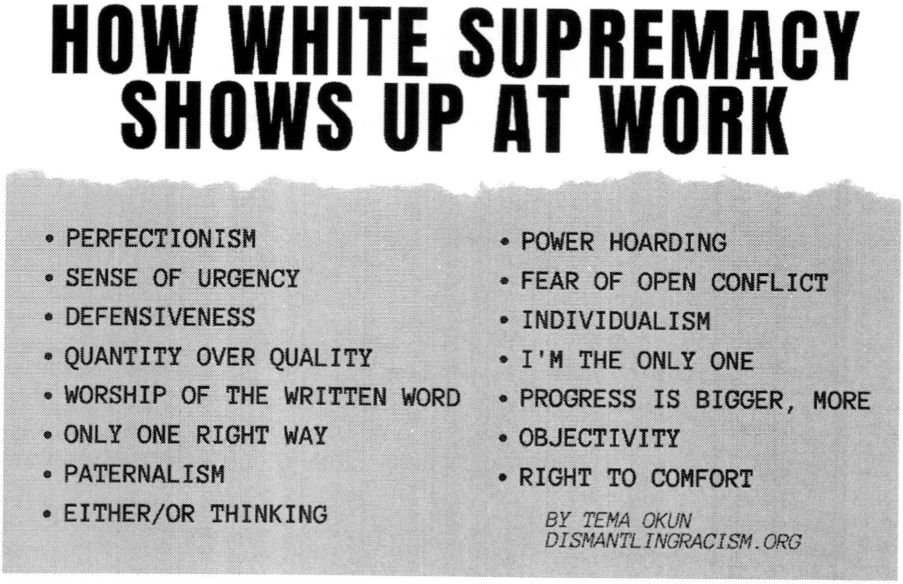

HOW WHITE SUPREMACY SHOWS UP AT WORK

- PERFECTIONISM
- SENSE OF URGENCY
- DEFENSIVENESS
- QUANTITY OVER QUALITY
- WORSHIP OF THE WRITTEN WORD
- ONLY ONE RIGHT WAY
- PATERNALISM
- EITHER/OR THINKING
- POWER HOARDING
- FEAR OF OPEN CONFLICT
- INDIVIDUALISM
- I'M THE ONLY ONE
- PROGRESS IS BIGGER, MORE
- OBJECTIVITY
- RIGHT TO COMFORT

BY TEMA OKUN
DISMANTLINGRACISM.ORG

Figure 11.1 The thirteen characteristics of white supremacy culture in the workplace

Note: Flores, M., Maxwell, R.C., Meredith, J., Murphy, A., O'Connor, Q., Smith, P. Y., & Waters, C. Hold, Please. Retrieved from https://howlround.com/hold-please

Source: From *Dismantling Racism: A Workbook for Social Change Groups*. Graphic by John Meredith, Courtesy of HowlRound.

URGENCY: SLOW DOWN

As the people with the stopwatches, stage managers keep an eye on schedules and breaks to ensure goals are met by the end of the day. With limited hours in the week, shrinking rehearsal periods, and the ever-looming deadline of opening night, it feels like compulsive urgency is, in fact, a necessity to create theatre. It's unshakably rooted in our ethos—just typing out the words "slow down" feels blasphemous in a way.

But when urgency is the driving force, it doesn't actually make our work better, it only serves to squander thoughtful decision-making and cultivate environments where oppression and abuse thrive. For example, stage managers may use urgency as a justification for discrimination by saying there "just wasn't time" to bring BIPOC people into the conversation. By choosing a quick solution over ensuring BIPOC people are part of the decisions that affect them, valuable insight is lost and solutions that favor white people and white-centric values are inevitably reached.

Many people are deterred from speaking out against microaggressions, harassment, and abuse during an individual project because it will be over soon and they don't want to be the one responsible for disrupting the already crammed process. Or, if they do speak up, it gets written off because there just "isn't time to deal with that right now." But there is, unequivocally, always time to address misconduct and we must drastically shift attitudes within ourselves to match this fact. Especially as people in a position of authority within the room, stage managers cannot allow ourselves to be complicit in placing the needs of a show above the needs of the actual human beings creating it.

But when urgency is the driving force, it doesn't actually make our work better, it only serves to squander thoughtful decision-making and cultivate environments where oppression and abuse thrive.

QUALITY OVER QUANTITY: RESCHEDULE

White supremacist culture contaminates the stage management process even before we step into the rehearsal room. Just three families own the majority of Broadway theatres, and across the country, leadership like regional **theatre boards**[5] skew heavily white, wealthy, and male. This leads to a labor structure that is directly driven by white supremacist ideologies that favor capital over the individual and quantity over quality. Theatres have a complex history of pushing against labor laws to continue working long hours—things like state requirements for days of rest or, recently, **California's Assembly Bill 5**.[6] For people with multiple jobs, people with disabilities that prevent long working hours, people with religious and cultural events outside of the Christian calendar, parents, students, and so many others, a capital-driven production schedule could be the final barrier barring them from a career as a theatre artist.

Many schedules, like the ones based on the **NEAT rulebook**[7] in New England, land at or just shy of a full-time schedule. But unless the production pays a steady income comparable to a full-time job—and most don't—it's quite likely these long hours are just a portion of an artist's workday. Rather than cramming in productions to maxed-out template calendars, we should standardize human-focused practices like tailoring schedules to the individuals working on a show and their specific needs.

There's an array of capital-driven standards that we can start dismantling. Non-theatrical companies across the globe are already exploring **the benefits**[8] of **a four-day workweek**,[9] while the United States theatre industry still hasn't yet caught up with decades-old labor reform, making us one of the few industries that still works six days a week. Just a single day off is simply not enough to rest and recover from the week. Providing a second day is crucial for people to see their families, work outside jobs, and even have a life as a human being. But cutting a day out does not necessitate tacking those hours onto another day. We are not obligated to try and puzzle every contractually allowed hour into our schedules.

One of the more egregious scheduling norms that has started to gain widespread scrutiny lately is the ten-out-of-twelve, a tech rehearsal where actors are generally called for twelve hours and get a two-hour break in the middle, and the production team typically works closer to fourteen hours or more. The rigor is compounded as these rehearsals take place during the longest week of the whole process—up to fifty-five hours on **LORT**[10] contracts. It's an exercise in diminishing returns and unnecessary burnout. At least from anecdotal experience, the last few hours of the ten-out-of-twelve often lead to the most frustration, most slip-ups, and work that will need to be redone the following morning. By focusing on getting the most hours rather than the best work and fair treatment of workers, we're putting people in a position to fail—on top of putting their health and safety at risk.

Our industry has instilled the expectation of artists to put the show ahead of everything else, and it's taking a massive toll on our safety and well-being. According to **the Center for a New American Dream**,[11] people who work eleven or more hours a day are two and a half times more likely to develop depression and sixty times more likely to develop heart disease. In addition, **multiple studies have shown**[12] long work hours and work-related stress to have adverse effects on a wide range of health impacts, including anxiety, sleep quality, substance use, mental health, physical health, and injuries. Prioritizing quantity over quality is a colossal tentpole of white supremacy that works to put organizational revenue before the physical and mental impact on the workers.

Change is possible. Places like **Baltimore Center Stage**[13] have already committed to eliminating ten-out-of-twelves and standardizing a five-day rehearsal week. Stage managers must use whatever authority we have in the scheduling process to implement human-focused scheduling. We can explicitly work against urgency-driven expectations by proactively having open conversations about thoughtful, realistic, and sustainable scheduling that creates room for a team of diverse experiences. We should make a point of using breaks to de-stress, and taking days off, and encouraging those around us (particularly assistants, interns, and those without union protections) to do the same. By finding new ways to structure our production processes and taking care of the individual, we gain a multifaceted, well-rested, better-functioning, and healthier team.

By focusing on getting the most hours rather than the best work and fair treatment of workers, we're putting people in a position to fail—on top of putting their health and safety at risk.

PERFECTIONISM & OBJECTIVITY: EXPECT AND ACCEPT MISTAKES

One step to start tackling capitalist-driven tendencies in theatre spaces is by reframing our view of mistakes in the workplace. For stage managers specifically, there is a pervading expectation that we aren't supposed to have any opinions or emotions—we are meant to be perfect robotic beings only around to serve the production. While it may be nice to feel omniscient and omnipotent from time to time, leaning into this idea can only set us up for failure since we are, in fact, neither of those things.

The expectation of perfection is explicitly taught in college programs like the one of our authors, John, attended—they were told a rehearsal should never have to pause on the stage manager's behalf. Even things like small typos or grammatical errors get called out as an unacceptable flaw. Phyllis, another of our authors, vividly recalled a time when colleagues called her out in the middle of a production meeting for a misspelling in a past report. And while precision can be helpful, if the meaning is still perfectly conveyed, this is often unnecessary nitpicking that redirects energy away from the overarching goal of communication and, notably, undermines the talented stage managers out there with Dyslexia.

The issues of urgency and perfectionism blend together into a culture many stage managers have created, where we commend overworking as a badge of honor and chastise not using every possible second to work as a failure. It's expected of stage managers to give up our free time by working through breaks or staying on call during our designated days off so we can respond to issues at a moment's notice. When we factor in setup, cleanup, creating reports, sending daily calls, updating paperwork, responding to emails, and any other tasks added to our plates, stage managers often work overtime without compensation.

Black stage managers are often isolated within their theatre community and must constantly work to prove themselves among a sea of white and white-assumed peers. The burden to be perfect is amplified for BIPOC, women, queer people, disabled people, and especially individuals living at the intersection of those identities. There is no room for mistakes—they have to be practically infallible to be given a shot.

Artists at these intersections must assimilate to professionalism standards of how to talk, dress, and carry themselves, turning on their "stage management voice" and toning down their Black, feminine, and queer mannerisms to be listened to and respected by their colleagues. These artists are told over and over again—implicitly and explicitly—that if they don't carry themselves in a way that makes white people comfortable, they won't get hired again.

Slipping up, showing emotions "incorrectly," or having opinions that conflict with the director could bar these artists from working at that theatre again. Not only is their own hiring potential at risk, but they have the additional weight of representing all BIPOC. "Stereotype threat"—the fear of acting in a way that confirms racial stereotypes—leads to a continual self-policing so that employers can't point to them as a reason to not hire BIPOC artists in the future.

For white stage managers, the standard of perfectionism furthers the idea that stage managers should be objective in their work. Objectivity is, however, impossible for human beings to achieve—we bring in our viewpoints and experiences wherever we go. White supremacist culture will always deem white beliefs as the norm and best option. If white stage managers act from a belief that they're just stating facts and following rules, they are ignoring the places prejudice is influencing their work and miss the opportunity to bring in new viewpoints.

Stage managers must question where their standards of professionalism are rooted and who they serve, and we must make space for forms of management and expression that are outside of our own. We can create a culture that gives everyone agency to speak up by embracing our mistakes and those of our colleagues as part of the generative process, and actively asking for the opinions of everyone in the room. Phyllis's biggest advice for young Black stage managers is: "Stop apologizing and know that you're enough. Practice taking up space without code-switching for other people's comfort. Be okay with voicing your opinions, even if they disrupt the current flow and need time to be processed."

These artists are told over and over again—implicitly and explicitly—that if they don't carry themselves in a way that makes white people comfortable, they won't get hired again.

POWER-HOARDING: REDEFINE THE PSM-ASM RELATIONSHIP

When brainstorming manifestations of white supremacy culture in stage management, the production stage manager (PSM) to assistant stage manager (ASM) relationship elicited some of the most potent responses from the authors of this piece. Many ASMs spoke about feeling disrespected, uncredited for their work, and given menial tasks outside their actual job duties in a way that gets brushed off as part of "earning our stripes." The concept of being seen and not heard is alive and well for ASMs in many rehearsal rooms.

On top of all the standards of professionalism outlined above, ASMs often have their input diminished further with a version of the "one voice rule"—a principle that information from the stage management team should always come from the PSM. Quinn, one of the article's authors, works as a female, disabled ASM, has often felt pushed into the role of the "quiet wife"—only speak when spoken to, and sometimes not even then. While this may create the appearance of a united front and streamlined communication, it often does the opposite. By shutting down other voices or requiring differing perspectives be filtered through one figurehead, it dismisses the ASM's autonomy and slows down the process.

On one project where another author, Miguel, worked as an ASM, the PSM required the team to turn in their paperwork a week before tech to be "reviewed." Miguel then got back a printed version with corrections in red ink, including notes on font choices (and what they should be) and an expectation of seeing "corrected" versions for review. This PSM and Miguel were the same age and working on a professional contract. We must always be on the lookout for infantilizing our colleagues—particularly BIPOC stage managers—in the guise of unsolicited "teaching" or "mentoring."

Figure 11.2 Chris Waters, during tech of *The Good Person of Szechwan* at California Shakespeare Theater

Note: Flores, M., Maxwell, R.C., Meredith, J., Murphy, A., O'Connor, Q., Smith, P. Y., & Waters, C. Hold, Please. Retrieved from https://howlround.com/hold-please

Source: Photo by Jay Yamada, Courtesy of HowlRound.

One antidote to this mindset is focusing on completion, not competition—a mantra passed down by stage manager Deb Acquavella. Each member of the stage management team is working to achieve the same goal of a safe and smooth production. Having multiple points of view and avenues to turn to for information doesn't reduce this goal but rather expands it. If an ASM knows an answer right off the bat, why wait for the PSM to dredge up the information just because they're the designated one voice? We need to stop viewing the ASM as working below the PSM and instead put value on each person's unique duties and expertise. We then become a collaborative team where everyone is valued for their contribution, rather than bolstering egos.

To that end, PSMs should welcome change from their team. Whether it's the formatting of paperwork or general methodologies, there is no singular right way to stage manage. Seeking to make those around us think and act in a singular way is part of white supremacy's binary focus on "right" and "wrong." What we learned in school or from past mentors isn't the only correct way to do things. If, for example, an ASM's paperwork looks different than the one we make, instead of automatically asking for them to conform to what is familiar to us, check if we can still parse out the information and if it still serves its essential purpose. There is, of course, room for feedback and growth, but don't let prescriptivism get in the way of new manners of thinking.

These ideas also encompass production assistants and interns who often replace the role of an ASM but are given a different title so they can be vastly underpaid or even unpaid regardless of the level of work and hours put in. This provides yet another financial barrier to entry in this field. While stage managers may not always have a say in the ASM hiring process, one step we can take is to require a paid ASM on any contract we sign. And if we do participate in the hiring process, it's important to not always turn to the same few ASMs we've worked with in the past. Nepotism, which is what this is when we get down to it, serves to give an insular bubble of the same people—often white—paid opportunities and creates an additional barrier for new individuals to gain experience.

WHAT ELSE?

There are so many places we, as stage managers, can be culpable in perpetuating white supremacy. These ideas are just a handful of the issues we need to reckon with. We hope this encourages stage managers to reevaluate the standards we set and take time to hold space for all artists. And we want to know: What else are our fellow stage managers doing to build a more equitable theatrical landscape?

NOTES

1. All content, unless otherwise noted, is free cultural work available by Howl Round, Theatre Commons, to our community of content contributors under a Creative Commons Attribution 4.0 International License (CC BY 4.0).

2. Flores, M., Maxwell, R.C., Meredith, J., Murphy, A., O'Connor, Q., Smith, P.Y., & Waters, C. Hold, Please. Retrieved from https://howlround.com/commons/miguel-flores

3. https://www.dismantlingracism.org/white-supremacy-culture.html

4. https://howlround.com/we-commit-anti-racist-stage-management-education

5. https://www.tcg.org/pdfs/tools/GoverningBoards2013.pdf

6. https://www.americantheatre.org/2020/02/21/californias-ab-5-not-as-easy-as-abc/

7. https://www.actorsequity.org/resources/contracts/NEAT/

8. https://www.huffpost.com/entry/the-health-benefits-of-a_b_10246982

9. https://www.henley.ac.uk/news/2019/four-day-week-pays-off-for-uk-business

10. https://www.actorsequity.org/resources/contracts/LORT/

11. https://newdream.org/resources/infographics-shorter-workweek

12. https://www.ncbi.nlm.nih.gov/pmc/articles/PMC6617405/

13. https://www.centerstage.org/about/social-accountability/

Part 2

Life

12

Stage Managing a Beautifully Complicated History

Nikki Hyde

SOMETHING UNEXPECTED

By the time we are doing run throughs of an opera in the rehearsal room, I endeavor to know the show like the back of my hand. But sometimes, something unexpected happens.

I was an assistant stage manager on the Los Angeles Opera production of Philip Glass's *Satyagraha*,[1] the second in his Portrait Trilogy, described by the American composer as portraits of people whose personal vision transformed the thinking of their times through the power of ideas rather than military force.[2] *Satyagraha* is a non-linear meditation on Mohandas Gandhi's life, specifically the time he spent in South Africa. After a week of pre-production and nearly four weeks of rehearsal, I was confident that the show was in my bones.

In the final scene of Phelim McDermott's production, the entire set breaks apart and disappears. Upstage, an actor portraying Dr. Martin Luther King, Jr. stands on an oversized lectern, silently orating to an invisible audience. Downstage, an aging Gandhi walks in slow motion, connecting with a small group of satyagrahi.[3] I had less to do at the end of the show, so I watched from the side of the rehearsal room. There is a moment timed with the music when MLK and Gandhi make eye contact, one non-violent revolutionary to another: a symbolic handoff from a previous generation to the next. That moment of eye contact, so

DOI: 10.4324/9780429321672-15

simple and brief, brought me to tears. It did not matter that I knew exactly what was coming or that I had seen that moment several times in different iterations, the confluence of the music, the symbolism, the hope, the tragic deaths of both men, and the history of the fight for human dignity across cultures was overwhelming.

That was in 2018. Less than two years later, America and the theatre industry would be grappling with a reignited fight for human dignity. From Black Lives Matter to We See You White American Theatre,[4] this reckoning mirrors the struggle that has been going on for hundreds of years for Black people in this country. That moment in that rehearsal room was the product of not only what I have experienced in my work as a theatre maker but also the generational stories I carry with me. In my career, I have had both the opportunity and the foresight to work on productions that have brought me closer to those stories. While *Satyagraha* was a fortunate assignment given to me by a company, I have strongly advocated for myself to work on shows that are meaningful to me and bring me closer to my identity as a Black stage manager, to my elders and ancestors, and to a history that I am sometimes able to shield myself from through my privileges. My work as a stage manager has forced me to confront this beautifully complicated history and I am a better person for it. Theatre has that power. We often think about how theatre can affect audiences, actors, and directors. But as stage managers, we live with these stories in a very intimate way. They affect us too.

BEING MIXED IN PWIs AND PBSs

A little bit about my background: I am Mixed. For my entire life, I have always identified as a Mixed person: 50% Black from my mom and 50% White from my dad.[5] Growing up in the 1990s, I had to choose between being White and being Black on standardized tests. My mother always advised me to choose Black. That made me uncomfortable, as if I was misrepresenting myself. But at that time, "mixed" was not an option, and even if I did not fully identify as Black, the world saw me that way.

I started doing theatre at a young age. My first role was as the littlest (and only brown) orphan in Meehan, Strouse, and Charnin's *Annie*, and several community theatre roles followed. I vividly remember playing the role of Raynell in a production of August Wilson's *Fences*. My mother played the role of Rose. While I spent most of my time backstage playing cards until my scene at the end of the play, I remember understanding that this was an important play, it was written by a Black playwright, it had an all-Black cast, and all those things made it atypical in my hometown. To this day, *Fences* is one of the seminal plays in my career, even if I engaged with it first as a ten-year-old who didn't quite understand the entire context. I remember wondering, why was Troy so hard on Cory? Why didn't Rose leave when Troy cheated on her? Why did life for the Maxsons seem so hard?

My acting career ended when I discovered stage management in college. At that time, my only stage management role models were White, but I am grateful for all the people who took me under their wing as I navigated my place in the industry. My first professional show was a world premiere called *Butterflies of Uganda* at Greenway Court Theatre. The play is based on the true story of a young girl who was kidnapped and indoctrinated into the Lord's Resistance Army.[6] Out of the gate, I was working on a show with an almost all-Black cast about a subject I knew nothing about. And the play was written and directed by a White American. At 22, I didn't question the idea of a White person in a Predominantly White Institution (PWI) telling the story of Black people. I also didn't question why I, a relatively inexperienced stage manager, was hired for this show. In her memoir, *More Than Enough*, Elaine Welteroth explains "No matter how much you try to blend in, your race walks into every room before you do."[7] My race, which I felt somewhat disconnected to, was already playing a role in my career.

One important thing I learned on that show was the concept of color privilege. One of the Ugandan actors told me that if I ever visited Africa, I would be proposed to by every man who sees me. She mentioned that her family celebrated when she brought home her mixed-race, lighter-skinned husband, because their children would be lighter than her. Twenty-two-year-old me mostly laughed this off but it made me hyperaware of my place in the world as a person of color. I am both light-skinned and ethnically ambiguous enough that I do not experience the same prejudices that my dark-skinned Black community does. Adding on the fact that I did not grow up and was not educated in any Predominantly Black Spaces (PBSs), I never felt comfortable claiming to be Black. That's why "mixed" was always my go-to identifier. I knew going into theatre, and even more so opera, would not increase my time in PBSs. So, after that experience on *Butterflies of Uganda*, I committed myself to seeking out work that put me in PBSs to tap into my own Blackness.

THE ONGOING FIGHT

As I am writing this, there are renewed protests in the greater Minneapolis area as the officer that murdered George Floyd stands trial,[8] and another unarmed Black man, Daunte Wright, was killed by a point-blank gunshot at the hands of a White police officer during a routine traffic stop.[9] What people of my generation and younger sometimes forget, or never realized, is that Black Lives Matter is fighting against the same things Black activists have been fighting against since the Jim Crow Era: institutional racial discrimination, disenfranchisement, and segregation. That was made visceral to me when I got to work as the deck stage manager on Universes's *Party People* at the Public Theater. *Party People* tells the history of the Black Panther Party for Self-Defense and the Young Lords[10] through an imagined reunion of its members at an art exhibit. When I saw the show on the Public's season schedule, I knew I wanted to—no, I needed to—be a part of it. I am embarrassed to admit how little I knew about the Party before this experience, and so much of what I knew was obscured by false narratives of domestic terrorism. The story of Fred Hampton, which you can now see dramatized in the film *Judas and the Black Messiah*, is enough to illuminate that what these movements were—and are—fighting for is the right to self-determination, to live without fear of dying at the hands of the state, to fully participate in the democratic process, and to live with dignity. I remember being enthralled every performance by a second act musical number called "Omar's Rant," a stream-of-conscious diatribe against Black oppression. Steven Sapp of Universes, who wrote and performed the piece, reposted the audio of "Omar's Rant" on social media shortly after George Floyd's murder and the start of the BLM demonstrations. I found myself repeating the opening refrain: "In the morning 'til the evening/ all day/ I'll be working hard all day/ 'til the evening/ since the morning/ I'll be working hard." There's a well-known adage that if you're a Black person in White America, you must work "twice as hard to get half as far." This doesn't only apply to social, professional, and financial upward mobility; it also applies to literal survival. We were in previews of *Party People* when Donald Trump was elected as the 45th President of the United States. Going to work the day after the election felt almost impossible, except for the fact that the story we were telling was vital.[11]

GENERATIONAL TRAUMA

A unique thing about *Party People* for me as a stage manager was that there were several other people of color on the creative team. That had not been my experience for the most part (other than my work with Cornerstone Theater Company, which I will discuss later). One stark example in my career of White artists telling a Black story is *The Scottsboro Boys*. I was a production assistant on a regional remount of the Broadway production. The book was written by David Thompson with music by John Kander and lyrics by Fred Ebb, and the show was directed and choreographed by Susan Stroman. On the original creative team, the only non-White person was the costume designer, Toni-Leslie James. And on the production team in this iteration, it was me: light-skinned, production assistant me.

I have thought about this production frequently in the years since for several reasons. The first is I am curious as to whether this show would have been produced at all if it had not been for Kander and Ebb (the musical duo behind big Broadway hits like *Cabaret* and *Chicago*), and Stro's star power to bring it to Broadway. While there likely were myriad ways in which Black representation on the creative team could have exceeded only the costume designer, I am grateful this story was being told. *The Scottsboro Boys* dramatizes the true case of nine Black boys between the ages of 13 and 19 who were falsely accused and repeatedly tried for the rape of two White women in 1930s Alabama.

Another reason I continue to reflect on *The Scottsboro Boys* is I had a core-shaking emotional experience during a rehearsal, similar to *Satyagraha*. We were in technical rehearsals and had just added costumes and makeup. At the end of the show, before the finale, the ensemble of boys runs offstage right (where I was posted) for a quick change into their finale costumes. The conceit of the entire musical is telling this historical event as a minstrel show, and the finale involves the boys wearing blackface. Almost the entire cast had done this show previously, so when they ran backstage that first time, they were harried but also confident in what they were doing. It was not until they were all lined up in the wing to re-enter that I took a good look at them. I felt a tightness in my solar plexus. It was hard to take a deep breath. The pain I felt seeing those actors I had grown to know was extraordinary. It was so shocking to me that once they went onstage, I had to close my eyes and collect myself. I had never experienced imagery as pain before. That was one of my first experiences with generational trauma. I didn't know I was carrying that type of humiliation and dehumanization inside me. I did not have to experience it firsthand. It was there all along.

There is a lot of discussion about the ethics of putting both artists and audiences through these types of potentially traumatic experiences in the theatre. In my opinion, it is imperative to tell these stories, or we risk losing our history. Or in my case, I will never be able to contextualize why I felt physical pain when I saw the actors in blackface. The discussion that needs to continue is not IF we tell these stories, but WHO tells them, and HOW we tell them to keep the storytellers supported and healthy. I was not wearing blackface, but I still felt harmed by that experience. But through it, I tapped into a deeper understanding of the world my great-grandparents lived in and how that has been passed down to my grandparents (one who is still living), my parents, and finally down to me. The mostly White audiences may have taken away a history lesson from *The Scottsboro Boys*, but that production, flaws and all, forever changed me.

SLAVE PLAYS

One history lesson we consistently avoid in the American theatre is arguably the most vital: slavery. In my career, I have not shied away from it. A few years ago, I was approached by South Coast Repertory to stage manage a world premiere play. I had never worked for the company or with anyone on the creative team before so, as I always do in those cases, I asked to read the play. The play was called *Little Black Shadows* and as soon as I read the setting, I knew I had to do it. Briefly, the play is the story of two slave children in 1850s Georgia who served two White children (one who is based on Martha Washington), sleeping under their beds, dressing them, and being "on-call" all day long. When theatre addresses slavery—which is rare—it doesn't usually show it from a child's perspective. Any portrayal of enslaved children is stark and horrifying, but my memories of that production process are full of laughter. Laughter through the pain, laughter through the constant use of the N-word, and laughter because I trusted my collaborators to tell this story well. There is a scene in the play where Toy, one of the "shadows," "reads" a children's book by looking at the pictures. In her interpretation, the book tells the story of a White man who looks

Black, and nobody will marry him. There are several interjections by the other "shadow," Colis, exclaiming how terrible that situation is. The self-hatred Toy's story reinforces—that White is good and righteous, and Black is dark and evil— and the repetitious, self-referential use of the N-word is gutting. But that same repetition, the shadow puppetry in the scene, and the matter-of-fact delivery of the story by the actors (who were adults playing children) made me laugh every single time. There was not a day in rehearsal or performance that I did not laugh throughout that scene. As uncomfortable as it made me feel intellectually, there was a release, a catharsis each time I watched it. I attribute that to Kemp Power's writing and May Adrales's direction. We can tell devastating stories, including stories about America's original sin, that also bring us joy, hope, and connection through laughter.[12]

CREATING COMMUNITY

I am a stage manager who thrives on challenging material. My introduction into professional theatre was as an intern for Cornerstone Theater Company, where I am currently a member of the artistic ensemble. One aspect I value about the work I do with Cornerstone is that we give members of various communities a platform to make art, tell their stories, and hear the stories of others. As a Mixed girl from Michigan, if I had only gone into "traditional" theatre, I would not have met the incredible community organizers, educators, veterans, environmental activists, migrant farm workers, prison abolitionists, LGBTQIA+ leaders, urban farmers, and rehabilitated gang members I have gotten to make plays with. One play that resonates with me in my journey as a Black stage manager is *Love on San Pedro*, a play about the Skid Row neighborhood in Los Angeles, which is just a few blocks away from where Cornerstone used to have their offices. The play (which was written by a White playwright, James McManus, who is now my partner) tells a beautiful love story in front of a backdrop of extreme urban poverty, poverty that disproportionally affects Black people, specifically Black men. The demographics of Skid Row have changed, and people experiencing homelessness has increased since we performed the play in 2013,[13] but working on the play opened my eyes to my personal biases about homelessness, poverty, and addiction. We all, in theory, could be one medical or financial catastrophe away from losing our safety net and needing assistance. If there is one thing to learn from the COVID-19 pandemic, it is that there are few government systems set up to help those in need, especially people of color.[14]

The process of stage managing *Love on San Pedro* and other community-based shows, including the non-political Public Works pageants at the Public Theater, has taught me about my own biases, my privileges, and my deep desire to connect with other humans in a collaborative way. I have little interest in telling stories that don't teach me something about myself, especially in connection with my own Blackness—the Blackness I don't always feel comfortable claiming; the Blackness that I am sometimes shielded from because of my light skin, my ability to code-switch, and the industry I have chosen to work in.

None of this work is easy. The journey I am on, professional and personal, is perpetual. Like art, it's messy and complicated and there will be missteps and regrets and joy and harm and pain and breakthroughs and revelations. Theatre brings us closer to our own humanity and the humanity in others, because of and despite the systemic inequity that exists in the industry. As an individual stage manager, theatre artist, and educator, I feel it is my responsibility to tell the hard, messy, complicated stories. If we shy away from them, it's impossible to learn from them. I will not allow my story, my elders' stories, and my ancestors' stories to be erased or, more likely, simply neglected or ignored. I will advocate for these stories to be told and if that requires me to take a step back from an industry that is avoiding this type of representation, I will.[15] But the theatre I know, I've experienced, I've dreamt of, with all its flaws, has the capacity to expose the humanity inside each of us so that a subtle glance between two historical figures on an opera stage changes us forever.

My name is Nikki Hyde and I am a Black stage manager.

NOTES

1. Sanskrit, loosely translated to "truth insistence" or "holding firm to truth." A particular form of non-violent resistance or resistance.

2. "Dunvagen Music Publishers, *Einstein on the Beach* (Recording)." Philipglass.com. Nonesuch Records, 1993.

3. Sanskrit for people who practice satyagraha.

4. www.weseeyouwat.com/

5. For this essay, I have chosen to capitalize "Black," "White," and "Mixed" when referring to race. This is a change from my previous practice of capitalizing Black and not capitalizing White or Mixed. For more information on this evolving topic, read K. Mack and J. Palfrey, "Capitalizing Black and White: Grammatical Justice and Equity," MacArthur Foundation, August 26, 2020, www.macfound.org/press/perspectives/capitalizing-black-and-white-grammatical-justice-and-equity; and K.A. Appiah, "The Case for Capitalizing the *B* in Black," *The Atlantic*, June 18, 2020, www.theatlantic.com/ideas/archive/2020/06/time-to-capitalize-blackand-white/613159/

6. A Ugandan rebel group that was designated a terrorist organization by the United States at its height of activity in the mid-to-late 2000s.

7. E. Welteroth, *More Than Enough: Claiming Space for Who You Are (No Matter What They Say)* (London: Ebury Publishing, 2019).

8. Derek Chauvin, the Minneapolis police officer who murdered George Floyd, was found guilty on April 20, 2021. I do not consider this justice. This conviction is the exception to the rule of police not being held accountable in the deaths of Black people. But it is a long overdue step in the right direction: see "George Floyd: Jury Finds Derek Chauvin Guilty of Murder," BBC, April 21, 2021, www.bbc.com/news/world-us-canada-56818766

9. "What to Know About the Death of Duante Wright," *The New York Times*, April 23, 2021, www.nytimes.com/article/daunte-wright-death-minnesota.html

10. S. Coffman, "The Young Lords and the Black Panther Party," Digital Chicago, n.d. https://digitalchicagohistory.org/exhibits/show/young-lords/young-lords-and-black-panthers

11. As of spring 2021, *Party People* has not been produced elsewhere since that production at the Public in 2016.

12. As of spring 2021, *Little Black Shadows* has not been produced elsewhere since that production at South Coast Repertory in 2018.

13. Los Angeles County had a homeless population count of 57,737 in 2013. That count increased to 66,433 in 2020.

14. As of spring 2021, *Love on San Pedro* has not been produced elsewhere since that Cornerstone production in 2013.

15. Thank you, Karen Olivo, for showing us how to enact change in our industry with integrity. N. Rosky, "Karen Olivo Will Not Return to MOULIN ROUGE!—'I Want a Theatre Industry That Matches My Integrity'," Broadway World, April 14, 2021, www. broadwayworld.com/article/Karen-Olivo-Announces-She-Will-Not-Return-to-MOU LIN-ROUGE—I-Want-a-Theatre-Industry-That-Matches-My-Integrity-20210414?fb clid=IwAR2kuIJL0TefODvCVivho5fM0zjyR0TnfIIm3aev6jHjG6-kqRGMX8mwbGU

13

Already Calm, I'm the Stage Manager
Michele Kay

WHO YOU ARE

There will be moments in your career when you doubt everything you know. When in doubt, remain calm, you're the stage manager.

You're sitting at the tech table for the biggest show of your life and you wonder, "How did I get here?" You question your choices. You doubt your worthiness. You are certain that at any moment, the production manager or director will realize that you are a fraud and don't deserve this seat at this table. This is the moment when you inhale deeply, exhale slowly, and you remind yourself that you ARE the stage manager and no one in the room is doubting your ability to guide them through the production. No one, that is, except you.

When I began college, I thought I was going to be a lawyer. It was the 1980s and that seemed like the thing to do. My intention was to get an undergraduate degree in history and then head to law school. As part of my Bachelor of Arts degree I needed to take a course in fine arts. I picked a class in the scene shop and was assigned to crew the musical *Shenandoah*. In my undergraduate program, we built the set onstage during the day, and then the show rehearsed onstage in the evening. One day, during the transition from the afternoon work call to the evening rehearsal, a student walked onstage whom you instantly knew was in charge. She took command just by simply walking into the room. She seemed to know

DOI: 10.4324/9780429321672-16

everything, and everyone seemed to know that she was important. I asked, "Who is that?" Our scene shop foreman informed me that she was the stage manager. After a brief pause, I said, "I want to do that." What did I think being the stage manager meant? I have no idea. But I liked her air of calm, cool control. I wanted to be a stage manager. I wanted to be THAT stage manager.

When you're starting out in the theatre and you say that you want to be a stage manager, people tend to step aside and let you do it. Why? Because no one wants to be the stage manager. People want to be onstage. People want to design the sets, lights, sound, makeup, and costumes. They want to build; they want to make. No one actually *wants* to be the stage manager. At least that's what people who are not inclined towards stage management think. I wanted to be the stage manager. I didn't know why or what it meant, but I knew I wanted to be one. And, now, decades later as a university professor who heads a prestigious stage management program, I meet lots of young people who want to be the stage manager. But what is it that drives us towards this profession? What keeps us in it? And what magic spell do we perform that convinces others that we are the right person for the job?

WHAT YOU THOUGHT YOU WERE DOING

At the beginning of my career, I had no idea *why* I wanted to be a stage manager, not really; I just liked the idea of being "in control" of something. Seeing that stage manager command the room, I thought that she was "in control" of something, and I too wanted that control. Like many young stage managers, I started out thinking that being in control meant to be controlling. It can mean that, sort of. If you look at the *how* of stage management, it's all about control. You control the prop placements and scene shifts, you control the rehearsal schedule, you control the cue placements. You can get very good at that level of control and that can feel very rewarding. You've become the embodiment of the phrase, "a stage manager knows everything." Knowing your show in intricate detail is critical to being a successful stage manager. Through knowing your show, be that an opera, a dance, a musical, an event, you can objectively demonstrate that you can be trusted with the details of the task. And it's easy to reward task-based accomplishments, and reward feels good. It feels successful. But a show is not made up of just props and scene shifts and light cues, a show is made up of people, and people are…squishy. People are wonderfully squishy. Yes, knowing your show, being a dependable resource of show-based knowledge is critical, but it is not everything. And without the second part of the equation, the *why*, it's nothing.

I was more or less self-trained in college; that is, I did not have a stage management professor or a class in stage management. I had faculty mentors who taught me *how* to stage manage from their perspective. Then I went into a wonderful, challenging, career-forming internship at a major regional theatre. As an intern I was assigned tasks appropriate to my level of experience. On my first show, I was in charge of getting rehearsal props for the production. We had a delightful closet of supplies to make or procure whatever was needed for hand props. I set my heart to it and pulled or made a prop for everything. I was very proud of myself. I preset everything accordingly and then I sat back waiting for a pat on the back for doing such an amazing job. What I got was a rude-awakening because in all my amazing rehearsal prop pulling and making, I had neglected to wash the dishes and I had given the cast dusty dishes. The stage manager, Deb Aquavella, walked over to my table, calmly yet firmly set a cup down in front of me and said, "never give an actor a dirty prop," and then, she walked away. I was defeated. My ego had been crushed. I had put so much effort into pulling and making the rehearsal props, and instead of accolades, I was told they weren't perfect. I was 22 years old and I just found out that I wasn't perfect. Although I did not realize it at the time, on that day, the second most important stage manager in my life taught me the most valuable lesson in management: that it wasn't about the things, it was about the people. By focusing on the things and proving how amazing I was at making rehearsal props, I had neglected to think beyond *my effort* to consider how my work was going to affect others. I had made every effort to show off my knowledge, and in doing so, I demonstrated my ignorance. From that point forward, if I wanted to be a successful stage manager, I had to learn how to shift my focus from the stuff to the people. For the record, I will be eternally grateful for that note from Deb who is not only my mentor, but also a colleague and friend.

After a year in the internship, I moved to New York, joined Actors' Equity Association, and found myself in the lead stage manager's seat more often than that of assistant. At the time, that seemed great to me, but looking back, I didn't have much opportunity to learn from an on-the-job mentor. When I was an intern, I was afraid to make a mistake. I had made one early on, and I held on to the sting of that embarrassment longer than I should have. In hindsight, I can see that as the beginning of my journey learning to focus on people, but at the time, I wanted to be good and be acknowledged for my skills, my hard skills, for the things I could do. So, I buckled down and pushed myself to not make mistakes. It's a good thing I was fun to be around, otherwise, I would have been insufferable. When I worked in New York, I struggled. More for the fact that I just was not cut out to be a New Yorker, but also, outside of a few fantastic assistant stage management positions, I needed mentorship. The funny thing about learning is that while you're doing a job, it's nearly impossible to reflect on the job you are doing. But there are moments, when the job is done, that you look back and you get to reflect upon all the things that drove you crazy in the moment from a distance. And when the moment is no longer pressing upon you, there is room for tremendous clarity, evaluation, and growth.

A NEW PERSPECTIVE AND A MOMENT OF DISBELIEF

After two years of feeling somewhat rudderless in New York, I decided to move to Chicago. At the time, I didn't know that I was looking for mentorship, I just knew that I needed a change. *(Life-tip: if you're not sure about something in your career, give it two years. That's just enough time to really explore a new job/location/co-workers, but not so much time that you've grown roots too deep to comfortably pickup and move.)* I had decided that the new Chicago version of me was going to become more involved in my union, so I went to my first meeting at the Actors' Equity office shortly after arriving in town. Through a chance conversation with one of the office staff, I was introduced to Cathryn "Bula" Bulicek, and unexpectedly landed my first opera job as an assistant stage manager for her on *The Tender Land* and *The Magic Flute* with the Chicago Opera Theatre. Honesty, I had no idea what I was getting into, but to this day, I have an incredible optimism that always tells me to say, "sure, I'm happy to give it a try."

Opera is different. The "stuff" side of stage management does not change much no matter where you are doing it; props are props, sets are sets. What changes are the people, and opera is a genre rooted in tradition and hierarchy: it is all about the people. In my time with Bula, I kept my eyes and ears open, and my mouth closed, except when I was cueing artists onstage (that's a little opera joke). But really, during my summer in opera, I learned more about patience and people management than I could have imagined. One day, we were in the final staging rehearsals for *The Magic Flute*, probably a run through. This was a tutti call (all call), including principals, chorus, and supernumeraries. Supernumeraries hold non-singing, primarily bit-part, acting roles, for example, waiters in *La bohème*, or in this case, temple guards in *The Magic Flute*. During the rehearsal, one of the guards knocked a spear into a fluorescent light causing it to crash to the ground. Rehearsal stopped, in part to clean up the remnants of the crashed tube, but really it stopped because one of the principal singers had left the room and refused to return while the vapors from the broken fluorescent tube were present. An impromptu meeting was called by the performers' AGMA (American Guild of Musical Artists) representative (the opera union), the affected performer, and the stage manager. While I cleaned up the broken tube, I watched the stage manager calmly navigate the choppy waters of a performer in peril: a performer who felt threatened enough by the environment to walk away from one of the final rehearsals before tech. At the conclusion of the meeting, I learned that this principal singer was not going to come back into the rehearsal hall for three days. I was in shock. I was in awe. In theatre, we'd stop, clean up the mess, and then get back to it, but in opera, where everyone knows that a performer's career hangs on the health of two thin flaps of skin at the back of the throat, this was big. I couldn't believe that the stage manager wasn't losing her mind. Basically, we would not see this principal singer again until we moved to stage a few days later. But the stage manager remained calm. She assessed the situation, recognized the needs of the performer, measured them against where we were in the rehearsal process, and calmly helped devise a plan that would work to the benefit of the performer and the production. Like the stage manager from my internship, she put the needs of the people first, and in doing so she most effectively managed the needs of the production.

A NEW BEGINNING

A few months later I received an offer to be the assistant stage manager on a production called *Nomathemba* (which means "Hope" in Zulu) that was moving from Steppenwolf Theatre to Crossroads Theatre in New Jersey, and then to the Kennedy Center in Washington D.C. They needed an assistant to join their long-time stage manager, Malcolm Ewen, at these external venues and I was in the right place at the right time with the right connections to get the job. Malcolm Ewen would turn out to be my friend and mentor for many, many years to come.

Shortly before we left to begin rehearsals in New Jersey, Malcolm invited me to meet him at Steppenwolf where he was turning over a production of *The Libertine* to the replacement stage manager. We met in the downstairs production office, then Mal asked if I wanted to follow him to the tiring house to wrap up his pre-show calls. I said, "sure" (see note earlier) and followed him through the maze of the backstage until I followed him ... onstage. And I mean, onstage, in front of an audience who was making their way to their seats and watching, what I then discovered, was the onstage pre-show. The pre-show that we just walked into. Onstage. And then, we walked up to the star of the show, a well-known movie actor, and Mal proceeded to have a conversation. Onstage. In front of the audience. At this point, I felt so utterly wrong. I wasn't supposed to be onstage. I'm a stage manager. I'm a behind-the-scenes person, and yet, there I was onstage, having a conversation with a movie star in front of an audience of a couple hundred people. But Malcolm was there, and he was calm and comfortable in this place, so taking his lead, I chose to be calm, though truthfully, not comfortable, in this place too. Choosing to be calm, and allowing this moment to unfold regardless of the internal jitters I may have felt about being onstage in front of an audience, taught me an invaluable lesson about choice. I chose to be in the moment, and I chose to not freak out at being onstage or talking to a movie star, and low and behold, I survived.

Outside of the usual challenges of remounting a production in multiple venues, *Nomathemba* had its share of unpredictable, squishy, human moments. Moments that, as the assistant, I didn't really have to address, but rather, as an assistant, I was able to step back and observe the stage manager at work. What I learned on this production was the art of negotiation, the value of a good laugh, and the many facets of trust. Stuff—props, costumes, and scenery—doesn't have feelings, or good and bad days, or opinions, it's just stuff. But people, wonderfully, squishy people are ever-changing, ever-evolving, and nearly always unpredictable. What we need, as stage managers, to be successful goes beyond checklists and paperwork, we need compassion, empathy, and we need to let go of perceptions of control in order to gain the confidence of our cast and our production team.

I had to learn to lose control, and for a stage manager, that seems antithetical to our very reason for being. Aren't we supposed to be in control of everything? Didn't I state that at the beginning of this essay? But I knew, going forward, to be the best stage manager I could be, I had to lose some control in order to gain confidence in managing people. Two significant things happened to shape my career during our run of *Nomathemba* at the Kennedy Center. First, I turned down an offer to return to New York to be the assistant stage manager on the then pre-Broadway production of *Rent*, and second, Malcolm asked in his wonderfully gruffly voice, "What are you doing this summer? Do you want to come to Vermont to stage manage at the Weston Playhouse?" I went to Vermont, and I've never regretted turning down that offer to do *Rent*. I mean, that was soon to be a huge hit on Broadway, and my career would have taken a very Broadway turn, but the choice to go to Vermont set me on a trajectory that, when looking back, has been wonderful.

VERMONT

When you're in Vermont but you're not from Vermont, you are a flat-lander—loosely translated it means you are not from the Green Mountains, you're from the outside, but that does not mean you are an outsider. Not in Weston. And not at the Weston Playhouse. In 1988, Malcolm Ewen with his two friends, Steve Stettler and Tim Fort, took over the producing and artistic leadership of the Weston Playhouse. By the time I had joined the staff of the Playhouse in the summer of 1996, they were known as "The Three Guys." My first summer in Weston, I was the stage manager on *Forever Plaid*, *Crazy for You*, *Arms and the Man*, and *Falsettos* which also ran as a fall tour in New England. Back then, The Three Guys directed everything. That summer I got to stage manage for each of them, Mal directed *Crazy for You* and *Falsettos*. I wasn't sure what it was going to be like stage managing for a man who had spent two-thirds of the year stage managing at one of the most reputable theatre companies in the country, but really, at the time, I don't think it ever occurred to me to compare myself to Malcolm or to think he'd judge my ability. You see, Mal had a way of making people feel at ease and at helping them to be, and do, their best without putting the pressure on them to be anything other than their authentic self. I have returned to the Weston Playhouse 15 times over the past 24 years and seven of those productions were with Malcolm as my director. Much of what I learned from him was through working with him as his stage manager. And so begins my dedication to my mentor, Malcolm Ewen.

HOW TO BE THE BEST STAGE MANAGER YOU CAN BE: SING TO STRANGERS WHILE DRESSED LIKE A COW

If you speak with anyone who has ever worked with Malcolm they'd say the same thing, he made you feel safe, cared for, and part of the family. As stage managers, we're taught to make people feel safe and cared for. We have our first-aid kits and our stage management kits stocked with such a variety of things a Boy Scout would drool with envy, but having the wares to patch a scrape or whip up a prop from gaffer's tape, a straw, and a binder clip only gets you halfway there. When you dig in, at the core of a safe and caring environment is acceptance, respect, and humility. What makes a family is patience, loyalty, and a touch of fun.

Three things are for certain in Weston: cheese, cows, and the Late Night Cabaret at the Weston Playhouse which follows every evening performance in the Playhouse. There are not a whole lot of options for late-night entertainment in Vermont, especially in a small town like Weston, so following the mainstage show many of the performers, the Young Company, and even the production and administrative staff will perform songs and sketches while audience members enjoy a late-night adult beverage and of course, some Vermont cheese. The songs and sketches come from show tunes, commercials, popular music, or are parodies of all these. Most shows involve references to cheese, cows, neighboring towns, and flat-landers. A beloved character of the Late Night Cabaret was Harlow Wilcox and his Green Mountain Boys. Harlow would come onstage wearing a straw hat, a t-shirt with some hilarious pun, and carrying his gut bucket which was a washtub with a broom handle and thick string or rope attaching the two. The gut bucket was Harlow's version of an upright bass guitar. He'd beckon the Green Mountain Boys to the stage, and then Harlow and his Boys would break into a melody eulogizing a lost cow, praising the cheese, or bemoaning a rivalry with a nearby farmer. It was fun and light-hearted, and it was quintessentially Malcolm. The first time I saw Harlow, I thought, what would the people back in Chicago think about this?! But this was Mal, playing a gut bucket and singing about cows to strangers—what could be more humbling? What was I to do but try it? At the Late Night Cabaret I've played a cow, a stage manager, and a leopard. I've danced to Olivia Newton John, and told stage manager jokes that I'm pretty sure no one got except me and the other stage manager in my comedy duo. Humility comes when someone recognizes you "from onstage last night" and you realize it wasn't your brilliant calling of *Guys and Dolls*, it was in the Late Night Cabaret. Humility comes in a cow suit.

When we can stand in front of an audience dressed like a cow, we must let go of our ego. When we stand in front of a rehearsal room full of actors or in tech in front of the production team we must let go of our ego. We must be humble in the face of judgment. It's not about us. It is not about the ego of any one of the members of the production team or the cast. When working on a show, we are one. We are symbiotic. We are all playing a critical part, and those parts make up the whole. When we, as stage managers, let go of our ego, we discover that stage management is about giving. It is about giving of ourselves, our time, energy, and expertise to lift a production to its highest. It is not about whether we are recognized for being the best, it is simply doing our best in the moment we are in. When we let go of our ego and we accept humility, we can come to peace with our raison d'être as a stage manager. In this world of ever more complex technology, we have to wonder, are we necessary? With technological advances are stage managers redundant? I say no, we are not redundant because we bring our humanity to a production. We bring our humanity to the rehearsal process, we bring our humanity to show calling, we bring our humanity to the experience of collaboration. We are the calm in the center of the creative storm. I have recently heard the calling sequence to the opening of *The Tempest* at Steppenwolf Theatre with Malcolm at the helm. He starts the sequence checking in all the players, calling a dozen standbys and receiving the responses of his team at the ready. And at the moment before the start of the calling sequence he says, "Hey, it's time to do a play, why not?" To me, this too is quintessentially Malcolm: "it's time to do a play, why not?" What exudes calm more than a stage manager, at the ready, standing by over 100 cues, and in a slow and steady voice saying, "It's time to do a play. Why not?" Why not? What else have we got to do but tell our stories? We're putting on a play. We're not curing cancer, but we're still important. We're a diversion. We're an education. We're a distraction from the woes of the world for the audience. Why not? What do those two words tell us? They don't ask the gripping question of "why?", but rather the taunting question of "why not?"

Collaboration is terrifying. At its finest, it is the most raw form of vulnerability. Where do we, as stage managers, fit into the collaboration? We are the calm at the center of the storm; we are the peacemakers; we are the translators; we are the record keepers. When we are at our best, we can provide a compass to help guide our creative colleagues through the messy business of collaboration: "Hey, let's put on a play." Collaboration is a beautiful thing, but only if the collaboration has a usable outcome. Although that makes theatre-making sound so business-like, there must be an end result. We are storytellers. But if we don't succeed in telling the story, then we are not theatre-makers, we are simply talking. Stage managers are essential to keeping the collaboration on track. To help our creative brethren rise above simply talking to the heightened state of collaboration of…storytelling. We create a space where people feel cared for, respected, and safe. Stage managers set the table for the creative energy to flow. Practically speaking, we tape floors and set props, but critically speaking, we do that to allow for maximum creative process to occur. We set the stage and we step aside. It is not about us; it is about them, and that is okay with us because we, the stage managers, are the caretakers of the creative space.

SLOW AND STEADY

We all need to pull on the rope in the same direction with [sic] a similar pace. We all need to go that way, and we all need to pull on the rope to go that way. We can't be pulling the rope to the left or to the right because that's not going to help us get to where we want to go. It's a process of moving through both the rehearsal process, but on a nightly basis, it's a process of starting at zero and getting to the end of the play, right, so you want to encourage people to pull the same way, because if there's an actor who's in another play, it won't be successful.

(Malcolm Ewen, in an interview conducted by Joe Drummond,
another Chicago legend of stage management,
for the Stage Managers' Association.)

In creating the collaborative space one of the most important edicts to remember is that we're all doing the same play. It is not us and them; it's just us. We, the cast, crew, creative and stage management staffs, are all doing the same play. We have different roles to perform in the production, but, ultimately, it is the same play and the result at the end will be the same: the Von Trapps climb over the Alps and escape, Juliet kills herself and Romeo finds her, the Youngers leave their apartment and buy a house in a predominantly white neighborhood. Although our roles are different, we are telling the same story; as stage managers, through our oversight of the production, we help our team pull the rope in the same direction. We call cues, we give notes, we watch, we listen, we learn: we captain the ship steadily and calmly through often choppy waters safely into the same port every night. Keeping our team on the track best serves the show. What my mentors have taught me is that in divorcing ourselves from a need to feed our own ego, to remain calm and, yes, in control, we provide the stable, safe space for collaborative creativity to flourish.

CURTAIN CALL

My friend, Malcolm Ewen, passed away in May 2019 after an arduous battle with cancer. At his memorial services in both Weston and Chicago, friends and colleagues spoke of Malcolm's life in the theatre and how he touched us as a mentor, a leader, and a stage manager. Chicago actor Cheryl Lynn Bruce best summed up Malcolm's gift to theatre-makers, "Malcolm, St. Do the Right Thing, epitome of unparalleled dedication to the management and care of his fellow human beings, of loyalty, of good humor, of excellence without incident." Excellence without incident—the calm at the center of the tempest.

Steady on, you are the stage manager.

14

Life in the Real World

Amanda Spooner

It was my first day of prep for the off-Broadway run of Paula Vogel's *Indecent* and instead of working in the office at The Vineyard Theatre, I was in a freezing operating room, no feeling from the torso down, separated from the lower part of my body by a curtain. With still almost two months to go, I had not really understood this was a possibility. I thought we had more time. Even after three days of labor, I felt sort of elated, completely disconnected from worry. I still made jokes with the nurses, I was still answering emails from my bed. When neonatologists came to my room and warned me of the risks of an early delivery, of a baby who might have brain damage from being deprived of oxygen, a baby who was tangled up in an umbilical cord with no water, whose heart rate kept dropping . . . I still felt like I was in my wheelhouse.

It was not until a nurse from the other side of the curtain yelled, "Time?" that it even occurred to me that my son might not have made it.

The whole world took pause. Life never felt so real.

I love being a stage manager. I am wild about all of it. I learned stage management from working on drag shows in San Francisco and eventually became smitten with new theatrical works, both genres requiring an appreciation for change and being present in the room. I spent all of college balancing professional experiences with school productions, once staying up for three days straight just to fit it all in. I took pride in having endless amounts of energy and resilience. I heard

DOI: 10.4324/9780429321672-17

over and over again how risky a profession in theatre could be, how thankless and possibly unrewarding. But I was all in. I live for the moments in which people care so much about a tiny detail of a play that they have to visibly restrain themselves. I love the chance we take when we share new works with the world. I love tech rehearsals. From the second I hit my stage management stride, I could not imagine doing anything else.

There were no matters of life or death getting in between me and the opportunity to be inside a theatre. Sacrifice after sacrifice in my personal life seemed to land me in all the wonderful places my professional life took me. I had heard countless negative opinions about stage managers trying to have time for children of their own, so much so that I cannot possibly cite all my sources. It is a widely accepted belief in our professional culture: stage managers cannot have children. Stage managers work long hours, must be available to fix everyone's problems, and rarely take breaks let alone have time for dependents. Even if they could afford children, they would never see them. For those who work consistently on higher paying contracts, we might *assume* it is an easier concept for them but they are still freelancers. There is no security, no certainty in our line of work. We are simply left with our community and all the places where our personal lives attempt to intersect with our career.

From the moment I met Rebecca Taichman, a director with whom I was paired to work on a new David Adjmi play, I was tuned into her wavelength. Her intellect both frightened and thrilled me. Our expectations of the world and ourselves were oddly similar. Being in the room while she was directing felt like standing in a theatrical frontier. Apparently, the fondness was mutual and before *Marie Antoinette* had even closed at Yale Repertory Theatre, she asked me to stage manage the very first reading of a play she had conceived with Paula Vogel. It was not just any play, it was an idea born when Rebecca was in graduate school, over a decade earlier. I happily agreed to make the commute back and forth between New Haven and New York City, to work on what was then known as *Rehearsing Vengeance* during the day and then call *Marie Antoinette* at night.

EQUITY MONDAY

My husband and I got married on an Equity Monday. I had my c-section on an Equity Monday. And if I had to guess, we made our son on an "Equity Monday" (meaning the one day off in the week). We were married in Las Vegas in December of 2014 but because of my work schedule (I was on seven projects at once, in various capacities), our trip was short and we had to postpone our honeymoon. After weighing every pro and con known to humankind, we committed to having kids, which was really the main reason we decided to get married in the first place. We could have spent our whole lives blissfully unwed but I had seen enough episodes of Judge Judy to decide I would like to be married before committing to a baby. In other words, I wanted a contract. Once my now husband did some reverse calculations regarding our ages, it seemed like the time was right to get married, have some years as a couple, and then hopefully have a child of our own.

I have stage managed a lot of readings, as I think most New York City stage managers will attest, but they do not all survive past their incubation. From 2012 through 2015, I think I was on eight readings and labs of *Indecent* before we learned we would have a fully-realized co-production at Yale Repertory Theatre and La Jolla Playhouse. Over the years I had seen many actors come and go, various combinations of casting tracks, tons of new script pages to fill my stage manager heart, at least three different titles, and loads of songs. The discoveries were tremendous and the idea we would get to do it with all the bells and whistles was glorious. And maybe in time, this one would find its way back to New York. Maybe in time we would end up on Broadway.

In July of 2015, between my stage managing Anne Washburn's *10 Out of 12* and the first production of *Indecent*, my husband and I went on our honeymoon. Still nervous about pulling the "baby trigger," I was simultaneously relieved and saddened by the fact my ovulation tests were indicating a baby might not be possible. We were really counting on time to establish ourselves as a married couple anyway, especially since *Indecent* was about to take me out of town for four months. And then who knows…? The sky was the limit, I had to see *Indecent* all the way through. Rather, I *wanted* to see it all the way through. It was not the time to have a baby. And without a single test result in the positive, I was all too happy to embark on a relaxing vacation with my wonderful new husband.

A couple weeks after I returned from my vacation, as we convened for the first rehearsal of *Indecent* at Yale, Paula Vogel came over to say hello. I had not seen her since April and just being in her presence feels like witnessing the wonder of the entire universe all at once. She is a magical human. We hugged and she stepped back, looked me over, and said, "You are glowing. I am going to Whole Foods later. What are you craving?" I was not offended, my weight has fluctuated throughout my entire adulthood. And little did she know, according to the ovulation test kit I bought at Duane Reade, my body was not operating as one might assume.

One week later, I had excused myself from table work to go to the restroom. Something was not right. Had I become pregnant on my honeymoon after all? Was this an attempt my body was making, to say, "Hey, lady, I AM actually trying here." Rebecca and Paula became concerned with my situation but I assured them I would see a doctor during a company BBQ the next day and meet them afterward at our evening rehearsal.

The next afternoon, instead of attending the BBQ, those two circled the health center in Paula's SUV, texting me throughout my appointment.

The doctor looked at my chart.

"So, let's see…it says here you're pregnant."

"No, ma'am, sorry for the confusion. What I was trying to tell the nurse is that I might have been pregnant but I don't think it stuck andthatisokaybecausewewerenotreallyt ryinganyway—"

"No, no. I am telling you. It is very early but you ARE pregnant."

I called Rebecca's phone.

"Alright…and you will forever have to pretend that I called you after my husband…I am pregnant."

"WE ARE HAVING A BA—"

"Yes, but shhhh…. it is very early and you cannot say anything. Tell Paula she was right. Now go eat meat and leave it alone."

But they never really left it alone. Instead, Paula showered me in snacks during rehearsal. Rebecca kept giving me woo-woo eyes while she insisted on taking prop furniture from me, that I was trying to reset. It took less than a week before the first cast member figured it out. I had not even really skipped a period. But Rebecca was right…it seemed we were actually doing it. It seemed we were having a baby.

The next few months were torture, waiting to tell the world at large our exciting news. I preemptively told a friend of mine, a director who already had a baby, and she said I should tell none of my colleagues. People would stop asking for me, assuming I was too complicated to employ with a child. That I would not be willing to work the same hours I always had. That I might ask for accommodations theatres would not be prepared to provide. It was true fear in her voice, fear and love for me, and despite her child already being in the world she seldom mentioned him publicly. The downtown and regional theatre scene was not built for a freelancing stage manager with a kid, she said. Was she right? Had we been too reckless? I was on a show I cared so deeply for and put so much work into…was I going to be dismissed from its journey, deemed a burden? She had examples, evidence. I hung up the phone and cried silent tears. I was stunned. It seemed the world was going to have an opinion about me having a baby, despite how invested I was in the decision.

I have always felt at home with the new and risky stories in the downtown scene. Those theatres are filled with thousands of cotton balls and naked people on roller skates. Those theatres are filled with simple enchantment. Those theatres seem to be totally focused on story over mass commercial viability—and if something is a hit, it might extend or head uptown. I had an affinity with that vibe and I was thrilled when, in 2016, an off-Broadway theatre, The Vineyard, committed to the NY transfer of *Indecent*. The space on 15th Street was the perfect container for our show. It was hard to ignore the possibility that this was the road to Broadway. Or maybe the wonderful Vineyard would be its last stop. Regardless, *Indecent* was being given a chance—it was still alive—and most of the company was a bunch of Broadway virgins along for the ride.

"WHAT DO YOU EXPECT? SHE IS A STAGE MANAGER."

Despite my excitement about the transfer, I decided to sit this one out. I was pregnant and while I was expected to make it well into tech before my delivery,

I had already assigned myself to the role of a nesting mother, washing and folding tiny little pants in anticipation of the baby's arrival. Thankfully the cast of *Indecent* reached out to me while we were in La Jolla and said, "You are a part of this family and we think you should come with us." When I talked to Rebecca about it, she made it my decision. I felt good. I felt energized. "Let's do this!", I said. She was relieved. So was I. I felt silly for ever imagining I would not join them. The plan was for me to take the show into tech and then just hang out, eating Paula Vogel's snacks and waiting to pop. With any luck, Paula would end up delivering the kid in the back of a taxi cab and I would have a great theatre story for years to come.

Aside from my doctor telling me to lay off the carbs, I was having a pretty fabulous pregnancy. I was busy with work the whole time but there was not a single issue beyond occasional heartburn. I was sleeping, eating kale, and even getting a little exercise too. I was looking forward to waddling around *Indecent* rehearsals, which were set to start in ten days. The 32nd week of my pregnancy hit at the top of what is known in New York City as Gala Season. In the midst of all my gala work I was stage managing a memorial service. It was St. Patrick's Day and we were in hour four of a venue walk-through in the Gym at Judson, right off Washington Square Park. As NYC is wont to do, the radiant heat was overcompensating for the chill and I was sweating profusely. The widow took one look at me and said, "You're not going to have that baby before Saturday, are you?" "No", I assured her.

The next morning, I woke up and just happened to tell my husband I was feeling funny. I rarely crossed paths with him in the mornings. I had an early *Indecent* meeting downtown and promised I would call my OBGYN afterward. Three meetings later, my husband had called me no fewer than ten times, wondering when I would get in touch with my doctor. Feeling tired or strange was an easy set of pregnancy symptoms to dismiss. I had tons of stuff to prepare for *Indecent*. After all those other readings that never saw the light of day, this might be the one that sticks. This might change everything. In the afternoon, my co-worker overheard me speaking to my husband and said, "Let's cancel your next meeting and head to the hospital. If it is not a big deal, we will not be there long."

Five hours later I was in a hospital room, in labor apparently, for how long was anyone's guess as I was not feeling any of my contractions. There was no water in my womb, and my son's heart rate was dropping. I listened to my husband on the phone with my parents. While the doctors were doing everything they could to keep me pregnant, I might have to deliver soon. They were trying to let the baby develop as long as they could, until the time was right. The OBGYN told us to choose a name. We picked Jack because it felt lucky and because we were watching the movie *Hook*. My husband said into the phone, that despite his stress I was perfectly calm. My dad said, "What do you expect? She is a stage manager."

THE GREAT PAUSE

Indecent opened on Broadway in the spring of 2017. I went with it, although it took Rebecca making sure that happened as I had never done more on Broadway than buy a ticket for a show. People still want to tell me how special the show was and I will always make time to hear them. I am proud of the risk and the investment that went into something I love so deeply. Every sleepless night of new pages and work lists was well worth it, it never felt like labor. I was in my wheelhouse. I felt very alive. During bows on opening night, the actor who had been on the show with me the longest just stared out into the house and cried silent tears. I knew exactly what he was feeling. He was stunned. We had both made our debut on Broadway in something we worked on for years and it was no longer ours. *Indecent* was out in the world where it belonged, for everyone to have an opinion about it.

A Tony, a tour, and one London production of *Indecent* later, Rebecca and I were working on our second Broadway show together when The Great Pause took hold—the pandemic. *Sing Street* is a new musical that started as a lab and, from day one, had set its sights on Broadway. We first developed the show downtown at New York Theatre Workshop, a place I had always dreamed of working. I was back in the off-Broadway neighborhood, in my comfort zone of new works, where we had permission to explore and learn, although the stakes felt higher than ever before. Tech was hard but I loved it. It felt good to be making magic again with Rebecca. Back in the trenches. Back to our shorthand. A little older, both of us. A little wiser. Our personal lives had grown and with that we had made more space for them.

When we moved uptown, to take *Sing Street* to Broadway, we were given time to reimagine the show's potential. I was thrilled to do it again. To have more time doing what I love. How lucky we were to take another step with the project, what some might consider the ultimate step for a new musical in New York City. On our first day of tech, five hours into our sound check, we were told we would be shutting down for the rest of the day because of COVID-19, a phrase familiar to us but what still felt like it was in the realm of SARS or Swine Flu. Speculations flew through text messages and social media, we went to the bar and sang at an overly-sanitized karaoke joint, comforted by the fact that 9/11 had only shut Broadway down for two days.

It has now been five-and-a-half months. *Sing Street* has been moved out of the Lyceum, put into storage, with a promise to bring it back out in 2022. I have never spent so much time at home.

After everything I heard about how hard it is to make it in theatre,
how impossible a kid could be for a stage manager,
I never really knew what it would be like for me until I took the risk.
To make theatre.
To make life.
To say yes.

"Time?" is what the nurse yelled to mark Jack's arrival.
Time is what the nurses and doctors took, to revive him.

Jack is what we called him because it sounded lucky. He is thankfully a healthy kid, a smart little guy at the age of four.

A lifetime will never seem long enough to know Jack, to be with him.

But I am grateful for the time we have together.

The whole world has taken pause.

I am still a stage manager.

I am a mother.

Life has never felt so real.

15

"Was That a Go?"

Lessons on Perseverance & Resilience

Jay Sheehan

"Was that a go?"

I asked in a heightened state of panic.

"No that wasn't a GO, it was a NO!"

He said over the garbled static of the walkie talkies. I still wasn't sure what he said…so I took the cue…

At that moment, the biggest rock band in the world was playing onstage at Qualcomm Stadium. The year was 1994 and I was working as the production stage manager for the San Diego Symphony. I had been introduced to a concert promoter by the name of Bill Silva, who I met when he did rock shows at Symphony Hall. Bill was looking for some help for the concert down at the stadium. I was looking for new experiences, so I was happy to offer my assistance where needed. For this show, I recall being on the chair setting crew. Six of us would help set up about 5,000 chairs on the field of the San Diego Chargers. It was an exciting time for me, as I was just learning the ropes of basic rock and roll management. I remember that weekend it rained as hard as I had ever seen it rain. Pelted by curtains of the downpouring water, we donned our ponchos and proceeded with setting chairs. I didn't care about the rain…this was my big break into the rock and roll business.

DOI: 10.4324/9780429321672-18

Now, being the biggest rock band in the world means you have the biggest production manager in the world. Taking care of this band and crew was an enormous responsibility, and I could see the seriousness in his eyes when he introduced himself to me. This gentleman's reputation certainly proceeded him wherever he went and many would shake in their shoes at the mention of his name. As I approached him for introductions, I remember telling myself…"Don't get intimidated, Don't get intimidated…Just do your job." His handshake was powerful and domineering. There was no doubt who was in charge, and he wouldn't let you forget it.

The day went on as planned. The rain miraculously stopped, and the opening act took to the stage. About halfway through the performance, the production manager for the band called me into his office. "I'm putting you on the house light cue at the end of the show." He barked. "It's really simple. Wait for me to say 'Go'…Don't screw this up or you'll never work in this business again." As I accepted my gig and turned away from him, all I could think of was that last sentence. "You'll never work in this business again."

I had always associated this saying with Hollywood. Something that only happens in the movies. Was he being honest? Was he just messing around with a new guy? At the time, I believed him. I was young enough and naïve enough to accept his answer as the truth. "Screw this up and you'll never work in the business again" The next three hours were a blur to me. The biggest rock band in the world had taken the stage about an hour earlier, with no incidents. Several times that day, I had to check in with myself and realize that yes…today, I am working for the biggest rock band in the world.

ROOKIE MISTAKE

My walkie talkie suddenly jumped to life. It was him, on the other end telling me to stand by for the house light cue for the end of the show. "Go get in the car with the electrician." New information suddenly jammed into my head. Panic set it. I got into the car with the electrician. "Where are we headed?" I asked. "Under the stadium through the opposite side tunnel." The electrician replied. At that moment I realized I hadn't walked the path to get to the switch earlier in the day. Rookie mistake #1.

As he took me to the house light switch buried deep under the stadium, I suddenly realized that I wasn't hearing anyone's voice on my walkie talkie. All I heard was the white noise contained in the static. "Oh no." I thought. The walkie talkie wasn't powerful enough to go through the concrete. "I won't be able to hear the cue being called." We didn't check the radios ahead of time. Rookie mistake # 2.

I headed to the switch, determined to not screw this up. The now garbled voices could barely be heard over the walkie talkies. I got enough to get the "stand by" from the production manager. So, there I was, one button push away from turning the house lights on after the last song of the biggest rock band in the world. Little did I know that the next 15 minutes would have such an impact on my life.

The walkie talkie crackled, the static blared. I heard a voice…"Was that a go?" I asked in a heightened state of panic. "No that wasn't a GO, it was a NO!" He said over the garbled static of the walkie talkies. I still wasn't sure what he said…so I took the cue…I hit the switch and suddenly the very bright metal halide lights blazed across the stadium. Except there was one problem. The show wasn't over. The greatest front man of the biggest rock band in the world was singing his most famous song. Rumor had it that he stopped singing to ask "Who turned the Fu★% king house lights on?" Well…that was me…

Hearing the commotion now intermittently over the radio, I could tell that something was not right. I heard a voice, his voice, barely audible say "OFF! OFF!" As more panic set in, I grabbed the switch and pulled it down successfully. The stadium plunged into darkness. All was fine and back to normal. Or so I thought. The issue now was that the show was over and the house lights needed to be turned on for the mass exiting of 60,000 people. Except for one problem. Metal halide bulbs need 15 minutes to cool down before being turned back on. Oh god…I thought, as I imagined the 60,000 people all leaving in complete darkness. It was a disaster of epic proportions in my mind. "Don't screw this up or you'll never work in this business again" was all that ran through my mind.

Once the bulbs cooled and I got the lights on (we used the stadium electrician's radio for the last cue!) it was time to return to backstage compound. I knew things weren't looking good for me when two of Bill Silva's staff met me about 100 feet before the backstage entrance. "It might be a good idea if you just gave us your radio and you went home. It's not pretty backstage right now." I couldn't believe what I was hearing. Go home? "Yes" was the resounding answer from my two colleagues. "Go home…he is blowing up and you shouldn't be here."

So…I left…like a dog running away with his tail between his legs. I felt like I had blown my opportunity to get into the business. Most of all, I felt that I had let Bill Silva down. Here he was, taking a chance on someone new, and I let him down. I literally thought I would never work in this business again. For the next several months, I had completely wiped out my self-confidence and my spirit. I was depressed and felt shame and guilt. My rookie mistakes their toll on me.

Despite the depression and anger that I felt, I remember my mentors telling me to always take the high road and not speak poorly about anyone that may have been involved in asking me to go home that night. That was a conscious choice I had to make. It was hard not to try and blame others, but over and over I would hear, "Take the high road and don't talk poorly about anyone." I finally accepted responsibility for my mistakes and moved on with my life.

SOMETIMES WE JUST DON'T SEE THE POSITIVE

Bill and I stayed in touch, despite my fears that I wouldn't work again. In 1996, I had heard that Bill was looking for an operations manager for his new venue.

I phoned him and asked if I could apply. I did and he took a chance and hired me. Little did I know that having that job would give me the knowledge and experience to then be hired by Universal Music Group as the director of operations at their new 20,000 seat venue in San Diego. From my experiences at the amphitheater, I was able to gain even more knowledge and I took on additional clients. "You'll never work in this business again" turned out to be incorrect all along. My mistake, my huge fail, turned out wasn't a fail at all…in fact it was a huge win. The evidence was clear. Sometimes we just don't see the positive possibilities in failing.

I ended up being down on myself and I lost my confidence because I allowed someone else to control the situation. I allowed someone else to instill fear in me. I allowed myself to fear failing. In fact, that "fail" really launched my career, which in turn provided opportunities to teach, which has turned into a 20-year run on the faculty at San Diego State University. Looking back now, I have a better understanding of what it means to persevere. To be resilient. To not be bullied with fear and intimidation … and to be steadfast in my self-confidence. So…that night, many years ago, under the stadium, my mentors were always right… "There is no such thing as a fail."

In addition to the lesson on failure, my mentors also taught me to not leave a job (or get fired) and start blaming others for the bad situation. Even if it was their fault, they told me to "always take the high road," and "Don't burn bridges, it can do serious harm to your career." Little did I realize that 17 years into the business I would find myself being tested by this very theory.

In 2000, I had been hired to be the production manager at one of the Native American casinos in San Diego. The concert industry was booming and we were doing about 100 shows over the five years I was there. It was a great gig, and I loved the venue.

I had been hired by my good friend, "Mr. X" (no need to mention names), who knew me from my days working with Bill Silva. Mr. X had risen to the top-level management at the casino. When he brought me on board, Mr. X instantly told me who to avoid on his staff. I was warned that one individual—"Big T"— was "not to be trusted," so "keep information away from him." That was the culture of the company. To hold information from others and don't trust anybody. It was an oppressive way to work.

Over the course of the 2000s, Big T started asking me questions about concert operations and venue development. I remember Mr. X telling me to not share any information with him, but I didn't care about that. In my eyes, Big T was a young and eager team member, trying to learn as much as he could about the business. I would go on to impart information on to Big T over the years and answered any questions he had, despite Mr. X's strong warning.

In 2006, a huge changeover happened at the casino. Mr. X had made a deal with a large concert promotions company that was eager to set up shop in San Diego. He and his entire staff would leave the casino and open a new promotions office in San Diego. With this one move, the dynamics of the San Diego concert industry shifted overnight.

With the departure of Mr. X, Big T became the casino's acting "Vice President of Concerts" until further notice. There were five shows left, and Big T asked me if I would stay until the end of the season, and train a new person to take my place. After that, I would have to leave my job of six years because "there were a lot of bad feelings," and as I was "one of Mr. X's guys," I was out. To be honest, I expected this as it happens in business all the time. New management means new people. This situation was no different and walking away at the end of the season would not be an issue on my part. Or so I thought.

The following week we had a show and Big T walked in and was holding an envelope in one hand and a cake in the other. I thought it was a little strange, but I didn't ask questions. As he handed me the envelope, he said "Here is a check for the last five shows paid in full, but we don't need you to come back." I was a little taken by surprise. He continued by saying, "Jay, sometimes the innocent gets killed in war. It's called collateral damage, and that is what you are at this moment: collateral damage." He continued by saying, "But we brought you this cake." I looked at the cake and inscribed on the top was "Good Luck Jay." I took a moment to take this all in. Was this really happening? I said out loud, "So I am being fired AND I am getting a cake?" Big T's response was simply "Yes." "OK," I said, and we all had some cake.

I left shortly after that and proceeded to drive home. I was emotional and wanted to let everyone know what had happened to me. I was the victim here. I was ready to fire off nasty emails about the casino and Big T.

"Always take the high road and don't burn bridges." I would hear my mentors' voices in my head repeat over and over, "Always take the high road and don't burn bridges." This was going to be hard work on my part. Our instinct is to get even, to get revenge in some way. I got home that night and sat in silence as I contemplated what had just happened. What I discovered was that I had to get to "acceptance" of what happened as quickly as possible. Once I accepted the situation, I could then move on. The problem was that I took this very personally. I knew I was a good production manager, and that I knew how to run a venue. "How could I be terminated like that?" I fell asleep hearing my mentor's voice again: "Don't burn bridges."

WORKING ON ACCEPTANCE

The next day I awoke and spent some time thinking about the situation. I worked on "acceptance" and somehow, after some time had passed, I got there with the help of some friends. "It is what it is," my friend Mike would tell me. "This isn't the end of the road for you, it's really a beginning, you just don't see that yet." So, with Mike's advice, it was time to move on. And move on I did. I went on to continue teaching at San Diego State, and began to concentrate on my freelance career as a production manager. I heeded my mentor's advice, and never spoke badly about Big T, or the casino, or my situation. I finally felt at peace.

One afternoon, I was sitting in my backyard when my phone rang. I was shocked to see Big T's name pop up on the caller ID. "What the hell does he want?" I thought to myself, as I contemplated not answering the call. It rang four more times before I would decide to pick up the call. "Big T," I said, "how the heck are you?" "Fine thanks," he said, followed by "I need you." After some perplexing silence between us, he continued with "We tore down the old venue and I am building a new event center, and I need you to help me." To say I was shocked would be an understatement. "Always take the high road and don't burn bridges." I replayed in my mind my mentor's lesson from nine years earlier. I realized that I HADN'T burned a bridge.

I DID take the high road, and here was the proof that the advice worked. "What exactly do you need?" I asked. "Well, I don't have a box office, a box office staff, or a seating chart. I don't have a security company yet or a security plan for the venue. Ushers, ticket takers, and stagehands are also needed." "Ok," I said, "but...you fired me nine years ago." His reply was most welcomed. "That was a long time ago. Come out and have lunch at least." So I did. The following week I headed out to the casino, the place I left nine years earlier.

Big T met me at the venue's construction site. "The stage is going right over there," he said. I looked across the way and saw a large pile of dirt. "Mix position here. Follow spots here. Alcohol bars here." The bus parking, truck loading dock, power as well as backup generator were all thought through in detail. "You really learned a lot since I left," I said out loud. "I learned from you Jay," he said. "You were my mentor, and you didn't even know it." I was touched by his comments and felt excited about the project. "When will it be done?" I asked. He replied, "Two years." "Well, why don't you call me in two years and we can have another discussion?"

Being a man of his word, Big T called me about two years later. "I need you" would be his opening line once again. "The venue is done, and I need you to help me run it." To be honest, I was shocked as I had almost forgotten about our lunch two years earlier. There was still no box office, a box office staff, or a seating chart. Still no security plan or security company chosen. We had a lot of work ahead of us. "When is the first show?" I asked. "July third," he said. "This is May now...you mean in six weeks?" I asked. His response was simply "Yes."

So, we got to work. Rolled up our sleeves and created the seating chart, security plan, usher plan, merchandise plan, and the plethora of other tasks that needed to be completed. We opened on time on July third to a sellout crowd for country award winning singer and songwriter Martina McBride. As the house lights went off for the first show, I couldn't help but have a smile on my face and a moment of gratitude as I recalled that now famous advice from my mentor, "Always take the high road and don't burn bridges." I listened to my mentors...it was good advice.

The lessons here are clear; you are your own best teammate. Be resilient and bounce back from adversity, persevere even in the darkest of times remembering that things will get better, and lastly, be steadfast in your own confidence.

Oh yeah, and always take the high road. Trust me...you'll be glad you did!

16

A Multiplicity of Identities, On Headset and Off

Narda E. Alcorn

With Copy Editor and Proofreader
Sam Tirrell

O n two different occasions in my life, I have been in a bathroom stall when friends and colleagues have entered and spoken specifically about me receiving a particular position because I am black. This is a good reminder to be discreet in washrooms, but it is also demonstrative of how people—white people, specifically—begin most job conversations with the color of my skin. In fact, skin color is often where the conversation about stage managers of color both begins and ends, making it automatically reductive. Discussions focused on race or skin color also, by nature, elevate the identity and standing of white stage managers. The silent implication is that their merit comes from skill, talent, and experience whereas the qualifications of stage managers of color are often left out of the conversation.

I received my very first job after lobbying for it for over a year as I finished graduate school at Yale. I had worked as an unpaid intern on its initial production in Chicago, facilitating script changes even after closing and striving to build strong relationships with the playwright and director. Finally, I was hired as the first assistant stage manager on August Wilson's *Seven Guitars*, directed by Lloyd Richards. The play, which chronicles the African-American experience in the 1940s, was scheduled to travel between regional theatres before arriving on Broadway. At the time, we did not know that it would eventually emerge as a mainstay in Wilson's Century Cycle. I was 25 years old, directly out of graduate school, and thrilled to be a part of it, feeling as though all of my hard work was finally paying off.

DOI: 10.4324/9780429321672-19

I did not anticipate, though, the way in which collaborators would initially dismiss me because of the dark brown color of my skin. In Boston, Chicago, San Francisco, Los Angeles—city after city, theatre after theatre—I would field questions by crew members, prop supervisors, and costume shop managers, all curious to learn whether or not I was the daughter or niece of the playwright or director. Their thinly veiled assumption was loud and clear: "How could you, a young black woman, possibly have a job like this without being related to a primary player?"

As someone who had always been extremely disciplined and hard-working, I was terribly offended by these remarks. I did not come from a family that had wealth or connections, and it has always been up to me to create my own opportunities. Two months into the tour, I had resigned myself to endure this assumption of nepotism. Eventually, as we moved from city to city, I learned that it was my consistent and distinctive stage management practice that had the greatest impact on curbing this perception.

My work was extremely detail-oriented. I was a clear and kind communicator, and I always delivered on my word. My graduate school training had taught me what it meant to be a professional, and it was essentially this—me doing exceptional work—that would eventually alter my collaborators' impressions of me and put a stop to the rumors of nepotism. I would notice the change occurring in tech as I managed the deck, instructing the crew while also empowering them. Colleagues who had initially dismissed me ended up trusting me, even relying on my expertise. The latter days of tech leading into previews and performances were often the most enjoyable and congenial experiences of the regional tour.

As such, I learned an important life lesson: to pay no attention to what others say about me and allow my work to speak for itself. My energy was better spent working hard and not worrying about what others were saying or thinking. It was an invaluable lesson to learn at the beginning of my career, just as *Seven Guitars* was beginning its Broadway run.

THE "REAL" SHOW

Fast forward to more than a decade later, and I vividly remember one unseasonably chilly summer evening in New York City. I was working on a Broadway revival that had recently triumphed at the Tony Awards, winning several, and I was thrilled when a colleague from the show asked to walk down Eighth Avenue with me. They would depart the next day for a much-needed vacation, and there were only a few weeks left of the show's limited run—it was likely that we would not see each other again until our next project. We strolled leisurely, chatting about the success of the show. When we reached the block of their office, we stopped beside a coffee shop, at which time I was expecting to finish the conversation. In actuality, I was about to be pitched another offer: "Narda, you are now at the level where you should be doing real shows." Unsure of where this sentiment was heading, I looked towards the sidewalk before making eye contact again. Meeting my eyes with smiles and enthusiasm, my colleague told me that an upcoming revival, written by a deceased white man with an all-white cast, was a "real" show that I could be working on. They affirmed that if I were to work on this legitimate production, my standing in the community would be solidified, and that I must be careful not to "pigeon-hole" myself. I nodded and smiled as we wrapped up the conversation, promising to check my schedule and be in touch. We embraced goodbye. Then I was alone, on the corner adjacent to the coffee shop.

Though race was never mentioned during the course of our conversation, the difference between the two projects in question was clear: my Tony-Award winning production featuring people of color and written by a person of color was not "real." I was struck by the feeling that no matter how hard I worked or how many Broadway credits I had, I would never fully belong to the community that I loved. I was suddenly cold and seething. I went into the coffee shop, ordered something hot, sat down in a corner, and silently cried.

I was angry that such an influential theatre-maker could possess such racist ideas and was unaware of the impact of sharing them. I was furious that they probably thought they were doing me a great service by telling me not to limit myself to shows by and about people of color. Most importantly, I was devastated that despite how exceptional our production was, there would always be people who would refuse to recognize the excellence because it had been achieved by people of color.

Even now, collaborators whom I admire and respect use veiled language with me to say that ethnically and culturally diverse projects are somehow less prominent, valuable, or "real." Perhaps even more troubling is the assumption that I can only work on shows with people of color. I recently received a surprised reaction when I mentioned an upcoming project by a venerable white playwright. My co-worker exclaimed, "Oh, I didn't know that they wrote about black people!" This particular project features an all-white cast, and I have intentionally cultivated a working relationship with the playwright in pursuit of this collaboration. Without knowing these details, the clear implication was that I am only considered for projects involving racially or ethnically diverse characters.

I wish I could say that on that chilly summer night, I pulled out my phone and called my colleague to expose their micro-aggressions and racist ideology, but I did not. In that moment in the coffee shop, cradling my hot beverage and reflecting on what my colleague had just said to me, the only thing I could have told you was that everything they said was bullshit. They were wrong. I loved my career, comprised of numerous Broadway shows, created by and focusing on people of color. I was proud to be a part of telling these stories. My standing in the community was just fine, and if others thought I was a lesser stage manager because I did work that spoke to my heart and soul about people who looked like me, that was their problem.

And this was the lesson. Truth be told, I find myself re-learning it again and again because of how our society has been socialized to think about what is legitimate or successful. There will always be people who consider the work that is foundational to my career to be less than because it looks at humanity through black people's eyes.

A TRULY INCLUSIVE ENVIRONMENT

The judgment that a stage manager of color's hiring is dependent on the color of their skin is always prevalent when stage managers commune to discuss who has been hired for what projects. Not long ago, I was discussing potential stage management hires with an assistant. I was taken aback when my assistant remarked that the theatre was going to hire a production assistant named Chris, but since I had been brought onto the project, the theatre "did not need Chris anymore." I do not know Chris, the production assistant in question, but I do know that Chris must be a person of color. I had come in to take over as the production stage manager, and my presence satisfied the organization's diversity quota: one stage manager of color per team.

I am concerned about how our theatre community discusses diverse team members because the current narrative perpetuates racism and tokenizes people of color, while also contributing to a growing animosity amongst white stage managers. On several social media platforms for stage managers, there is often backlash when someone posts that they are looking to hire a stage manager of color. The vitriolic attack that ensues against the person of color who has not yet been hired maintains the institutional racism that this country was built upon. These baseless accounts assume that belonging to an underrepresented group is the person of color's only qualification and they are taking a job away from a qualified white stage manager.

Discourse like this has dominated the conversation around the composition of stage management teams in recent years, particularly as the country's awareness of racial and ethnic inequality deepens. I do believe that the intent is appropriate, but the results of this conversation are, more often than not, uninspired practices that show minimum compliance without any systemic or organizational change.

I have learned that there are ways to achieve inclusion when there is a genuine desire by a group of individuals who are profoundly committed to the cause. I have attended workshops offered by artEquity[1], for example, and have learned that communities move through stages towards diversity and inclusion. The theatre, and specifically stage management, is no longer exclusionary or club-like, wherein only the majority culture can participate. We are at the stage that artEquity calls "Compliance/Token Organizations." Supervisors and managers are careful to ensure that they hire gender-diverse or ethnically diverse people, specifically in entry-level positions; however, the values foundational to the organization have not changed and the commitment to diversity is dormant at the organization's highest levels. The diverse people who are hired and begin contributing to workplace culture tend to feel like tokens or badges that the organization can point to and take pride in.

Despite how I sometimes feel like my inclusion on a team or in an organization is perfunctory or symbolic, I certainly do not want to return to a time when the consideration of diversity was not in the forefront of our field. My aspiration for the theatrical stage management community is a truly inclusive environment that values diversity and views the field as abundant instead of scarce, making room for all types of stage managers and celebrating diverse hires. My dream extends to the wider community, too. Imagine if the general management offices in New York that manage Broadway were committed to diversity and inclusion in every decision made in their day-to-day work. Their practices, policies, and cultural norms would reflect this commitment regardless of whether or not diverse people were represented in the organization. They would regularly and openly examine their culture and management styles to see how their procedures may negatively affect the staff, especially historically excluded groups. The leaders of the organization would commit to combating white supremacy culture.[2] Characteristics like perfectionism and power hoarding would be actively replaced by a culture of appreciation, collective power sharing, and an acceptance that there are many ways to achieve the same goal. I am looking forward to a time when production managers in not-for-profit theatres across the country are not satisfied with having a yearly intern of color. Instead, these offices would become committed to recruiting and hiring people from diverse cultural groups and then supporting these individuals in their ascent to higher positions.

A MULTIPLICITY OF IDENTITIES

In my first month at a new university, I was embarking on a listening tour. I was conducting individual meetings with the students in my stage management department to hear about their dreams and aspirations, what they thought was working well in the department, and what needed improvement. One student in their final year—a student of color—voiced concern to me about being assigned to the "people of color" show in the season. They said that they did not want to "pigeon-hole" themselves. A thousand thoughts ran through my mind upon hearing this, and I quickly asked the student stage manager if they thought the white students in the department were pigeon-holing themselves when they worked on a show with an all-white cast.

"Of course not," was the response. "That's different."

"Is it?"

After a moment, I saw my question register and the stage manager realized the irony of the conversation. We sat in silence for several minutes.

"Is it wrong that I prefer to do the 'ethnic' show or the 'Black History Month' show? Am I hurting my career by focusing on this type of work?" I could not help but register that 20 years ago, I had been struggling with identical thoughts and questions. I was reminded of how powerful white socialization is and how it has permeated all generations. I asked myself, "Have we made so little progress?"

I felt grateful in that moment that I would have the opportunity to mentor this student, remarking the following:

> It is not wrong that you prefer to tell stories by and about people who look like you. That is never wrong. In fact, it is beautiful. You are not hurting your career by preferring this type of work. You are following your heart and soul by wanting to stage manage stories by, for, and about people who look like you, and that passion is what can make a great stage manager.

I am no longer offended when someone asks if August Wilson or Lloyd Richards were my family members and if that is how I came to work with them. Both men were dear to me, and it was a great privilege of my career to serve their work. I am also not shy about inserting myself into conversations when I hear white stage managers citing the race or ethnicity of a stage manager as a qualification and ending the conversation there. I will often make the observation that if the discussion were about a white stage manager, their experience, skill set, education, or past collaborators would be considered, so why not voice those same qualifications for stage managers of color? Lastly, I no longer remain silent when my white colleagues and friends presume that I was hired for a particular job because of my race or conclude that a project by or about people of color is less significant than another. These conversations are difficult to navigate and my intent is to broaden perspectives. I believe that several colleagues and friends have benefited from my interruptions because they have led to the consideration of language used when discussing diversity and hiring practices.

I have a multiplicity of identities, both on headset and off: wife, mother, family member, best friend, mentor, and educator, among others. Still, in my 25-year career as a professional stage manager, no other identity marker has been as significant as my race and skin color. I am black, a person of color, African American, a member of the African diaspora. As a black woman in the American theatre, from the beginning of my career to today, and in spite of the narrow definition that the community has attempted to impose upon me, I have come to uncover, recognize, and embrace what makes me authentically *me*: my love of the production process, my talent, my skills, my professionalism, my spirit, my dark brown skin, my naturally curly hair, and even my giggle.

Though it is a historical truth that the majority defines the minority, it is the act of learning to define myself—of relinquishing control over how others perceive me and embracing all aspects of who I am—that is the most bolstering and rewarding step towards genuine acceptance.

NOTES

1. artEquity is an organization founded and directed by Carmen Morgan. Training topics address structural and systemic issues of identity, power-sharing language and communication, team building, and strategies to initiate and normalize equity-based approaches in organizational and community culture.

2. Tema Okun and Kenneth Jones, *ChangeWork*, 2001, https://pfc.ca/wp-content/uploads/2020/12/dismantling-racism-workbook-en.pdf

17

The Fallacy of Figuring It All Out

Finding Grace in the Imperfect Attempts at Balance
Jonathan D. Allsup

This essay is not academic, by any means; it is actually a message to my younger self. By conveying the challenges that come with finding times of balance and appropriate imbalance, and between work and non-work life, I hope my writing will spark a conversation. I also hope that it can make a difference in others' lives.

As I write, I also ponder what would make me more qualified than anyone else to produce a chapter on finding a good "work/life balance." Truth be told, I dislike the very phrase. It is not a helpful concept, it is an unhealthy premise, and difficult to achieve. It is misleading, as though the scales can be equally balanced on each side of the equation, and as if our task is to try to secure and maintain that thin-line of a perfectly equal balance.

DROP BY ANY TIME!

My wife and I have many apps that make our home life more efficient. We have a doorbell that connects to our phones and alerts us to any front yard movement (often, it's just leaves blowing around our porch). We have a vacuum cleaner that self-vacuums on a schedule or by command. We have a centralized smart-home

DOI: 10.4324/9780429321672-20

device that will answer every query we have. We own designated dishes for parties only. We keep food and beverages on-hand, ready to serve at a moment's notice for impromptu gatherings—feel free to drop by any time! We are not rich. We work hard to pay off the enormous amount of debt we incurred from educational costs and poor decisions early in our careers, but our home is the epitome of efficiency; it's somewhat to be expected. My wife, Maegan, is a professional stage manager, and I am a stage manager recently turned production manager, yet we struggle to find the right balance between work and rest. I live a mile from the theatre where I work. Maegan is a freelancer, and most of the theatres she works at are 40 to 90 minutes away from our home. We both do what we love, and we both love what we do. We do our best to have a balanced relationship with each other and accomplish the myriad of things that need to happen in our house. We don't have any kids yet, but we do have a dog and a cat. We wonder how we will ever be able to accommodate the structure that children require.

SUCCESSFUL CAREERS AND LIFE OUTSIDE OF WORK

I believe that a successful career in the arts is possible and sustainable alongside a fully lived and appreciated life outside of work. There's not a universal magic bullet, elixir, medicine, or formula that can work for everyone. The remedies are as unique as the individuals who discover them. I believe sustainability of the individual is possible. This is true for freelancers and those who work full-time within an organization. However, organizations can't be relied on to recognize the needs of individuals seeking more balance. Their needs are personal and true to them. All they can do is to ask for the theatre administrators to have a conversation, true and honest communication, humans relating as humans, meeting to find ways to be more human. What resources do both parties possess that can work towards the betterment of all? When all involved begin seeing each other as allies, searching for meaning, hoping for fulfilment, aching for connection, then all can engage in both dialogue and production of high-quality work that profits all. It says in the Gospel of Matthew: "What does it profit a man if he gains the whole world but loses his soul?" What does it profit a theatre if it has the best productions but loses its people in the process?

THE PROBLEMS YOU SOLVE, AND THE ONES YOU CREATE

We can be our own worst enemy in the pursuit of balance. I think we all, from time to time, fall into a trap of loving the adventure, the recognition received from saving the day, and the ability to create something from what others falsely perceive as nothing. This can happen in both our home and our work lives. It feels good, thrilling even, when people recognize us as the problem-solver. As Mike Murdock said, "You will be remembered for two things: the problems you solve, and the ones you create,"[1] and we want to be remembered for the former. We often receive little applause for our work, but we tend to receive even less when our projects are delivered early, under budget, and without complaint. Perhaps that shouldn't be the case. Maybe delivering early, under budget, and not worn out should be rewarded. I'm not implying professional theatre is a dysfunctional system or that theatre administrators are tyrants. Even as a current member of theatre administration, I struggle with this very thing. Individually, often we can be our own worst enemy in this regard. Some of us need to advocate for ourselves, and others need to advocate for ourselves against our own selves.

For some, taking on an administration role provides opportunity for a steadier income and a more reasonable schedule. However, the opposite can also be true. While the paycheck, benefits, and more consistent schedule holds appeal, the constant stress and strain can counteract any benefits. In *A Christmas Carol*, the character Marley is weighed down by chains and cash boxes. We attempt, as artists, to fool ourselves, thinking we are immune from Marley's fate, because we work in the arts. We are easily blinded, and just as susceptible as Marley, to our own modern chains of cell phones, spreadsheets, regulations, work hours, etc.

GIVING YOURSELF GRACE

Recently in a text exchange with my supervisor I wrote:

> I'm actually, this very minute, considering how I can have a week with family in the quiet of my home around Christmas in a way that doesn't cause so much extra work to prep for family that it doesn't make it worth it. We, as a culture, have allowed our very basic human instinct, to be with other humans, to become laborious. How can we regain [the instinct to be with other humans], spend time with each other, unplug from the constant hum of the world continuing to spin, and not wear ourselves out but rather refuel our physical, mental, and spiritual selves? Maybe that's the struggle we have, until we figure it out, hopefully with enough time to enjoy living in that realization before we die. And maybe those that figure it out sooner get to live longer in that space they have created?

I wish I had struggled with these questions earlier in my career. I wish I hadn't sacrificed my grades in other classes to achieve more in production. I wish I hadn't spent so many hours in the theatre, hoping and wanting to be needed, when I was wanted and needed at home. The biggest fallacy we believe as humans, and possibly as artists, is that all other people have it figured out and we haven't. We then perceive the failure as a shameful reflection of our own shortcomings.

I think my supervisor says it best when she says, "No one in our organization thinks they have it figured out." She means we are all growing and changing, and she implies that we are all actively trying to be better. We must also give ourselves grace. We must be willing to give both ourselves and others grace when perfect balance isn't achievable in our lives.

In my life I've mistaken excuses for grace. I've given excuses to loved ones, choosing to believe that I was so important or needed at work that I couldn't possibly choose home-life over work-life in a particular moment. There's a day in my past, quite a few, frankly, when I chose to be too busy, when I chose to think that I was more important at work than I was at home. I thought things couldn't get done without me. I suspect my choice that day cost me, and many others, to give up things that were dear to us. For some of us, poor choices brought pain, and our actions produced wounded relationships. Those choices also brought about turns-of-events which have made my and others' lives so much richer and more meaningful. I wouldn't trade those experiences for anything, but I want to learn and grow so I can mitigate the amount of pain and grief my actions can cause myself and others. We in theatre know that process is just as important as product. *Christmas Carol*'s Ebenezer Scrooge won't become a good person if he doesn't himself learn from the three ghosts: one past, one present, and one future. I do find it somewhat telling that his transformation was brought about by what essentially is a long night's sleep. I suppose a long night's sleep could do us all some good on the road to transformation!

Processing the issues involved for personal development is tiresome. It takes concentrated awareness to maintain distinction between enjoying life at work and life at home and even more effort to integrate those experiences into our future action. It is hard. Some people make it look easy. I encourage you to ask anyone you perceive as having achieved balance how they do it. They will likely tell you about the hard work, intentionality, struggles, and sacrifices they continue to experience.

I do believe it is possible to have a conscious, balanced, purposeful, and satisfying life within the arts. Some external events may force us to gain new perspective: major life changes, medical issues, death, birth, losses, and additions. These things affect everyone; no one is immune. Do we give ourselves enough time to deal with them? In between rehearsals, meetings, performances, and other obligations, do we allow ourselves the time we need to process, not just attend to, these events? Do we feel compelled to give our all at our jobs, to find the tender, vulnerable place in the rehearsal hall or the design meeting or the struggle for high-quality production values, and leave ourselves without enough energy and vulnerability to deal with our own personal concerns? What do we do to address this? Are you, like me, feeling too daunted by the task of self-betterment? What's the bite-able chunk of this elephant? I don't know. I really don't know. I'm on the same path. Maybe the next step is simply to recognize each other on this path, to say hello, to encourage each other, pick each other up, and walk together.

THE PERFECT BALANCE QUESTION

How do we find perfect balance? We won't. In our own reconciliation with our inability to secure and maintain perfect balance we gain perspective, like a slowing pendulum, coming closer to finding our center with each swing. How do we find perspective? Grant, give, donate, love yourself and others, and give yourself time to reflect. We cannot, we will not, be able to find perspective in a vacuum, or a meme, or a GIF, or an emoticon. We will not be good at achieving consistent perspective early in our journey towards finding our own personal ability to create balance. It will take effort and care and intention. But we can only start at the beginning, opening our eyes, minds, and souls…connecting with others; looking up and listening to our surroundings.

Here are some ideas to try:

take a walk—in the rain, in the sun, in the breeze, on the beach,
invite a friend and walk with them,

foster a dog,
foster ideas,
develop a pattern of prayer and meditation,

give encouraging high-fives,
give consensual hugs,
give authentic smiles,

look at someone in the eyes,
look at yourself in the mirror,

take a train,
journal, reflect, write,
listen to music, explore what draws you to it,

love,
be patient,
give grace to others,
give grace to yourself,
give up on the things you can't change,

read your favorite chapter—twice,
reflect on you—discover what makes you special,
reflect on others—discover what makes them special,

throw parties—and enjoy them,
pay your bills with thanksgiving,
clean out your closets,

give compliments to others,
give compliments to yourself,
believe the compliments you receive,

listen, think, respond,
wonder, pause, appreciate,
then, if necessary, take a picture,

share, like, cry, and comment in real life,
treat yourself to something authentic,
forgive,
give,
plan,
find joy in plans that change,

find fulfillment in the simple and mundane,
take a sabbath,
enjoy a year of jubilee,
plan a gap year,
travel,
grow,

work hard,
celebrate the work of others,
make the toil fun,
address it when it's not,

be kind—it costs nothing,
support one another,
collaborate,

find a mentor—a leader—someone you admire,
emulate those parts you admire,

dress up,
put on comfy clothes,
cook a meal,
light a candle,

love hard,
cry hard,
laugh hard,
give of yourself,
give yourself a break,

listen,
find a listening partner,

acquire what you need,
don't hold on to it too tightly,

try,
fail,
try again,
be someone's safety net,
by doing so, you're creating some safety nets of your own,

and when none of that works,
do something else,
keep trying.

STRIVING COMMUNITIES OF PEOPLE

I struggle with the varying degrees of success I've found in creating my perspective on balance. I believe success at achieving perspective requires more than passive accountability. We are a community of people striving towards the same goal. We can help each other by being open with each other, willing to share our successes and failures. It's a strangely personal thing and, in the end, we alone are our own arbiters of how we can feel rested, rejuvenated, and have gained better perspective, but if we open the conversation, if we talk about it openly with friends and co-workers, if we address problems in the moment, if we speak out loud the truths of successes and failures, might we learn from each other much in the same way that we learn from watching theatre?

At one point, several months ago, I thought I could easily write this chapter. Yet I procrastinated writing it for weeks and months. I thought and talked about this subject many times with friends and colleagues, and I created vulnerability during those conversations so much that I thought I had a perspective that was worth sharing. I don't necessarily know if it is true or not as I reach the end of this chapter, but what I do know is that the balancing struggle continues for me and for others. I do know that the struggle is worth continuing. I do know there are moments in my life at work that are rewarding and there are moments in my life at home and with loved ones that are rewarding if I choose to recognize them. In this bizarre world of multi-screen, over-saturated visual content, we must struggle to find the simple and curate those simple moments of perspective into our home lives and into our work lives.

And thus, I invite you to join with me on this journey towards a new perspective that I hope will provide time to appreciate, live, rest, and rejuvenate. Our tenacity makes us better artists, friends, family members, co-workers, adjudicators, and arbiters of our own future abilities in all those areas.

NOTE

1. Cited in John Thomas, "Colin Kaepernick a Good Role Model for Our Children? Let Parents Decide," April 17, 2014, https://guardianlv.com/2014/04/colin-kaepernick-a-good-role-model-for-our-children-let-parents-decide/

Part 3

Career

18

A Matter of Perspective

Ramón Valdez

THE FIRE HYDRANT

On the corner of the street where I grew up there lives a fire hydrant. It's been there for years. You'd only know it was there if ever there was a need for it to wake up. Otherwise, it just sits there, a piece of set dressing actualizing the space, just watching the world unfold. It's odd how that happens. How, something so pedestrian instantly completes an image inside our heads. It becomes exactly what is needed, offering its unique perspective. We see it, we know where we are. It's comforting, isn't it?

On our way to some errand, my mother, going on about something or other, quipped in "Are you listening?" with her eyes fixed on the rearview mirror knowing full well she had an extra 30 seconds left of the red light for me to plead my case. "Yes. I can grow up to be whatever I want to be." It was the same monologue I heard almost weekly. At only seven or eight, thinking about what I wanted to be when I was older wasn't something I was particularly interested in defining, but I certainly knew I needed to figure it out. Growing up in a Mexican household, getting an education and getting a job were two things that were not up for discussion. My mother is a first generation Mexican American, and my father was an immigrant from México. And they, well they had certain expectations of my brother and I, expectations that were rooted in what my grandparents expected of

DOI: 10.4324/9780429321672-22

them and what my great grandparents expected of my grandparents and so on and so forth for the history of my existence.

Then, it hit me. What I wanted to be when I grew up. Well, that and the drops of water flicked off the fingers of reveling children. Someone must have opened the fire hydrant. Again. I saw them through the window, the children, playing and cavorting about. Resembling me in age and experience, the neighborhood children and I had very little in common—our personalities were just too different. They wanted to marinate in their youth; I wanted to get back to my reading. Where they excelled in an active amalgamation of amusement, I took comfort in watching the world unfold. Truly, I had no desire to join them. To be out there, in the rain. Besides, it had been just about 30 seconds now and the light would soon turn green.

The car begins to creep forward. It moves faster now, and faster still. Soon, in the rearview mirror the image comes into focus of the water jumping, the children laughing, and the fire hydrant guffawing but the farther we move the smaller they become, disappearing now entirely like the sun behind the horizons divide. We're at another red light. This corner feels different. There's no fire hydrant here. It's quiet here. No water. No children. I don't like this corner. How could it be that this thing that I forget is there, can so forcefully disturb space and time to bring about such a distinct pull and attraction?

The errand is over. We're almost home. Stuck waiting at the red light that lasts just 30 seconds too long. Back to where the fire hydrant lives—it was the first thing I noticed. But it's quiet now. The children are gone. It just sits there like it has for so many years. Waiting to be useful.

I didn't think about the fire hydrant again for the rest of the weekend. It's easy to forget important things like a fire hydrant when you're not thinking about them. Then Saturday became Sunday and Sunday left to go get Monday. My weekend was gone. It was time to go to school. We're at the red light now. I look out the window and there it is; so content in just existing.

SCHOOL SHARING

"Ok, is everyone ready to share?" asked the teacher when we all took our seats.

Share? What are we sharing? We're supposed to be sharing something? I lean over, "Kiara, we're supposed to be sharing something?" "Yea," she said, "we were supposed to come up with what we want to be when we grow up."

Suddenly I'm in the backseat of my mom's car looking at her in the rearview mirror, waiting at the red light where the fire hydrant lives on the day it decided to speak. Now I understood our conversation.

One at a time my classmates started sharing. So far, we have three astronauts, two teachers, four cops, an archeologist, and two doctors. It's my table's turn. I still hadn't figured out what I wanted to be when I grew up. All I could think about was the fire hydrant, the water spewing, and the children having so much fun at play. I should be thinking about the assignment. It's almost my turn. "Veterinarian,"

I hear Kiara say. I'm next. How did we get here so fast? Aren't there more people at my table? It's my turn. Say something. "Fire hydrant." Yes, that's it! "I want to be a fire hydrant when I grow up" I say confidently. "You mean a firefighter," responds the teacher. Kiara's face translates the puzzled tone of the question. "No, I mean a fire hydrant. You know, the yellow things on the street corners. A fire hydrant." The class laughs. The teacher nods and moves on to the next person. "*You can grow up to be anything you want to be.*" I hear my mom's voice linger as the rest of the class shares what their future holds.

My mother is a liar. I very quickly realized that you can't grow up to be whatever you want to be. There are rules. Science. The fact that humans cannot become inanimate objects and stay alive. Well, there goes that dream (*was* it a dream?). Beyond that, I didn't think much about what I wanted to be when I grew up. Not for a while.

NOT BY CHOICE

Fast forward to eighth grade. That's when I got into theatre. Not by choice. Our homeroom teacher had decided that the whole class was going to put on a play. That's great I thought, but I don't act. After class, I let the teacher in on this tiny detail she seemed to have overlooked. And that is how I became the stage manager. The eighth-grade version of a stage manager looks very little like stage managing. It wasn't bad though. *Could this be the start of something?* I kept doing theatre in high school. Then college. Then after college. And then, now. How I got here is beyond me. I went to the University of Southern California to major in print journalism. I graduated with a theatre degree. It's funny how that happens. How the world keeps moving you forward once you decide to get out of your way.

So, what does that have to do with this? Well, the longer I've stayed in theatre the more I realize that as a stage manager I tend to sit quietly in the corner, watching the work unfold, just waiting to put out fires. Hmm. As it turns out, after all these years, I managed to become a fire hydrant. My mom wasn't a liar. You really can grow up to be whatever you want to be. With a not-so-subtle shift in perspective, it all made sense. Looking back, what caught my attention wasn't the fire hydrant itself but rather what the fire hydrant was doing. It was bringing together the neighborhood children, providing them with a space and the conditions where they could surrender to the present moment and just have fun. That's what I wanted to do with my life, to be able to facilitate an experience for others. All it took for me to have this realization was to listen—I had the answer all along.

LISTENING WITH ALL YOUR SENSES

Listening. Now, there's something you spend a lot of time doing as a stage manager. If you stick with it, you learn how to listen with all your senses. You learn how to hear what is not being said, the energy in the room, the rhythm of an actor's breath, the processing of information, the execution of an intention, the landing of a realization. It's a special thing to be let in on a private moment of discovery, into a rehearsal space where artists are asked to bring into the space their whole authentic self, their lived experience, and the history of their existence as they delve into the work to infuse their characters with roots in a diorama of reality. This vulnerability is magnified when you consider that not all spaces are equipped or built with the intention of amplifying all voices—especially those of the BIPOC and LGBTQ+ communities. And that is something that must be actively addressed. But what does this mean for me? I must acknowledge that I personally have never *felt* that my existence within the industry was ever at risk, that I was ever looked down upon because of who I am. But to be clear, that is *my* perceived experience and that does not take away from or diminish the experiences of others nor does it signal that it doesn't happen. Is it possible that I have been able to navigate this space and community because of my privilege as a cis gendered male with fairly light skin who is in a position of relative power? Yes. I recognize that. And if I am to honor the work of a stage manager, I need to be prepared to listen to the moment, to what is happening, and to encourage and support growth. Growth can be painful. That's why it's called growing pains. Your body is quite literally breaking itself, expanding, evolving, transforming. It's almost like watching an actor become a character, isn't it? This is the weight that comes with being entrusted with a rehearsal space—especially when you're dealing with new work.

In my professional journey, I have primarily worked with two companies— Rogue Machine Theatre and the Ojai Playwrights Conference, both right out of undergrad. At the root of these companies is a commitment to play development and new work and all the effort that comes with fostering that growth. Now, it's one thing to stage manage a published piece, you have, after all, a completed script and with it, all the answers; the collective just needs to figure out what questions to ask. When developing a new work, however, not only are you coming up with the questions, but you're also helping come up with the answers. And that is what makes it so exciting.

SACRED RESPONSIBILITY

Theatre practioners are a special breed of human. It is not enough for us to see the world; we must share our observations with the world. That's why the art form is so alluring for so many. It is a platform upon which you can invite others to bear witness to what you have discovered. And this is the sacred responsibility that stage managers are entrusted to take care of, to nurture and facilitate. It is this responsibility that has shaped my understanding of what it means to stage manage—to encourage and support. To harbor a space where actors, directors, playwrights, and creative team can safely and bravely engage in discovery. The act of making theatre is a willful surrender to vulnerability, self-reflection, and an embrace of our inherent humanness. It is an act of resistance, revolution, and engagement. And it starts with the words.

Playwrights, in my experience, are uncomfortable staying silent and are compelled to find the right words, the right turn of phrase until the language tastes familiar and is suitable for consumption. Directors then take the text and assemble an ensemble of players to absorb the meaning of these letters, to embody the message, who are jumping at the chance to give themselves over to an audience. The designers and the production team come in to enhance the entry points, to give the seeping stew flavor, texture, light, and sound. Collectively proclaiming proudly, "Look! Look at what we have made!" And "what will you do with it now?"

Oh, and the stage manager? We're the ones methodically, diligently, patiently stirring the stew, letting it breathe, giving space to all the assembled ingredients so they can draw out their unique offerings and give us a taste of the necessary. This is what makes all the effort it takes worth it. From scheduling and coordinating rehearsals to printing out new script pages, copying the new script pages, recycling the still warm copies, and printing out new script pages because the new script pages you originally printed and copied are now old script pages. Keeping track of the world while the world is being created is a lot. It takes a lot. It can feel overwhelming when you have so many people depending on you to stay calm, centered, and attentive. It's not called growing pains for nothing. That's when I learned one of the biggest lessons of being a stage manager. The only way you can genuinely enhance something is by bravely bringing your whole self to it. I needed to understand my *part* in the process, not get bogged down by what that means, get out of my way, and do the work.

Early on in my career I was fixated on being perfect, being what everyone else needed me to be and any mistimed cue or mistake bothered me. Until I decided it didn't. I realized that anyone could do my job. Anyone, in their own way, could do my job. But nobody could do the job the way that *I* can do the job. And that was the commodity that I was offering—*my* way of doing things. Theatres weren't hiring a stage manager to work on a show, they were hiring *me* to stage manage their show. That made all the difference. That shift in my thinking, that shift in perspective, allowed me to give myself permission to accept the humanness of me, worry not about the job but focus on why the job exists and my part in that process. And remember why I got started in the first place.

A COMMUNAL CONVENING

My parents were never concerned about what I wanted to do when I grew up, not really. Their expectation was that I would figure that out as I decided who I wanted to be. The type of life I led. The way I claimed my space—even if it was just sitting in the corner. They knew before I did, as parents always do, that I was capable of being what I *needed* to be. Some are called to be a thundering crackle of excitement; others are destined to be that pocket of breath as the thunder fades and the rain dissipates and a calmness blankets the ground. Working in the theatre is a lot of work, but it is also fun. It is a gathering space, a communal convening of creatives spewing talent and grace. It is a marvel to see the articulation of curiosity and the embodiment of wonder. But even when that innocence of play is mired by the heaviness of the outside, it's important to recapture that *feeling* of play. That brazen indulgence of the rain on a street corner where the red light takes an extra 30 seconds, so the beat can really land. That's why it's important for me that the last words I tell the actors when we're at places is "Have fun!"

I saw it the other day. The fire hydrant. It's still sitting there, after all this time. Holding in torrents. Building up so much potential. Disciplined and selective. Strategic and intentional.

And here I am, thankful, ready to keep dancing in the rain.

19

Maxwell, Brown, and Co.
Learning from Corporate Management
Christopher Sadler

During the summer of 2005, I found myself browsing the Management section of the Borders bookstore in Boise, Idaho. I had recently been appointed as the new professor of stage management at the University of Oklahoma (OU) School of Drama and one of the first classes I was to teach was Advanced Stage Management. I had previously taught basic stage management, but an advanced course? What was I going to do? I knew I could get through the stage management process in an introductory course, so I wanted something different; something that would expand the students' learning outside the world of theatre, yet keep it tied to the art form. I was always interested in the human side of stage managing, how we form relationships with fellow artists and how we work together to achieve a common goal. So, while on a day off from my last production at the Idaho Shakespeare Festival, I sat on the floor in front of shelves filled with lots of books by the same author: John C. Maxwell.[1]

LOTS of books. "This guy is prolific," I thought. And the size of many of them intrigued me: not very thick and only 5" x 7". I liked the compact size, so I got to work. The first two I perused turned out to be the ones I bought: *The 17 Essential Qualities of a Team Player* and *The 21 Indispensable Qualities of a Leader.* I like the symmetry of the pair—same format, same size, but they tackle the two different concepts that are in essence what a stage manager is: a team player AND a leader.

I have my original copies, still in good condition even after re-reading them dozens of times while exploring their contents with, at this count, over 50 students.

DOI: 10.4324/9780429321672-23

So that trip to Borders worked out. Maxwell inspired me to take corporate business ideas and apply them to stage management in order to deepen my students' working relationships and give them new perspectives.

JOHN C. MAXWELL

Maxwell covers 38 managerial qualities in the two aforementioned books, and in class, students write a response to each, and read those papers to the other students. Then we discuss the quality, both in the context of stage management and in their individual lives. Some qualities inspire more discussion than others and certain Maxwell concepts have become ingrained in the OU stage management culture.

Charisma is one of the first chapters in the *Leader* book and it comes as a surprise to many readers that it is a quality that one can learn and develop; it's not something you're born with. In the chapter, Maxwell tells us to "Put a '10' on Every Person's Head."[2] This lesson has stuck with so many that some younger students have thought it was an older student's idea! Maxwell is telling us to expect the best out of people, even if you've had a negative encounter with them before. This concept helps develop trust in collaborators and reminds college stage managers that everyone is growing and learning and changing; a bad experience with a first-year crew member shouldn't influence your attitude when working with them as a designer a year or two later.

In the *Team Player* book, Maxwell discusses being Communicative. Here I've found another long-lasting lesson: the "Twenty-Four Hour Rule." Maxwell tells us not to let more than 24 hours go by if you have a disagreement with a teammate. Many stage managers are uncomfortable with conflict; here we are reminded that more harm comes from letting things fester. He tells us: "Without knowing both sides of the story, people tend to give the benefit of the doubt to themselves and to assign negative motives and actions to others."[3] Only good comes when we undertake the effort not to make ourselves the protagonist in the drama, and instead to empathize with others. It's a theme that reoccurs in most of the works mentioned here, not only Maxwell—you can't be successful unless you realize that most people aren't reacting to you directly; you have to attempt to understand their point of view.

There are numerous other examples from these books, but there's not enough room to expound on them here. Some "fit" better for us as stage managers, some we have to bend to make sense of them. But the through line in both texts is that your attitude is your choice and that affects more than you realize.[4]

DR. BRENÉ BROWN

While Maxwell's works form the bedrock of the class, after a few years I wanted to discover new ideas and other authors to assist in the students' (and my) education.

I can't recall exactly when, but I first found the work of Dr. Brené Brown through a couple of YouTube videos from RSA (the Royal Society for arts, manufactures, and commerce). These animated shorts take on Empathy and Blame. Dr. Brown breaks down what empathy truly is and how it differs from sympathy. She tells us, "Rarely does an empathic response begin with 'At least'."[5] Stage managers want to "fix" things, but displaying empathy rarely results in a problem solved. The humor in the video nails the concept she's explaining; the students at Oklahoma have an inside joke from this video: "Umm, nope. Wanna sandwich?" (the reaction of a character who uses sympathy, not empathy). Through a self-depreciating story, Brown teaches us that blame is "simply the discharging of discomfort and pain. It has an inverse relationship with accountability."[6] These shorts are quite accessible and contain such valuable lessons for anyone in a collaborative environment that I show them at workshops and during our Introduction to Design and Production class as well.

After finding these, I was determined to know more of Dr. Brown. I discovered her first TED talk and it has become as integral to the Advanced Stage Management course as the Maxwell books. "The Power of Vulnerability" is a great introduction to her most famous concepts. For many, it's the first time they encounter the idea that shame and vulnerability are essential to empathy and creativity; that what we have believed as negative or weak is actually necessary and strong.[7]

In 2019, Dr. Brown posted on Facebook regarding perfectionism. As a recovering perfectionist myself, and knowing that many stage managers are often similar, I shared it with all the OU stage management majors at the time. I asked who felt called out, and all of us raised our hands. It's such an important reminder than we are allowed to be fallible (and the fact she employs a phrase I've used my entire teaching career: "strive for excellence"), that I'm going to quote it in its entirety:

Rolling into 2019 with a little perfectionism reality-check (because I need it).

Perfectionism is not the same thing as striving for excellence. Perfection is not about healthy achievement and growth.

Perfectionism is the belief that if we live perfect, look perfect, and act perfect, we can minimize or avoid the pain of blame, judgment, and shame. It's a shield. Perfectionism is a twenty-ton shield that we lug around thinking it will protect us, when, in fact, it's the thing that's really preventing us from being seen and taking flight.

Perfectionism is not self-improvement. Perfectionism is, at its core, about trying to earn approval and acceptance.

Most perfectionists were raised being praised for achievement and performance (grades, manners, rule-following, people-pleasing, appearance, sports). Somewhere along the way, we adopt this dangerous and debilitating belief system: I am what I accomplish and how well I accomplish it. Please. Perform. Perfect. Prove.

Healthy striving is self-focused – How can I improve? Perfectionism is other-focused – What will people think?

Lay down the shield. Pick up your life. Let's keep 2019 brave, kind, and awkward.[8]

I've used one of her books in an independent study with a student (a great way to explore new works!), but I find videos make her concepts easier to comprehend; plus, she's an engaging and impactful speaker.

SIMON SINEK

More recently, I discovered Simon Sinek—once again, through videos and then written work. Sinek feels like a combination of Maxwell and Brown; he is definitely talking to a corporate audience about corporate issues, but delves into the importance of empathy in leadership. In a TED talk, he remarks: "Leadership is a choice. It is not a rank."[9] This stuck with the class and we discussed that though stage managers may not always have authority, they can be leaders, sometimes even more effective leaders than others on the production. Sinek says in another video, the "real job of a leader is not about being in charge, it's about taking care of those in our charge."[10] This also resonated with us, as many times younger stage managers may struggle with their leadership and what it means. Does it mean being "in charge"? Does it mean, being "the boss"? Sinek clearly says "No." Leadership is about creating safety for those to whom you are responsible. I think this approach speaks to stage managers in a direct way. We create the positive work environment where, when risks are taken and vulnerabilities exposed, people can feel safe.

A couple of students and I recently read his book *Leaders Eat Last*. In it, Sinek explores leadership from basic human brain chemistry (the role of oxytocin, dopamine, etc.) and the beginnings of human society and how those can make us better leaders today. He gives us thought-provoking concepts to consider: "The cost of leadership…is self-interest."[11] In other words, that is the reason we stage managers sacrifice. If we wish to lead, we must care for others first. He brings up the ever-popular theme of work-life balance:

It has nothing to do with the hours we work or the stress we suffer. It has to do with where we feel safe. If we feel safe at home, but we don't feel safe at work, then we will suffer what we perceive to be a work-life imbalance.[12]

But if we have good relationships at work AND at home, it does not matter what the percentages are. There is, of course, much more to the book, but after diving more deeply into Sinek's thinking, we ended the semester agreeing that this was a text to keep in the curriculum.

LEA BERMAN AND JEREMY BERNARD

One semester, the students in my process-based, introductory course on stage management suggested I find different homework assignments for them. They had been creating mock paperwork examples, and they told me it felt repetitive considering what they create during their production assignments. I saw their point and went searching for a substitute. Happily, I stumbled on *Treating People Well: How to Master Social Skills and Thrive in Everything You Do* by Lea Berman and Jeremy Bernard. Unlike Maxwell and Sinek, they are not corporate-based, nor are they research scientists like Dr. Brown. Berman and Bernard come to their topic via a route not many of us take: Social Secretaries in the White House (Berman during George W. Bush's term and Bernard in the Barack Obama administration). Through their unique point of view, Berman and Bernard take our childhood lessons in manners and give us an adult reminder. In this day and age, we can sometimes forget the simplest of teachings—listening, loyalty, diplomacy, calmness, and owning your mistakes.[13]

The COVID-19 pandemic forced me to get creative when I had a class full of dancers and actors expecting to be working backstage for crew credit. I turned again to this book and it worked well. Many students remarked that they found it relevant and that it would assist them in their career goals and finding new approaches to facing adversity. Some, though, disagreed with Berman and Bernard on certain points and I was pleased to see them analyzing concepts and justifying their thoughts. Not always agreeing, not taking everything as gospel just because it was the required text, demonstrates the development of independent thinking.

AND CO.

Having explored these authors, I am always searching out new perspectives. I've enjoyed sharing P.M. Forni's work on modern civility, and successfully included Abby Wambach's *Wolfpack* in the most-recent Advanced Stage Management class (it will remain in the curriculum, but read in the first year). I also have Louise Evans's *5 Chairs, 5 Choices* (exploring the options we have in our behaviors) and *Radical Candor: Be a Kick-Ass Boss Without Losing Your Humanity* by Kim Scott in the pipeline. I'm excited to see what these will bring.

INTERPRETATION

These works require stage managers to develop/improve our skills in interpretation. We weren't the authors' intended audience, so we have to take their corporate business context and translate it for our world, our needs. Maxwell spends a significant portion of the chapter on Generosity discussing charitable financial contributions—not something early-career artists can afford—so we talk instead about generosity of spirit, volunteerism, and the like. Sometimes this "translating" is simple, sometimes difficult, but rarely impossible. This can be especially true with the Maxwell books, as they were written in 1999 and 2002 and have a strong, almost singular, white male perspective. It can be challenging, but ultimately rewarding, to see what value one can find in them.

I couldn't sum up this concept better than an alumna of the program here. She wrote:

> By asking students to take a book that is meant for a different audience and find the ways that it works for them encourages students to absorb the information in a deeper way. The answer to the question of what makes a good stage manager is not conspicuously presented—students must find the answer for themselves. It also spurs students to view stage management in a new perspective—it is leadership, and leadership is a universal language that anyone can speak.[14]

In a time where self-discovery and critical thinking are highly prized, I am grateful to have spent time in that Boise Borders, discovering a way to assist stage managers in finding new perspectives. The answers they encounter in their path to becoming successful collaborators and leaders allow them to form relationships with fellow colleagues and work together to create.

SUGGESTED ADDITIONAL WORKS

Louise Evans, *5 Chairs, 5 Choices* (Independently published, 2020).

P.M. Forni, *Choosing Civility: The Twenty-five Rules of Considerate Conduct* (New York: St. Martin's Press, 2002).

Kim Scott, *Radical Candor: Be a Kick-Ass Boss Without Losing Your Humanity* (New York: St. Martin's Press, 2019).

Abby Wambach, *Wolfpack: How to Come Together, Unleash Our Power, and Change the Game* (New York: Celadon Books, 2019).

NOTES

1. John C. Maxwell is a #1 *New York Times* bestselling author, coach, and speaker who has sold more than 26 million books in 50 languages. In 2014, he was identified as the #1 leader in business by the American Management Association® and the most influential leadership expert in the world by *Business Insider* and *Inc.* magazine. Source: https://johnmaxwellteam.com/john-c-maxwell/

2. J.C. Maxwell, *The 21 Indispensable Qualities of a Leader* (Nashville, Tennessee, Thomas Nelson, 1999), 11.

3. J.C. Maxwell, *The 17 Essential Qualities of a Team Player* (Nashville, Tennessee: Thomas Nelson, 2002), 33.

4. In fact, Maxwell believes personal attitude is of such importance he wrote an entire book on the subject: J.C. Maxwell, *The Difference Maker: Making Your Attitude Your Greatest Asset* (Nashville, Tennessee, Thomas Nelson, 2006). At OU, I have first-year stage managers read and respond to it.

5. RSA, "Brené Brown on Empathy," YouTube video, 2:53, December 10, 2013, https://youtu.be/1Evwgu369Jw

6. RSA, "Brené Brown on Blame," YouTube video, 3:25, February 3, 2015, https://youtu.be/RZWf2_2L2v8

7. TED, "The Power of Vulnerability: Brené Brown," YouTube video, 20:49, January 3, 2011, https://youtu.be/iCvmsMzlF7o

8. B. Brown, "Rolling Into 2019 With a Little Perfectionism Reality-Check…" Facebook, January 8, 2019, www.facebook.com/permalink.php?story_fbid=2435104106 504684&id=188471851167932

9. TED, "Why Good Leaders Make You Feel Safe: Simon Sinek," YouTube video, 11:59, May 19, 2014, https://youtu.be/lmyZMtPVodo

10. S. Sinek, "Most Leaders Don't Even Know the Game They're In," YouTube video, 35:08, November 2, 2016, https://youtu.be/RyTQ5-SQYTo

11. S. Sinek, *Leaders Eat Last* (New York: Portfolio/Penguin, 2017), 81.

12. Sinek, *Leaders Eat Last*, 71.

13. L. Berman and J. Bernard, *Treating People Well: How to Master Social Skills and Thrive in Everything You Do* (New York: Scribner, 2018).

14. Kaitlyn Souter, letter of support, November 30, 2019.

20

On Networking and Making Connections

A New, Empty Rolodex

Elynmarie Kazle

"This needs to be filled."

That was the note left for me on the Rolodex in my new office at Weathervane Playhouse. The year was 1997, where Rolodexes were miniature files containing small cards and alphabet tabs that contained people's contact. I had brought my own, a supersized version from Los Angeles—stuffed to the gills with press representatives, government officials, grants and fundraising executives, and friends. While now, we carry most of this information in our phone or in our laptops as scanned in and carefully labeled business cards, at this point, I had a brand-new challenge at hand: a new, empty Rolodex!

I had left LA in search of a more family-friendly place to raise my two-year-old. Having given birth to my son, I returned to freelancing in a variety of stage managing, producing jobs—serving in a variety of technical positions in the LA area. When a Weathervane Theatre job opened up, I applied out of curiosity. It turned out the chair of the board had grown up with one of my dear LA friends. Jimmie and I had served on the LA Stage Managers Committee together for nine years putting together networking events, creating the Lucy Jordan Award, and working with our small but mighty group of LA union stage managers to create community for those living in greater Los Angeles County. Eileen had reached out to her childhood friend Jimmie to ask if he knew me (bypassing the carefully

DOI: 10.4324/9780429321672-24

chosen references on my resume), and he gave the nod. I got the interview and the job in Akron, Ohio. The rest is nearly 20 years of interesting history.

But to return to the original question, how did a girl who grew up in Saint Paul, Minnesota, get to Akron, Ohio, home of the blimp, derby downs, and the birthplace of the marble? Honestly? It was that Rolodex—the connections I had made in that round file of contacts.

In 1984, I was working as an ASM with the Old Globe Theatre in San Diego, fresh out of grad school. I had a crappy little garage apartment and there I created my first "wall," filling one side of my square apartment with postcards from friends, flyers, playbills, actual photographs, notes, calendars: a two-dimensional Rolodex. Looking back at it, I realize now it was a non-digital facsimile of what Facebook would become in the digital age—I have often said that it was invented for me—with me in mind, anyway—it's our modern Rolodex. That wall was a daily reminder that the world from which I had come and the one I was now entering was big and at the same time very small—if you knew how to navigate it. And I came to find out, networking and connecting the web of people I know has always been my bag.

NETWORKING

In this business we move around. A lot. Job changes, relationship changes, and going from project to project make it hard to put down roots. But sure as it will rain on a Tuesday, you will see those people again. In the pre-internet days, we used the telephone and US mail—I even had an answering service while in New York City. But my favorite thing to do was to send postcards. I used these not only for friends and family, but for all of my business contacts as well. The advantage of a postcard was that you could send a greeting and keep in touch, but the person you wrote to was not under any obligation to respond. They were aware of your activity and it kept you in their mind. Facebook, Instagram, and other social media are a little like that: you can post, you can follow, you can comment on someone's posts, send a congratulatory greeting on an opening or on a personal celebration, and keep touch in a way that requires no response. If you keep that in mind—the concept of requiring no response—you will be able to retain many more of the contacts you make as you move along in this business.

Opera is one of my favorite genres ever. I started right out of grad school serving as the first female PSM for two different companies: Opera Columbus and San Diego Opera. While attending Ohio University, I was fortunate to work with a spectacular director, Chris Alden, on a production of *Cavalliaria Rusticana/I Paliacci* at Opera Columbus. I kept in touch in my own way, and 15 years later, my friend John Sadler (a contact I made through the University of Georgia, where I attended for only one semester) calls with an opportunity for me to stage manage for the Long Beach Opera on an interesting new production, *The Hoppers Wife*. My first day, also the first day of tech, I found out the director was none other than Chris

Alden, who I had so enjoyed working with in Columbus all those years ago. A territorial issue regarding who was in charge arose between the stage manager who had originated with the production in NYC and myself. I knew I would have to speak with the director about it, a potentially dicey situation. However, staying in contact had kept the relationship with that director alive. When I sat down in the house to discuss it with him, he said, of course, he would take care of the problem. It might have been a real issue that would have hurt the production, but since we had tended of our relationship, the director supported me while respecting the NYC SM, and I was able to take the reins and go on to have a very successful run.

This was a reminder that keeping those working relationships alive by communicating regularly with past colleagues is essential. Whether or not they responded in kind, it was still well worth my time. I recall that Chris even spoke of my little notes and cards and was rather apologetic about not responding. I let him off the hook; I mean, it was to my advantage to continue to keep in touch—especially so early in my career. It makes the job so much more of a pleasure when you walk in and see a colleague who is also a friend. The contacts you make are of no use if you let them get cold.

I would have to say that there were numerous times, when visiting a former colleague, or seeing a show and running into someone, that I walked into some lucrative job situations. This has worked by extension for students, mentees, and friends, who I have connected to internships that have spawned lifelong jobs, finding their way into overseas teaching and directing opportunities.

BUDDING STAGE MANAGERS

When those of my generation were young, not many of us had specialized programs through which to learn our theatrical craft. Those that studied theatre ended up in actor-centric programs, often with professors who had no idea what to do with budding stage managers. For advice, we relied on senior students—or any one of the trusted teachers or staff—who were charged with helming the productions so that we could learn while running performances. If we got decent advice, we were told that we would need to pay our dues.

The path to "paying dues" started in small ways in the summer repertory system. Most colleges and small towns offered this option. In summer rep we learned things about problem solving and that the show must go on. In some ways this was a very good system; it encouraged us to keep an open mind, let us know that there was more than one way to solve a problem on a show, in a rehearsal and on the stage. But I also wonder if it has not in some way encouraged the oppression of the artist, and the fear of saying something that would jeopardize our position. We were told at a very young age, and I think that it is still so, that there is very little money available to create these shows. We must make sacrifices to ensure that the show goes on. For some, this created unimaginable opportunities. For others, the low paying situations have not allowed us to move along the path but have encouraged bad practices for producers. It has been a hard road back to keeping in mind the value of human capital and relevance of safety practices.

Is it possible that the old school "dues paying" mentality creates an unwillingness of the mid-career individual to help someone else along the path? There are questions that come up in your head when someone contacts you out of the blue to ask for a favor, a reference, or advice on starting some coursework. Why do I have to share what I have, what I have created with another individual—give away the keys so to speak? This is where knowing when and where it is appropriate to "sell" yourself, to share with someone who may someday be in a position to return the favor, and when it is just "good to meet you" comes into play. For instance, when you shadow someone else's show, they are sharing their job, their company, and in some cases, their headset. This is not an appropriate place to bring out the resume or lobby the crew or PSM for a job. Be polite, friendly, quietly enthusiastic, and appreciative. This plants the seeds of good will and makes a good first impression. But if you are in an internship situation, take advantage of the opportunity. Don't forget to put their card in your Rolodex—add them to your network, if appropriate.

I can remember walking into the head office at the Old Globe to ask if they had a minute. Introducing myself politely as an intern (especially when unpaid) got me a valuable five or 15 minutes with someone who has very valuable knowledge or advice. As an intern you are there to learn, not only work; it is important that you take opportunities as they present themselves.

GIVING GOOD ADVICE

I created the United States Institute for Theatre Technology (USITT) Stage Management Mentor Project (SMMP) to create the opportunities for this type of connection. Knowing when and how to do this is difficult when you are first starting out. Students who move into stage management may work alone for the entirety of their undergraduate career. Even as a newly initiated member of the work force I knew this, so I thought if I could connect a student to a professional, and to a team of students across the country, it could help them take the first steps towards building a network of their own. And through all of the changes, including six changes of leadership, this is where the USITT SMMP has always exceled: connecting students to professionals and to each other as they move along the path to bigger and more complicated parts of their careers.

"She generally gave herself very good advice (though she very seldom followed it)," is one of my favorite quotes from Lewis Carroll's *Alice in Wonderland*. While believing that keeping in touch is a must, there have been times when it was a little overwhelming. It was hard to keep up.

In the final year of my MFA program, I was fortunate to have three separate apprentice-type experiences and in one of the summers in the midst of grad school I served an assistant production manager internship with Great Lakes in Cleveland. These were all interesting opportunities and as I was of the opinion to try anything, these led to some interesting circumstances. On graduation night I was on a cruise ship with my friend Ben. We had opted not to travel back to Ohio from San Diego and had secured positions with the Old Globe there for the summer. After that contract was over, I interviewed and was hired as the first female stage manager for the San Diego Opera. On a break between contracts, Ben and I decided to take a jaunt up the coast; stopping in Santa Maria to see the artistic company of Great Lakes, who had relocated there following Vincent's departure from the Cleveland Company; he asked that we both come on to assist him and Olwen in getting acclimated to California and this new company.

During the month, the PSM resigned and I took over the job, spending a year on the central coast. During that time, I continued to communicate with the stage managers I had worked with in Cleveland as well as an actor friend, Brian. We were all hoping to work together again at some point. Postcards flew back and forth from Santa Maria but then I got the opportunity to return to my hometown area for a production of *A Chorus Line* which I took.

The day my contract ended with *ACL* I truly did not know what to do. I had relocated solo, was living in Minneapolis, and started the application process for unemployment. A few days later, my phone rang. It was Alan, a playwright from grad school; he was working with a playwright who needed an Ohio University producer to do a showcase production in NYC. It was an interesting opportunity, but one I had no idea if I could afford. We agreed to speak in a couple of days and literally the next day I got a call from Andy, the stage manager whom I had worked with during the season at Great Lakes in Cleveland. He was doing a Robert Wilson piece at Brooklyn Academy of Music (BAM) and wanted to know if I would be interested in interviewing. I said I would and might just be traveling to the city for another production and I would get back to him. That night the phone rang again, it was my actor friend, Brian, wondering if I was still interested in stage managing *Strange Snow* for him in Los Angeles. Now I was in a quandary: I did have one airfare that the *ACL* company was going to provide me back to LA. Brian said I could stay with him and he would provide a car. But I also had these other two offers. I said I'd call back in a day.

This was all good news but I had no idea how I would work it out. But with some help from family and also the Actors Fund (a spectacular organization) I was able to get on my feet, make the multiple jobs work, and ultimately spent September in NYC, October and part of November with Brian in LA, then back to NYC to bunk at the Y in Brooklyn and do the performances for Civil Wars and two more contracts at BAM. I was broke, but surviving and happy. And had a lot of support from family and friends. But the connections would not have happened if I had not been using that "Rolodex" keeping in touch regularly with the great theatre folk with whom I had worked, even this early in my career.

STAYING IN THE PRESENT

In the days before Facebook with limited email and cell phones, my "Rolodex" kept me in touch with opportunities. These days, my graduated students do this with me and with their other contacts in many different ways. Using Facebook, via some open and some closed groups, as well as when they or I travel, we try to see each other's work. Some send out monthly updates; I have a student in Korea who has been doing a monthly "newsletter style" update on their life traveling and working overseas with the Fulbright program. This is the type of personal marketing we should do to keep ourselves present so that when a job or opportunity arrives, we can be the someone who comes to mind. It may also be a good spot to always ask contacts to be references, if you want them to be. And to keep asking over the years.

Letters of recommendation play an important part as well. I have had a long and varied career and some recommendations are better than others. Personally, I am not a fan of "To Whom it May Concern." I will always write a letter of recommendation for someone that I would recommend for a position if asked for. I also want to write it specifically for that person and that position, and I would want to highlight the things that I believe would help the potential employer the best. In the long run, a specific call, letter, email recommendation is always best.

There are many supporting groups on the net, but I truly believe that the Stage Managers' Association (SMA) does this best for stage managers across the board. It is an association primarily for professionals. Networking events called SM Go (SMs go out) are held in cities across the country, 50–100 each year. SMA also sponsors formal and more informal speed dating events so that SMs can get to know producers, production managers, and general managers, who do the hiring during the season.

One of the ways you can meet stage managers you do not know is by shadowing or observing on a show. "Operation Observation" is the SMA's oldest program. It was the first program to offer observing on Broadway productions. Through the SMA as an early career stage manager, I had the opportunity to shadow an ASM at Radio City, to meet Broadway legends George Rose and Loretta Swit on a production of *Edwin Drood*, to be sitting next to the illustrious stage manager, Bob Bennett, while he called a show recently in the intimate booth at the Signature in NYC, was invited by the local stagehands to hang out in the spot booth at *Sweet Charity*, and had the opportunity to share an intensely funny moment with Mickey Rooney, courtesy of stage manager Joel Tropper, during *A Funny Thing Happened on the Way to the Forum* in Hollywood. I even got to share Arturo Porazzi's book recently on the Broadway production of *Come From Away*, sitting on headset in the back with the electricians, Arturo's book open in front of me.

OLD SAYINGS

Looking back at it, I realize now that my Rolodex was a non-digital facsimile of what Facebook would become in the digital age, and it allowed me to keep in touch. So, stay in touch, whenever or however you can. An old saying goes, "When it's bad keep it in the dark, but lift up the positive in the light." This goes double for social media: when you are constantly "woe is me" in public, privately people decide not to work with you. And don't think employers are not investigating you on your platforms. While it has made it much easier for us to communicate, social media has also made it easier for employers to check out our "non-reference" information.

Stay connected, keeping social occasions social, creating a good contact list, asking for specific references, doing your research, and most of all, treating every job like it is the most important one by doing your very best job every time. Be that person everyone wants to work with, and soon they will be tracking you down!

21

From Stage Management to Production Management
One Path
Cary Gillett

HOW STAGE MANAGEMENT FOUND ME

Like so many young people, I was exposed to theatre by way of performance. I did theatre camps at a young age and by high school I was hooked. Acting was everything! When it came time to choose a major in college, I said in no uncertain terms that I would major in theatre. Luckily, my parents agreed, though I knew they were worried about what job prospects I'd have upon graduation.

I have a memory of someone serving in the role of "stage manager" my senior year of high school (though to be honest I could not have told you what he did). I recall standing backstage next to my friend who was on run crew. I asked what they talked about on headset and he shrugged and said "nothing important, the stage manager keeps saying numbers. I have no idea what they mean." We were not taught technical theatre in high school, despite having a theatre class. I graduated only knowing acting and directing. A shame for sure.

My first year of college opened my eyes to the fact that there were SO MANY positions in theatre! Not just actors and directors, there were designers, dramaturgs, technicians, playwrights, and much more. I vowed to learn about all parts of the theatre while I was in college, and I'm happy to say I did just that. I was told repeatedly that I was "really organized and should try stage management." "Sounds

DOI: 10.4324/9780429321672-25

good to me!" I thought, so I signed up to assistant stage manage, having no idea what I was getting myself into.

MAKING STAGE MANAGEMENT MY CAREER

I quickly discovered I loved stage management because I loved seeing a production come together and being a part of it every step of the way. I was in fact "really organized" and found out I was good at communication to boot. My acting background came in very handy as I was able to relate to the performers and anticipate their needs. For example, I knew how much inconsistency can throw an actor off, so they need things the same way each time, such as how their props are set or what pre-show calls they are given.

After graduating I spent a year touring with the National Players where I was able to both act and stage manage. That tour taught me a lot about myself and about theatre, but the biggest thing it taught me was that I did not want to be an actor, I wanted to be a stage manager. I took an internship in stage management at the Olney Theatre Center in Maryland where I got my first true taste of full-time stage management work. What they did not teach me in college was how to survive an EIGHT HOUR rehearsal every day and still stay focused and on task. Upon completion of my internship, I was asked by Olney to stage manage a main stage production and signed my first Actors' Equity Association contract. At age 23 I had done it—I had become a professional stage manager! I expected the job offers to come rolling in, but then I learned one of the biggest lessons in theatre—it's all about who you know. I did not know many people yet. I had only worked at one place! Olney did hire me again to stage manage more shows, but hardly what would be considered full-time. I started getting my name out there and other offers came in here and there. I needed a full-time job to make ends meet.

During this time the general manager for the National Players vacated the position, so on a whim I applied—and I got it! I had one asset: I had toured with the National Players, but other than that, I had not a clue what I was doing. I spent two years in that job making it up as I went along. Guessing at budgets, making touring schedules, supporting the members of the tour from back home. But this was just my day job, most nights and weekends I was stage managing and loving it. By the end of these two years I had made enough connections that I felt confident leaving the day job behind and stage managing full-time.

While I was working my National Players day job, I continued to stage manage on the side including working at Olney and other theatres in the Maryland/ Washington DC area. Part of what helped me make the decision to jump headfirst into stage managing full-time was that Round House Theatre offered me three shows in one season. Fast forward one year and I was their resident stage manager, stage managing all five of their main season shows! I could not believe my luck. I was now 26 and had landed something many spend a career trying to achieve. I felt grateful and proud.

WHEN PRODUCTION MANAGEMENT BEGAN KNOCKING

During my time as resident stage manager at Round House Theatre, the production manager asked me if I would step into our newly vacated associate production manager position. They could hire another stage manager or two to take over the rest of the shows much easier than they could hire someone to jump in as associate production manager. I said yes, taking one for the team, but only through the end of the season. I did not dislike the work of production management, but I did miss being in the room watching the show come together. I found myself visiting rehearsals often during this time, eager to get back to it. At the completion of that season the current production manager was asked to step into an associate producer role and the job of production manager was offered to me. I expressed my gratitude for the offer but graciously declined. I was a stage manager, not a production manager.

During my time at Round House Theatre I fell into another gig each summer working with the Potomac Theatre Project (PTP), a small company with a short summer rep season. My first summer I stage managed two of their three shows. I loved the company, but not the production manager. To be honest, this person was in over their head and was not committed to the work or the company. I found myself picking up slack simply to make sure I had the information I needed to do my job properly. At the end of that season, the producers thanked me for my hard work and asked if I would consider coming back next summer as the production manager. I really had no desire to do this, but loved the company and the work they did, so I agreed, but only on the condition that I also got to stage manage one of the shows. So, the next summer I was back, this time wearing two hats—not something I would recommend—but I did not know that at the time. I was able to do both, but wished I had another person to turn to as a sounding board or to play bad cop to my good cop. Afterwards, I knew doing both again was a bad idea, so I resigned myself to doing whatever job they needed of me, which they decided was production manager. I agreed, with some resignation: I was a stage manager, not a production manager.

MAKING THE SWITCH

After eight seasons working as a stage manager, the schedule started to take its toll and I could barely see my husband. Plus, we wanted to start a family and I knew I did not want to be away from home so many evenings and weekends, so I needed to make a change. I started to think about the ideal next job. It would need to be full-time so I had paid time off given the desire to grow our family, it would need to be in the theatre (no way was I going anywhere else), and it would need to be a position that was involved in every part of the theatrical process. It didn't take long to realize the answer was production management and clearly had been for a while, I just had to get over my thought that I could only be one thing. The truth was I did not have to give up stage managing, I just had to allow myself to pursue production management while keeping my stage management options open. I would take my love of theatre and the process, my skills of communication and organization, and take them to the next level!

Honestly, the jobs of stage manager and production manager are very similar. Management positions of any kind are not at the top in a hierarchy, instead, we are at the bottom supporting the team from below and there to catch them if they stumble. Both positions require a wide and varied knowledge of the work it takes to get a production on its feet. You have to speak all languages and know all terms; you have to know what information people need to do their jobs and you have to anticipate any potential challenges along the way and avoid them if possible.

If stage management is the microcosm (focusing on one show at a time) then production management is the macrocosm (focusing on all shows at once). If you find yourself working full-time with a company as I have done, you will likely be working on multiple shows at once. At the time that I wrote this, I recently closed a show and opened another, am in the planning/implementation stages of four more, plus still wrapping up finances on a show from last season and starting to do early cost outs for six shows being considered for next season—that's 13 if you lost count. I did not initially find it easy to widen my focus from one show to many, but over time found the ability to do just that. It's hard work to help these projects to stay afloat. Every day is an opportunity to revise my to-do list and create new priorities based on where we are in each step of the process.

WHAT I WISHED I HAD KNOWN, AND WORKING WITH STAGE MANAGERS

I have learned that every production manager starts their first job not knowing what they are doing. That was certainly the case for me. I remember quite clearly sitting at my desk in my office (my first time having my own office), staring at my computer and thinking to myself "Now what?" I have come to discover that this feeling repeats with every new job. Despite years of experience, there are still moments that I doubt myself. Impostor syndrome is a real thing. You will inevitably feel it at some point in your career, if not multiple times. Breathe deep and work through it. Trust your instincts, they are what got you this far in your career. Take solace in the fact that someone hired you to do this job which means they believe in you. Let that be enough to make you believe in yourself.

The hardest thing I found in the transition from stage management to production management was dealing with budgets. I wish I had some formal finance training, everything I know I either gathered from others or made up myself. If I had it all to do over again, I would have gotten an MBA before making this change in my career. It's all guesswork, especially budgets—those that have been at it longer than you guess better because they've had more experience guessing and their guesses are more informed.

Each organization and therefore each production management position is different. Don't ever make assumptions—be adaptable. Work closely with the people and the systems to best know how you will fit in and what changes you might need to make, but don't rush it. Change is hard—you cannot turn a ship around overnight. (I strongly recommend the book *Switch: How to Change Things When Change is Hard* by Chip and Dan Heath if you find yourself in a position to make a big organizational change.)[1]

Inevitably, if you find yourself in a production management position, you will work with stage managers on a regular basis. If you have ever stage managed, you know how supportive (or not) a production manager can be and how that affects the process. I strongly urge you to support your stage managers the way you would have wanted to be supported. Be the production manager you wished you had worked with or emulate the ones you loved. I promise you it will make all the difference. Both positions can feel lonely at times, but they don't need to be if you form a strong supportive bond for each other. Be in alliance, not in opposition to each other.

Not every stage manager will be like you and that is OK! Don't micro-manage, there are so many ways to do the job well. Instead of standing in their way, be a sounding board for them. Use all your stage management history as a way to share knowledge and brainstorm solutions. Don't let you or them view your experiences as anything other than a benefit. When you find yourself working with stage managers younger or less experienced than you, don't lecture, but guide. They will learn from you in an informal way. Keep sharing, suggesting, and encouraging. If they do come to you for advice then of course give it, but still in support of their growth not your ego.

MY ADVICE (FOR THOSE WHO WANT TO PURSUE PRODUCTION MANAGEMENT)

Don't stop learning. Study as much as you can about all aspects of theatre and other fields within the performing arts. I myself took on production managing for dance after having only worked in theatre. My learning curve was steep, but I reminded myself that while the discipline might be different, the support system was not. It's still a show! The field is changing so fast that it is impossible to fully keep up, but you need to try. Find opportunities for professional development when you can. Attending the United States Institute for Theatre Technology (USITT) annual conference is a great place to start. Learn about yourself, what makes you tick.

Find the joy. Stay connected to the parts that you love—for me it's being in the rehearsal room, or in the tech process. I find every excuse to sit in rehearsal whenever I can. I benefit from watching the art come together. It reminds me why I do this work. I also love being on book and sweeping/mopping. If things are behind getting the theatre ready for the cast to take stage I will be the first to offer to sweep so the stage management team can do the parts of the space prep that require knowledge of the show, plus I secretly love doing it! There is nothing more satisfying then a well swept stage and I find the process of sweeping very Zen.

Value the people. Surround yourself with smart, talented, and passionate people that you can trust to do good work and that can advise you on the things you don't know. It's the people who do the work and make it worthwhile. Make those people feel special. Celebrate small wins. Create a collaborative spirit amongst your team.

Be honest. Know what you don't know and don't hide it. Defer to others when they have more information or ability to decide. If no one on your team has the skills to get a project done, then find someone who does. Be transparent with your work, your process, your abilities, and your decisions. It's okay to show vulnerability, you are a person like everyone else and you have flaws and weaknesses. Look at the work of Brené Brown to tap into this idea more.

Trust others and be trustworthy. In my experience there are two types of people, those who trust right away and those who need their trust to be earned. I fall into the first category. I find that this business is one that necessitates fast relationship building. If I trust you right away, then I can more easily connect with you and the working relationship is stronger. I trust that people are in the positions they are in for a reason. Someone decided they deserve to be there and that is enough for me. I also find it necessary to be trustworthy. Don't let people down. As Don Miguel Ruiz states in his book *The Four Agreements*, "your word is your vow."[2] Keep your promises and if that is not possible explain why and find another way to right the situation.

Know that you are not alone. There are hundreds of other production managers in the United States alone, let alone overseas. Grow your network so you have a support system to learn from and turn to at a time of need. Look for mentors who have established themselves in the business already and learn from them. And when it is your turn, provide mentorship to others who are breaking into the business. We should all help each other get better at what we do.

As a wise person once told me—"When you reach the top, send the elevator back down!"

NOTES

1. C. Heath and D. Heath, *Switch: How to Change Things When Change is Hard* (London: Random House Business Books, 2011).

2. D. Miguel Ruiz, *The Four Agreements: A Practical Guide to Personal Freedom.* A Toltec Wisdom Book (San Rafael, CA: Amber-Allen Publishing, Incorporated, 2018).

22

Unemployment
The Other Side of Being a Freelance Stage Manager
Erin Joy Swank

Let's face it. As stage managers, we like to work. We like to get paid well and to be appreciated. We look forward to the ebb and flow of a production, from pre-production to rehearsals to tech week to closing. What we don't usually like—particularly as freelance stage managers—is the search for the next job and figuring out how to make ends meet between gigs. Sometimes having down time between productions can be refreshing, invigorating, and full of sleep or vacations. However, it can also make you worry about finances. Depending on what kind of work you've done in the past, you may very well be eligible to file for unemployment compensation benefits.[1]

I want to make a caveat here, I will only talk in broad generalities and offer some advice for how to prepare for filing unemployment, so you can see if you are eligible. Every state in the United States handles unemployment slightly differently, and the rules may change from year to year, so please consult with the appropriate government agency as to the current protocols. That said, I have had experience filing for unemployment in multiple states over the years, and hope that this chapter will help you set yourself up for success in making it through the lesser-employed times.

GOVERNMENT "BOXES"

First and foremost, we theatre people don't fit well into government boxes. Frankly, I'm not sure we really want to, except when it comes to dealing with our income and the government, as during tax time and when filing for unemployment. Benefits are usually thought of for people who "through no fault of their own" have been let go due to a downsizing of a manufacturing company, or a similar non-freelance scenario. These are people who thought they had a full-time job and were suddenly let go, with perhaps two weeks' notice. We, on the other hand, often know exactly when our upcoming job will end: the closing performance (or perhaps after load-out/archival). Like those factory workers, we still do not have any more work to do for the company after that. We can use the same terms as the others do when filing for unemployment—**"lack of work"** or **"laid off."** If we had worked on the right kind of job that fits within their boxes, we can file for unemployment just like those factory workers, because the opportunity to work has stopped.

ARE YOU ELIGIBLE FOR UNEMPLOYMENT?

Stage managers in the performing arts generally fall into one of two contract situations: employee or contractor. As a **wage-earning employee**, Federal Form W-4 is filled out at the beginning of the contract, taxes and social security are taken out appropriately on your behalf, and come tax time, you receive a W-2. The company sends unemployment insurance taxes in to the government, and unemployment compensation is paid from these funds. If the job is filed as an **independent contractor**, on the other hand, you fill out a W-9 form, no taxes are taken out, and then you receive a 1099 at the beginning of the next calendar year. Just because a 1099 contract may have a higher wage on paper, there are other monetary factors for the future to consider when taking a job. With a W-2, you'll have taxes taken out throughout the year, instead of being stuck with them later, and the company is also footing the bill for some of the taxes (which you have to pay yourself when working as an independent contractor). If you do both types of jobs, you may want to claim a lower deduction than usual on the employee contract, so that more taxes are taken out to offset your 1099s, rather than be surprised at tax time. All union work is also W-2, so it may go towards pension and health (if applicable) and occasionally 401(k)s. W-2s have so many benefits, and unemployment compensation is only one of those![2]

Technically speaking, independent contractors are supposedly given more leeway to do jobs on their own terms, but there are many of us who do not believe theatre workers should really qualify as independent contractors, particularly stage managers. The theatre will likely dictate exactly when I am to be at rehearsal, and certainly tells me when performance times will take place. There are also protections built into employee contracts; it can be a gamble if you work as an independent contractor when it comes to things like workers' compensation for accidents, overtime calculations, and…unemployment benefits. To collect unemployment, all of your earnings are based on the W-2 salary figures. If you only worked 1099 independent contractor gigs, you are likely not eligible for unemployment.[3] If you did a combination of 1099 and W-2 work, you likely are eligible, though you'll get better returns if you did more W-2 work. Everything is based on a formula of how much you worked on the right kinds of gigs, over a certain amount of time. And every state is different. More on that later.

PREPARING TO FILE THE FIRST TIME

Filing for unemployment is work in itself. There is no free ride; the government wants you to earn any money they give you, and you can probably understand that looking from the other side. However, sometimes it can seem like an enormous pain to jump through the hoops. Here's how to set yourself up best for the process:

First and foremost, start making a list of every single show, benefit, and lecture you've ever done. Trust me, when you get a couple decades into this business, you're not going to remember everything. I started my process a little late in the game, and it's been fascinating to find old programs of shows I'd forgotten I'd done, like a one-week staged reading of a new work. These can be great references when you suddenly want to do more new works; perhaps not in the resume itself, but mentioned in your cover letter. And if you want to apply for unemployment between gigs, you're going to need a lot of evidence you worked somewhere. I keep two documents, one an MS Word document listing at bare minimum the show, theatre, my role, and dates (even if rough); this list goes all the way back to college. Include conferences you attend (especially if you're a speaker) and awards you've received, if you may ever need to create a CV (curriculum vitae) for education. For more recent shows—those I'll reference for taxes and/or unemployment—I create a spreadsheet with many more details.

When you file for unemployment, they're going to want information for every **wage-earning employee (W-2)** gig you've done in a given recent time period. Each state looks at a year's worth of wages, but can vary how far they look back to find that year. To be safe, you'll likely need the last 18 months. If you've only had one or two long-term jobs in the last 18 months, you're in good shape. If you do a lot of short stints (a six-week contract or even shorter opera—or yes, one-day gigs), the sooner you start gathering this stuff, the better off you'll be. If you're about to file unemployment, concentrate on the W-2 jobs. I tend to over-supply and give them too much information, but this last time I was told I shouldn't have turned in any of the 1099 for the **initial** claim. You will definitely need this same information for your later weekly claims between gigs.

Following is a comprehensive list of what the IRS wants to know for each job (both W-2 and 1099, as can be answered):

1. **Name of Employer/Company**—Note, this is the payroll company as listed on your check. If you work at a theatre on a university campus, it's likely the name of the university, not the theatre, for instance.
2. **Payroll Address**—Again, this is what is listed on the check/paystub.
3. **Physical Working Address, if different**—If I worked both at an office and a venue, and the office is the same as the payroll address, I don't bother with a second address; however, many times there is a payroll address that is quite different, perhaps not even the same state. [This can get very funky if you're on tour. Contact your HR person to find out how folks file, as you're likely not alone. It's really about where the employer turned in unemployment taxes.]
4. **State**—In my working spreadsheet, I add a separate column to reiterate the state name (physical location), so I can sort by this later if needed, a common requirement for government forms.
5. **Employer/Company Contact Person**—You'll want to record the name, title, and phone number of your direct supervisor (or contract signer).
6. **Reason the job ended**—Get used to the terms **lack of work** and **laid off**, depending on the state in which you file. The other options would be that you were fired, terminated, or discharged (you weren't, if you worked all the way through closing/end of contract). Other terms that fall under lack of work include temporary layoff/furlough, the position being eliminated, or the business closed. Each of these may also be your answer.
7. **Date you knew you were going to be laid off**—I usually say "the day I was hired," and include a brief explanation describing theatre schedules with known final performances.
8. **Was anyone else laid off at the same time?** My standard answer is, "Yes, the entire cast and crew."
9. **Do you have a return-to-work date?** This is something you really hope for; one time I've known I was going to be returning to a theatre a little later in the season, which fit in the time period unemployment requires. As a result, I didn't have to look for as many job searches in the interim, which was a great relief. It can be hard to find enough jobs to satisfy requirements.
10. **Are you union?** In my case, yes, but some states then follow up with a question similar to, "Are you a union member who is currently seeking work exclusively through a union hiring hall?" (Some states also continue with "or business agent?") Oh, how I wish I could answer that follow up question as a yes.[4] IATSE (International Alliance of Theatrical Stage Employees) members have this benefit and only need call into the hiring hall to say they're ready for work. In some states, actors or others with agents get a bit of a job-searching reprieve too…not so much for stage managers.
11. **Your rate of pay**—Go back to your contract for the exact amount per hour or week; don't worry about any overtime amount, just the base

rate. The last unemployment customer service person told me that when I report 1099 work, I report the net gross AFTER taxes, but that was news to me. She confirmed that with W-2, however, you always report gross earnings BEFORE taxes. Confusing, eh?

12. **The hours you worked per week**—This is easier to research if it's an Equity or other union contract where it's written down. Make your best guess for others, and record for yourself what you put as your answer. It'll be especially important if you work a partial week and have to report one day's pay by figuring out the ratio worked.

13. **The start date and end date**—Self-explanatory.

OTHER THINGS TO KNOW

The work week for every state that I have filed in runs from Sunday through Saturday. Of course, a theatre/opera/ballet week is usually Monday through Sunday. You will nearly always have a partial week to deal with.

Most states have a waiting period—mine has always been a week—between the time you file and when you can start receiving money.[5] Start your claim as soon as your job ends. Some states go on a daily basis, or from the last day of work, but some are to the "closest Sunday" to which you filed. If you wait until later in the week, you essentially lose a week. From what I understand, some states may pay you for this "Waiting Week," but I don't think I've ever received money for it. If your work history takes a while to verify (freelance theatre artist with multiple states) it may take several weeks (or months!) to solidify before you see the money, though you should eventually be issued anything after that waiting period.

While filing unemployment, you must be available for work, able to work, and pursuing work. It's not a free ride and there are hoops to jump through, and weekly requirements to receive the money. However, there are (usually) funds available for you. Unemployment claims are good for a year—and you can take jobs during that year, then go back on the claim—but they must be "re-upped" every year after that.

I'VE GATHERED MY WORK HISTORY, NOW WHAT?

If you have worked in multiple states, you should do an online search to see what formula each state uses to calculate wages, and what the maximum weekly benefit will be. It is often easiest to file in the state in which you live, but I've had times where I worked so much in other places that I didn't earn my state's minimum to file. The maximum amount of money you can receive each week also varies from state to state, by hundreds of dollars. Generally speaking, I'd say it's best to go with whichever state can give you the most money per week. They all may end up at the same maximum cap they'll give you in a year; if you're getting less per week, you'll have to spend more weeks on unemployment to get all of that money. I'd rather run out of unemployment benefits—having collected everything I could—than wind up getting more jobs than I expected and losing the opportunity to see some of the money from not working. Do your research in advance to see which might be better. Some may start their lookback on a different quarter, or use a different formula for averaging your salary (for example, some base off your two highest earning quarters, some take an average of the whole year).

Finally, different states require different hoops to jump through each week that you are filing, especially as to the number of required job contacts per week. Do some research to see what the options are for your state(s), and file where you think it will work out best for your circumstances. I've been lucky that a state will usually let me know, "Hey, did you know you could earn more (or less) money if you filed in this other state instead?" However, getting the unemployment claim to transfer can sometimes be a bigger headache in red tape. It once took three months before I saw any reimbursement, with multiple phone calls per week until it was settled for one state to release the claim and another to accept it.

More states are moving their unemployment systems online, but when possible, I prefer to get a real live person on the phone.[6] We do not fit their boxes as well online. The guidelines I gave you earlier will help you understand some of the terminology, but I find it best to talk to an actual human being. I try to joke with them to understand our business, and it's really great when you get someone who "did theatre in high school" or somewhat understands the business. That said, if you have multiple jobs to input, do your best to make the experience pleasant for them as well. It will go a long way.

CONTINUING YOUR UNEMPLOYMENT CLAIM

The hard part has only just begun. Now, you have to keep earning your money. The government does not want you simply sitting around reading books or going on vacation while they send finances. First, you'll likely need to send back some sort of verification form, including your signature, and may have a short turn-around time for returning this.[7] They also want to see that you're trying to stop taking money from them. Job-seeking requirements vary from state to state. I've had to look for anywhere between three and five jobs per week, and keep a record of it. (As mentioned, there was that one time when I was going to return to the same employer within ten weeks or so, so my requirements were waived.) Massachusetts in particular was very difficult, and in addition to having three "job contacts" per week, they also had to be on three different days of the week. If I found three jobs to apply for on Sunday, I played the game of whether to apply immediately and not miss the opportunity, or whether to send my resumes on three different dates, in order of the job I wanted the most. Also, if I hadn't located any jobs by about Wednesday—stage management job listings are not exactly frequent commodities—I started to panic a bit and look at what other ways I could fulfill the requirements.

Luckily, many states include a variety of other activities that fall under job-search activities. You usually need to file with the state's "workforce center" to receive job listings. Most of the time, that can count as one action your first week. Some states allow networking events and job career fairs to count. If the Stage Managers' Association or Actors' Equity Association is having a gathering or seminar (in person or online), this can count for many states (but not all). Some states count the first time you upload your resume to LinkedIn or Monster.com or another job-seeking website. Seek out all the opportunities you can for your particular state's requirements. There are a few where you can only submit for a job *if* you know they are hiring, too. That means you can't send out cold submissions, which can truly hamper your prospects. Keep track of what you did each week in another spreadsheet. Record most of the same information about the job as you did for your employment history—if nothing else, this can be your own great resource if you are asked for an interview several weeks later. Added information I like to keep includes how I found the job, how I submitted for it (in person, phone, snail mail, email, or website, and the corresponding contact information), the salary rate if known, and whether I received any response (oh, how I wish every job posting listed the salary rate, too!). States can vary how they want you to send them your weekly actions, too. Some will have you submit all the information online weekly or biweekly, while others will have you simply file to say "yes, I want money, and no I didn't work," but then spot check you a couple weeks later regarding the required job contacts. Make sure you keep your records up to date and do the work every week. It's also good to set yourself a calendar reminder to file for unemployment regularly.

If you have to contact an unemployment office because you have questions, be prepared to have a lot of patience. It can be notoriously difficult to get through to a live person. Some states only allow you to call on a specific day of the week, based on your last name. The hours for service can also be incredibly limited, and awfully early in the day for a theatre person (especially if it's for a state in an earlier time zone). You can be on hold for a long time; I got to know which classical music piece I would hear on repeat for one state—only to be told in the end that "they're working on it." Be as patient as you can, and use your theatre charm of being a novelty that doesn't fit their boxes. You may just get someone who did plays when they were in high school who has a bit of understanding.

WHAT HAPPENS WHEN I GET ANOTHER JOB?

Ah, this is where it can sometimes get even trickier. Because unemployment claims are usually delayed by a week, you also have to keep thinking about them when you start working again. I have fallen victim to being too consumed with a new job that I forgot to file that last week of unemployment. There are a few states that allow you to continue to keep a claim open while you are working—I know of a friend who simply made it part of her weekly to-do list to sign in to her state's unemployment online, tell them she was working, and carry on with her life. I have never had that opportunity. Sometimes, I'll say that I worked a particular week, and I'll get a notice that I'm not getting payment for that same week, as the amount is more than they would have given me. In some states, they continue to let me file, especially if that gig was only a couple days long. However, in my most recent state, as soon as I made more than their weekly limit, they closed my claim. I nearly lost a week of unemployment payment because of the lag time, and luckily checked in again to re-open the claim. Sometimes, I say, "oh well," and decide that week wasn't worth the hassle.

I try to refile for unemployment as soon as the next job ends, sometimes even the same night. Unemployment usually starts on Sunday, as mentioned, and shows usually close on Sundays. If I know of a potential job prospect already, I may hold off on applying for it until that evening, so that I already have one job-seeking action finished for that week.

Remember, if you take any kind of job after you have started to receive unemployment benefits, you have to report that as income, including 1099 contracts. Depending on the amount of money earned, the length of the job, and each state's requirement, your claim may be closed. [8] If it's a shorter gig (working part-time during the week), your claim may be able to remain open, it will just change the amount of benefits you can receive that week. Keep track of the jobs, including how many hours you worked, and the payment per hour, and file that in your weekly claim.

WHAT IF I'M OFFERED A JOB, BUT DON'T WANT IT?

This is so hard to gauge, in my experience. I try not to apply for jobs that I don't really want, but sometimes I'm stuck needing those job contacts per week. Then again, many theatre job postings unfortunately don't list the salary range—something many of us are fighting—and it takes until the job offer for you to find out it's below your usual asking price. As you're weighing the pros and cons of negotiating or accepting the offer, another thing to consider is how it will affect your unemployment. You'll need to check with your state on what counts as **"suitable employment**," wages comparable to your past employment, with duties that fit your education level and work experience. The longer you are unemployed, your ability to turn down the not-great jobs will decrease.

HOW LONG CAN I COLLECT UNEMPLOYMENT?

If you follow all the rules for your state, a claim is active for a full year. It may be closed if you start working again (for example, you have an eight-week contract including prep week and performances). As mentioned earlier, be sure to re-open that claim as soon as the job ends. You may also run out of unemployment money, either because you hadn't worked enough of the W-2 projects the previous year, or because you haven't worked enough the current year—and thus had many weeks of unemployment. The maximum monetary benefit is often 26 weeks of unemployment, though for many recipients this was extended by another 13 weeks during the 2020/2021 COVID-19 pandemic. You generally cannot file for any additional compensation until your year is up. When those 12 months have passed, start this process all over again, seeing which state may be your best bet this time around.

As I said at the start of this chapter's essay, sometimes having down time between productions is welcomed for a freelance stage manager. While it can also make you worry about finances, you may very well be eligible to file for unemployment compensation benefits, depending on what kind of work you've done in the past. Being on unemployment does not mean you have failed in your career, either, though it can feel that way. You earned the money that was put aside when you worked for an employer (though not as an independent contractor in most circumstances). Make it part of your "job" to collect these earnings, rather than let them go to waste. I've seen reports that in an average year, only 50% of eligible people collect unemployment. Granted, many states have made it particularly difficult to get through the system. Hopefully, the information in this chapter can make your filing go a bit smoother!

NOTES

1. During the late Spring of 2020, the federal government allowed USA states to change their unemployment benefits laws. It allowed them to provide unemployment benefits for situations related to the COVID-19 pandemic. Link: www.careeronestop.org/LocalHelp/UnemploymentBenefits/unemployment-benefits-finder-help.aspx

2. For further details and the most current information, please visit www.irs.gov.

3. The CARES Act of 2020, in response to the COVID-19 pandemic, allowed independent contractors and other gig workers to claim unemployment benefits not usually

available. Some who had both 1099 and W-2 work got caught in a rough middle-ground as, once again, they didn't fit the normal government "boxes." W-2 work was considered first, and sometimes negated any additional compensation possibilities for the 1099 work.

4. There are some states where Actors' Equity Association can be counted as a union with a hiring hall, but I have never experienced this myself. The follow-up government box will ask for the number of the union local, of which there isn't any. When in doubt, contact AEA directly to find out what number can be used for that state, often a zero or one.

5. This waiting week was waived for unemployment benefits during the 2020 CARES Act.

6. During the 2020/2021 COVID-19 pandemic, it became increasingly obvious that several states' unemployment systems were archaic, perhaps in order to discourage those seeking benefits. Many used near-extinct COBOL programming, and often claims were best received when sent by fax, rather than by submitting phone or internet applications. While faxing was already an out-of-date form of communication at the time, a workaround was to send document scans through free fax service websites, watching page limitations. This wound up being one of the best ways to get through to a human when you couldn't get through on overwhelmed phone lines.

7. On these verification forms, take the time to make sure they include every job that you reported. If you are a freelancer, many of the jobs may slip through the crack, especially if in multiple states. Check that you're getting all the credit you deserve!

8. Occasionally I have had an issue where I start and finish a job within the time period between biweekly claims. If I work a new job, it may close my claim as of that date, and then start the new one on the date I am filing. On paper, I suddenly am out at least a week of unemployment benefits, as it starts over on the date of the "new claim." I have had best results by calling in—or faxing—and explaining my situation, especially if it is only for a one-day job. Be prepared to spend some extra work explaining your freelance life, but often someone can make you fit the boxes a bit better.

23

These Skills Are Made for Walking

Tina Shackleford

The art and craft of stage management involves a particular set of skills for success. Those skills are valuable and applicable in many positions beyond theatre. These are things stage managers know, at least in theory, and most of the time, when stage managers change directions in their careers, it is a voluntary choice, arrived at after a time of contemplation and decision-making. The COVID-19 pandemic of 2020/2021 created a different situation, as many who would be happy to spend their entire careers in stage management found that the production opportunities vanished seemingly overnight.

This chapter was originally envisioned in a time before COVID, when the examination of transferable skills one could take from stage management to other fields was an embrace of opportunity, not of desperation, when the choices of "when" and "how" were not so limited. Yet it was reinforced again how those fundamental stage management skills are not unique to theatre. Although these abilities may seem second nature to good stage managers, it is gratifying to find that they are applicable in many other professions. But no matter the reason, it can be difficult to know how to consider moving these talents to a new place and to anticipate how they might be valued in a different work environment. Talking with a few former AEA stage managers who have taken their expertise successfully into other areas reveals much about the portability of stage management, connections and surprises, and even how they would do returning to the field.

DOI: 10.4324/9780429321672-27

THE PATH OUT

Trevor Long, associate director of production at the Guthrie Theater[1] in Minneapolis, says the decision to leave stage management, which happened during a gig with a high-profile Cirque du Soleil[2] show, was simply a matter of "'OK, I am done with this now.' The makeup of the people, the makeup of the job, what I wanted out of it didn't mesh in the same way." Long started thinking about "going the complete opposite of where I was," but ended up looking at production management jobs, where he would serve the production in a different way. Even so, he found his stage management skills coming into play:

> One of the main reasons I was hired for this position was that they were looking for someone who could be very relational to everyone: the run crew, wardrobe, technicians, designers. Someone who was capable not only of listening but also responding, a facilitator and a mediator.

For Kristen Manning, a former stage manager and now Senior Paralegal at Wolf Group Los Angeles,[3] it wasn't about being done with stage management as much as a life change. "I got married and the lifestyle and the crazy paycheck and the looking for jobs wasn't fitting with my married life," Manning says. "Ironically, the idea of law started with the business law class in my MFA program. I kind of grokked everything taught, so I was confident I could jump into the intellectual part of being in the legal world." Her acceptance of long hours also meant she could jump right into the field of law:

> My normal day is around 10 hours, no lunch break. Sometimes when getting ready to go to trial it's like a week of 10/12s. However, the weekend of two days does always exist, even if you don't always get to take it.

Lifestyle changes also came into play for Jamie Luther, now senior media manager for Hearst Magazines, where his responsibilities are spread across all digital titles as well as advertising support:

> I met someone who is now my husband while I was working in theatre and stage managing on the side. He wanted me to move to San Francisco with him; this was kind of an adventure and I took him up on it. I wound up with a role in Event Management with the San Francisco Chronicle, which was like stage management. I got a taste of a 9-to-5 week, a consistent salary and benefits, and I liked it. When we moved back to New York I kept that mindset.

And some people simply realize they want to do different things. Deborah Gilboa is now a Pittsburgh-based parenting expert, family physician, international speaker, author, and media expert—but there was a time when she had a steady job stage managing for Second City. "There was no stage management gig better than the one I had," Gilboa shares. "And I loved it. But I did not think I could do it for 30 years and still love it." She had been volunteering as an EMT and thought about going to school to become a paramedic until a friend gave her some insight into herself:

> He said, 'That's a terrible idea. You really like to be in charge of things and to change systems and to make things run more efficiently.' And that's definitely all of my stage management training. Then he said 'You'd make a terrible paramedic; you should just go be a doctor.'

She listened to his advice and now has a thriving practice.

Amy Bender had a long career as a stage manager, but found similar concerns:

> I've been doing Stage Management since I was 15, and I have two degrees. I felt like the schedule and the number of hours was overwhelming after 30 years of doing it. And I wanted to try to find something to give me a more normal schedule. I just felt like I wanted to experience a normal life, whatever that is.

She first left to pursue a degree in accounting:

> I was looking for a way to have my own business, to supervise myself. I enjoyed the mental part of it but less the actual work. To go from such a social profession where you're interacting with people all day long to sitting at a computer not talking to anyone, was too big a switch for me. And I realized I was leaving one job with high hours for a job with even more hours, particularly during tax season.

She returned to stage management for five seasons, but has left to pursue nursing. "I felt like if I was going to be helping people, I could be where people actually need help. The variety and amount of opportunities was why it was also appealing."

THE JOB IS ALWAYS WITH YOU

No matter what they are doing now, all former stage managers still relied on skills they honed in theatre. For Long, time management is still a crucial skill. "That's the cliché answer, but it's true," Long says:

> Managing the clock as much as managing the people. Because the different groups are going to look at the calendar and the clock very differently. Trying to ensure that they're all talking about it in the same fashion is often more difficult than it sounds.

Organizational skills are at the top of Gilboa's list. "The ability to keep 27 peoples' schedules, personalities, needs and fervent desires in order and prioritize them is very much like triage," she says. "The ability to figure out what is a true emergency and what someone just perceives as a true emergency is also crucial. A lot of lessons that stage managers know are really germane to medical training and medical practice." Long finds organization a natural asset in his job. "I tend to have a very quick turnaround with things, and I don't let things fall off my plate very often, or if I need to, I am very deliberate about delegating to someone else."

Luther echoes the importance in his current position:

> Where I work best is the intersection of creativity and organization, so it wasn't completely new. The core of it is, how do I create a system? How do I make this process, this organizational work, often so someone else can run it? Starting out was like starting any new show, a little politics and learning procedures.

He also saw other skills come into play. "I learned that I was very good at multi-tasking and that skill translated. I had a strong grip on the artistic more often than not. My technical background was solid, enough to be dangerous."

Gilboa also credits her theatre work ethic for making her a better doctor:

> Drama training teaches you really two things. One is if you can't find a solution, it doesn't mean it can't be done; it just means that you're not looking at it from the right angle. There's no such thing as can't, it might be more expensive than you think; it might be more time-consuming; you might need more resources or different people or a different approach, but there is almost nothing that can't be done. That's really helped me as a physician. The other thing I learned is that when you finish something, you say, that's done, what else can I do? That ability to solve problems in an unrelenting, persevering way and the ability to have an excellent work ethic really sets us apart.

Other important soft skills include the ability to read a room. "Something big that transfers from stage management is how to understand people and what they are saying and reading body language," says Manning:

> If you're not used to taking the temperature of a room and trying to make sure everyone is playing nicely with each other, you don't think about doing it. When you have a client who doesn't understand why something has to be done a certain way, and you have to pick up on the miscommunication and find a common thread, you realize it's like translating the director's desires to the designer. Being able to figure people out is also where the job really translates.

Long adds:

> As a stage manager, that's part of the deal anyway, and I think that much of my experience with Cirque in particular helped out in a lot of different ways, primarily in dealing with a lot of different cultures. Because you really have to be in tune, whether the issue is something that's individual to the artist, or something cultural between two artists. It puts another layer of complexity in those relationships.

Public speaking continues to be a valuable skill. "The sheer act of interpersonal communication" is important, says Luther. "Being able to be in front of essentially strangers on the first day and establish tone, to talk to different people and to code switch to speak their language." Yet the terminology can be the biggest challenge:

> I work with finance so I have to speak in billing terms, internal sales language. Understanding the technical parts of theatre and the curiosity about it is important. It gets you a very long way with people, instead of just saying give me this, you ask for it in someone else's terms. Often we're essentially saying the same thing in different terms, and I use both terms in paperwork.

Bender adds:

> You always learn about listening to the room and paying attention to what is needed without anyone asking, and I feel like that's something I try to do as a stage manager, but it really applies to nursing. Listening to people and watching to see what's going on, to sense what they need before they ask you or before they realize they need it. That's important to being a SM but it really applies to health care.

Most managers interviewed emphasized the perspective they have gained in the years since leaving stage management. "I feel like I spent my day helping people as a stage manager; that's what we do, help people" says Bender. "Creating a work environment for them to do their best work, there are things they need assistance with, but it's not like there are people dying, who need your assistance." Luther stressed the management of his time and position. "I work in media, I don't cure cancer. The work can wait. The email can wait until the next day. Setting boundaries sets an example for a sustainable life." The size of his organization helps. "Moving to an organization of 2000+, you are no longer the center of the world, there is a bigger corporation available. Which is humbling in a sense."

The ability to speak in public, so fundamental to stage management, is sometimes a rarity outside of it. "It's borne out of having to command a room and convey information quickly, efficiently, and with courtesy," says Luther. "I had a boss who was terrified of public speaking which was terrible for them but great for me. Any time an issue came up, I became this public speaking wonder kid."

Manning sees the same things in court: "There is a performance aspect, definitely, particularly in front of a jury. Last year we had a case where the jury didn't like one side in trial; sometimes if you're there, you can give notes!"

And Gilboa adds:

> In general, doctors hate speaking in public. I had no idea. In med school there were opportunities to present things and everyone said to me, go ahead, we'd all rather have a root canal. I had been hanging out with people who would throw their grandmothers under the bus for the opportunity to speak in front of people.

A DIFFERENT VIEW UPON RETURNING

But it's not just a one-way street. The new paths stage managers take teach them things about stage management as well. "The truth is there's a big cultural push to not be judge-y, and yet using judgment is a crucial part of doing a good job, as a physician and as a stage manager," says Gilboa. "You don't get to feel good about not judging, at the price of their life or their child's life."

As far as returning to the field, "There would be a great learning curve to get back and remember everything," says Manning, but she also thinks she would definitely be better at it:

> I think I would be more self-confident and less concerned about making sure everyone was perfect and happy. What I have gained as a paralegal is the ability to be more confident in my decisions, because I am directing more at this office. If I make a decision, I can rest assured it is the right decision. Before, stage management mattered so much to me that I worried about not getting it right and it would make me a wreck about almost everything.

The focus of the work would be different for Luther:

> The work I would choose would be a passion project, not just to further my career. I'd bring in a little more rigor, a little more process. There is a lot of chaotic energy in stage management, and I'd try to work against it rather than immerse in it. My tolerance for shenanigans would be much lower.

Long also thinks his decision-making would be different thanks to his time away from the position. "As a stage manager I used to think that I was very globally minded, that I was aware of all these things happening around me," Long shares:

> And as a production manager, I have taken that up a couple of notches. It would be interesting and also be very difficult to rope some of that in, and not get into areas where the stage manager is not supposed to tread. But on the plus side, I think I would be much more in tune with how what

the director or actors want to do right now has implications for other departments. I would be better at that level of detail than I was before.

Not losing sight of the big picture, Gilboa says that she would "feel stronger about negotiating my own contract, and that's the difference 20 years makes." It's not all about the paycheck, though:

> I would be able to focus on the work and feel less susceptible to getting drawn into people's personal drama. Also, I happened into a lot of jobs that I enjoyed, but I wasn't at all strategic in choosing the things that I did. When you're starting out you never think you're going to get another job. Now I think I could recognize that and take jobs that I had a great reason for doing.

Bender hopes to keep her options open:

> I can see myself as wanting to do it again, even as a nurse. It's something I can do at a moment's notice; I don't feel like it will get rusty. There are some really enjoyable things about the job; actors are really fun to work with, you don't feel like work when calling a show, running a fight call, and so on.

However, the viewpoint would be different, since:

> nursing would give you access to real problems as opposed to creative problems. Having that distinction would make you a better SM as to what you are bothered by, but I feel like I'm like that anyway, I'd have more perspective about what's important.

As a production manager, Long can keep his hand closer:

> One of the things that I'm trying to do this year is to spend a couple hours in the rehearsal room, maybe not every week, but certainly over the time, just to hang out. With no agenda, simply to watch the relationships going on. Knowing how the director is talking to the actors really informs what kind of tech process you're going into, in a way that sometimes the Production Manager doesn't get to see.

KNOWING WHEN THE TIME IS RIGHT AND HOW TO MOVE ON

How does someone recognize the right time to move on? When a life in the theatre can seem all-encompassing, how can one find a quiet moment to see beyond that? When giving advice about changing fields, some former stage managers think the path can be clear. What's crucial is to recognize the skills one has, and how they translate into other disciplines, and then to have confidence in molding strengths and expertise coupled with a drive towards a new direction. Luther advises: "Look for roles that interest you. You're coming from a passionate background, that interests you. Treat your theatrical resume like a job description. You have real world experience; you just have to show that."

"There's nothing scary about changing jobs," agrees Manning:

> If you want to do it you should think about it and figure out what you really want to do. But don't be afraid to do it, because you have a huge skill set that is going to be valuable to an employer in some other field. You're not tied down and you're not second class; you are ahead of the game in a lot of ways.

Bender reminds us of the common skills: "It may take a little while to figure out what's important, it's got to be exciting. Stage managers make such good employees because you're managing other people's time, they are on time and reliable." It may be largely about presentation:

> For somebody who was looking for another career, you can always sell yourself by talking about those qualities which make you a good employee no matter what you're doing. Reliability, attention to detail, problem-solving. So much problem-solving. That kind of skill translates to anything.

It may be tempting, at the most stressful part of a production process, to wonder what else one can do other than stage management. Most of the time these are fleeting flashes or escapism. But it's important to recognize when they are not. In theatre we are often convinced that no other profession embraces as much devotion and commitment as ours, or conversely, that our skills and talents are only applicable to the current circumstance. Neither is true, and it is important to remember that stage management abilities and instincts move easily to other kinds of work.

NOTES

1. The Guthrie Theater was founded in 1963 and is dedicated to producing the great works of dramatic literature, developing the work of contemporary playwrights and cultivating the next generation of theatre artists. Link: www.guthrietheater.org/about-us/

2. Cirque du Soleil is a Canadian entertainment company and the largest contemporary circus producer in the world. Based in Montreal, Quebec, Canada, and located in the inner-city area of Saint-Michel, it was founded in Baie-Saint-Paul on June 16, 1984, by two former street performers, Guy Laliberté and Gilles Ste-Croix. Link: www.cirquedusoleil.com

3. Wolf Group LA is a law firm providing personal service and attention to clients in the Los Angeles area. Link: www.wolfgroupla.com

Afterword

Moment of Pause—Tech, 09.26.20
Evangeline Rose Whitlock

This moment of pause is coming to you from *inside a theatre, while my students are teching a show*.

I can't tell you how good this feels. Ok, we're all wearing masks. Ok, I'm sitting a row behind and six seats over from my student stage manager instead of right next to her. Ok, so the actors can't hang out in the green room and instead have to stay in their own private dressing room when they are not onstage. Ok, so there's no communal basket of tech candy. Ok, we'll never invite a live audience into the space, and the show will be recorded and streamed ...

But we're in tech.

These students have been working in a socially distanced and mask-wearing rehearsal room for the past five weeks. They've sacrificed the usual college kid stuff like going to parties in order to try, as best as possible, to keep themselves and each other safe and healthy. It's been a challenge. It's been exciting. We've all learned about the reality of Zoom fatigue, and now we're learning the realities of mask fatigue. We're learning how hard it is to break the habits to which our bodies are so accustomed, like peeking over someone's shoulder to clarify a line in the script or demonstrate a particular stage left to right cross.

And now we're in tech.

Tech, or more formally, technical rehearsals, is the part of the production process where all the various elements that have been in development in separate rooms and studios and shops come together. The actors put on costumes and work on a physical set that used to be lines of tape on a floor. The lighting designer creates sunsets and sunrises and settings like shopping malls and diners with hundreds of lighting instruments. We add in the soundscape, projections, props. What used to be some plastic cups and a spare coffee carafe is now that expertly designed elaborate porcelain-looking tea set. And the stage manager pulls the whole thing together, the key strategist in this complex interconnected web of disparate elements that somehow, magically, beautifully, and with a whole lot of time, patience, and creativity, become the fullest expression of the story we are trying to tell.

Tech involves many, many, many moments of pause. The stage manager calls out "hold, please" whenever something needs to be sorted out, and then everyone works together to sort it out, and then the stage manager tells everyone where to start, and then finally, to start again. Sometimes these holds—these moments of pauses—are less than a minute. Sometimes they are upwards of 20 minutes. Or even longer. It's erratic and methodical all at the same time. But here's the interesting thing: those moments of pause, those holds that can feel so tedious, are usually the moments that are full of the *most* action, because that's when the beautiful magic you see in the final performed product is happening. The work that goes on in a "hold, please" moment is often unseen. The riggers need to make an adjustment in the grid. The wardrobe crew needs to go repair a costume. The lighting designer has to fix some internal programming.

If the most common phrase you hear in tech is the stage manager's "hold please," the second-most common phrase is the chorus of questions a couple minutes later: "What are we still holding for?"

I know we're all asking that right now, as the world continues the slow crawl through the pandemic and we all tire of wearing masks, staying six feet apart, not being able to hug our friends ... erratically and methodically working our way through these strange days.

What are we still holding for?

I've said this before, and I will say it again: there is *always* work going on in a "hold please," even when we don't see it. And that work ... that work is some of the most beautiful, the most collaborative, the most rigorous, the most joyful. We're still holding. And that's ok.

We're in tech, after all.

Biographies

Narda E. Alcorn (she/her/hers) is a professor and stage manager who has worked on Broadway, Off-Broadway, regionally, and internationally. In 2019, Alcorn was appointed Chair of the Stage Management Program at Yale School of Drama. She has been Head of Stage Management for New York University, DePaul University, and State University of New York at Purchase. She received DePaul's Excellence in Teaching Award in 2015 and The Robert Christen Award for Excellence in Technical Collaboration in 2017. On Broadway, Alcorn has had collaborations with the Tony-winning directors Kenny Leon, Bartlett Sher, and George C. Wolfe. She premiered four of Pulitzer-Prize winning playwright August Wilson's Century Cycle plays, and stage managed

Photo Courtesy of Photographer Shelli Aderman

two Broadway revivals of his work. Her New York and Regional credits include productions with Denzel Washington, Viola Davis, Billy Crystal, Kevin Kline, Annette Bening, Phylicia Rashad, David Schwimmer, and Richard Foreman. Narda was a long-time stage manager on the Broadway production of *The Lion King*, and she has collaborated with the celebrated MacArthur Fellows, composer George E. Lewis and playwright Tarell Alvin McCraney. She has recently co-published, with Lisa Porter, *Stage Management Theory as a Guide to Practice: Cultivating a Creative Approach* (Routledge, 2019) and the essay "We Commit to Anti-Racist Stage Management Education on HowlRound" (2020; https://howlround.com/we-commit-anti-racist-stage-management-education).

Photo Courtesy of John Gary
Brown, Creede Theater
Photographer

Jonathan D. Allsup (he/him/his) is the Production Manager at Paramount Theatre in Aurora, IL. Jonathan was a freelance AEA stage manager serving on stage management teams at Paramount Theatre in Illinois, Curious Theatre, Lone Tree, Denver Center, Arvada Center, and Colorado Shakespeare Festival in Colorado. Jonathan served as production stage manager and managing director for Creede Repertory Theatre from 2007–2014 where he stage managed over 500 performances spanning over 30 productions. Jonathan holds a BA in theatre from Northwestern College in Orange City, IA and an MFA from University of Idaho. Jonathan also teaches theatre workshops and classes across the nation.

Photo Courtesy of the author.

Alana Clapp (she/her/hers) began her career with Cirque du Soleil in 2009 with the show *O* at the Bellagio. She joined the stage management team of *Mystère* in 2012, and is currently the General Stage Manager for the company's longest running Las Vegas production. An advocate for arts educational programs and youth mentorship, Alana has presented at various universities throughout the country including Emerson College, Chapman University, University of California – Irvine, and Carnegie Mellon University, her alma mater. In addition to her work with Cirque, Alana is a guest lecturer at the College of Southern Nevada, instructor for the USITT Elite Stage Management training program, advisory panel member for the Stagecraft Institute of Las Vegas, mentor with the USITT Stage Management Mentorship Project, and has worked on a number of events for film, television, and comedy specials.

Joseph Drummond (he/him/his) retired as Production Stage Manager after 42 seasons and 133 productions with the Goodman Theatre. His credits include *The Iceman Cometh* (also at Brooklyn Academy of Music in 2015), *Death of a Salesman* (also on Broadway in 1999 and at the Ahmanson Theatre in Los Angeles in 2000), *Glengarry Glen Ross* (also on Broadway in 1984), and *White Snake* performed in China in 2014. He received the Joseph Jefferson Award for Lifetime Achievement after 25 years of stage management at the Goodman and the Del Hughes Lifetime Achievement Award from the Stage Managers Association in 2011. He serves as the Central Regional Representative on the board of the SMA.

Photo Courtesy of the author's spouse.

Cary Gillett (she/her/hers) is currently the Director of Production at Baltimore Center Stage. She also teaches at the University of Maryland in College Park and at the National Academy of Chinese Theatre Arts in Beijing. She is a proud member of the Actors' Equity Association (AEA) and the United States Institute for Theatre Technology (USITT). Cary heads the Stage Management Mentor Project at the annual USITT conference. She is the co-author of *The Production Manager's Toolkit* with Jay Sheehan from San Diego State University. The book was published by Routledge/Focal Press in 2016 and the second edition will be out in 2022.

Photo Courtesy of Photographer Lauren Hyland

Photo Courtesy of HowlRound Theatre Commons. Creative Commons Attribution 4.0 International License (CC BY 4.0).

HowlRound is a free and open platform for theatremakers worldwide that amplifies progressive, disruptive ideas about the art form and facilitates connection between diverse practitioners. HowlRound's creation was a direct response to: 1) research that suggested artists were increasingly distant from the center of theatremaking within not-for-profit institutional infrastructures, and 2) the new possibilities created by technology to influence theatre practice. HowlRound's founding came at a time when too many voices were left off our stages, not represented inside of our institutions, and not recognized for their substantial contribution to our past and present. HowlRound set about to create a group of tools that would amplify voices and issues chronically underrepresented and unheard in the theatre. HowlRound found an organizing principle in the "commons"—a social structure that invites open participation around shared values. HowlRound is a knowledge commons that encourages freely sharing intellectual and artistic resources and expertise. It is their strong belief that the power of live theatre connects us across difference, puts us in proximity of one another, and strengthens our tether to our commonalities. Website: https://howlround.com/about

Photo Courtesy of the author.

Tom Humes (he/his/him) Assistant Professor, Kent State University/AEA Stage Manager/I.A.T.S.E. Stagehand. Tom currently serves as an assistant professor for the School of Theatre and Dance at Kent State University. He teaches Stage Management, Theatre Management, Production and Stage Management, Graphics for the Theatre, First Year Experience for the design/tech and production students and serves as production stage manager at Porthouse Theatre. Tom's primary background is in stage management for venues such as: Cain Park, Cleveland Play House, McCarter Theatre Center, DOBAMA Theatre, Beck Center for the Arts, Karamu House, Cleveland Orchestra, and Opera Cleveland. He also has a background as a theatrical electrician and lightboard operator for Cleveland Play House in the Bolton Theater and in the Allen Theatre complex. He is a member of Actors' Equity Association and local 27 of the IATSE. He received his BA in Theatre at Bowling Green State University.

Nikki Hyde (she/her/hers) is a stage manager who is passionate about storytelling. She is a faculty member at California Institute of the Arts, an ensemble member of Cornerstone Theater Company, and a frequent stage manager at Los Angeles Opera. Some favorite credits include *Voices from a Pandemic* (Notch Theatre Company), *Eurydice, Satyagraha* (LA Opera), *The Box* (Pulitzer Center), *Highland Park is Here, Love on San Pedro* (Cornerstone Theater Company), *Carmen, Three Decembers, Rigoletto* (San Diego Opera), *Little Black Shadows* (South Coast Repertory), *A Trip to the Moon* (Los Angeles Philharmonic), *The Pirates of Penzance* (Pasadena Playhouse), *The Pride* (The Wallis), *Party People*, Public Works' *Twelfth Night*, and *The Odyssey* (The Public),

Photo by Dillon Artzer Photography.

and *Lost Girls* (MCC Theater). A member of Actors' Equity Association and American Guild of Musical Artists, Nikki has also worked for LA Theatre Works, Ojai Playwright's Conference, New Dramatists, Center Theater Group, New York Musical Festival, Merola Opera Program, Cincinnati Opera, Opera San Antonio, Houston Grand Opera, Oregon Shakespeare Festival, Shakespeare Center of Los Angeles, and Opera Grand Rapids. In her free time, she enjoys cooking vegan meals, running, practicing yoga, and taking long road trips with her partner, Jim, and dog, Bella.

Rafael Jaen (sounds HA-EN) (he/him/his) is a practicing costume designer, associate professor of theatre, and author with 30+ years of experience. He has received multiple design accolades for his costumes and his teaching, including the *Kennedy Center Golden Medallion for Excellence in Theatre Education*, the Salem State University *Life Achievement in The Arts Award*, and the UMass Boston *Manning Price for Excellence in Teaching*. In Fall 2020, he was inducted as a USITT Fellow. He also serves as the USITT VP for Communications, and he is a past National KCACTF Design, Technologies, and Management (DTM) Chair. Mr. Jaen is the author

Photo Courtesy of UMass Boston and Firestarter Interactive.

of *SHOWCASE* (2011) and *Digital Costume Design and Collaboration* (2017) by Focal Press/Routledge; he has also contributed journal articles to the *Theatre Design & Technology (TD&T) Journal* and the TD&T Portfolio. He is the main editor for the USITT/FOCAL Press *Backstage* series. He is currently the Performing Arts Department Chair at UMass Boston in Massachusetts. Websites: www.rafaeljaen.biz and www.umb.edu/academics/cla/faculty/rafael_jaen

Photo Courtesy of USITT. Photographer Andrew Barker of Hello Headshots.

Michele Kay (she/her/hers) studied theatre and history at Miami University in Ohio. Upon graduation she began a career in stage management that has spanned 30 years and has taken her from Broadway to opera, musical theatre, and drama; dance to production management; from Chicago to Vermont, and many places in between. In 2003, Michele landed back in her hometown of Cincinnati, Ohio where she is an associate professor of Stage Management and the Chairperson of the Department of Theater Design and Production at the University of Cincinnati's College-Conservatory of Music (CCM). Michele is a proud member of Actors' Equity Association, American Guild of Musical Artists, Stage Managers' Association, and USITT where she has been a mentor with the Stage Management Mentor Project since 2012 and a Gateway Program mentor in 2019. Michele loves being a stage manager, a teacher, and a mentor, but she has probably learned the most from being a mom to Karl and Parker.

Photo Courtesy of the author's spouse.

Elynmarie Kazle (she/her/they) is a stage manager and production manager (Akron School for the Arts) who has created stage management mentoring programs and curricula for institutions across the country. Recent productions include: *The Match Girl* (Columbus Dance Theatre) and the Regional Emmys (2019) for NATAS. Credits include Brooklyn Academy of Music, Deaf West, Pasadena and Cleveland Play Houses, LA Classical Ballet, San Diego Opera and international touring. She served nine years on AEA's WC Stage Managers Committee, and three years with the directors union. A founder of LA's Ovation Awards as well as Arts Alive (Akron), she was recently named to the National Theatre Conference. She is one of the youngest fellows to be inducted into USITT. She holds a BFA from University of Minnesota, Duluth, and she received her MFA at Ohio University in Theatre Management. An active adjudicator for International Thespians, she has been an adult leader for BSA Troop 1 for 15 years and is the proud mom of an Eagle Scout.

David McGraw (he/him/his), a proud AEA member, has stage managed for over a dozen theatres in his 27-year career. He created the Stage Manager Survey and the SM2030 Project and authored "The Epoch Model: An Arts Organization with an Expiration Date" (2010), the training film, "Standby Cue 101: An Introduction to Calling Live Performances," and the "Stage Manager's Kit" blog for *Stage Directions*. He serves as a director-at-large for the Stage Managers' Association. He was one of the first stage managers on the Fulbright Specialist roster, working with the South African State Theatre

Photo Courtesy of Shelli Craig Photography

on *FREEDOM: The Musical*. Mr. McGraw has taught for 18 years and serves as the Arts Administration Program Coordinator for Elon University.

Joanna Obuzor (she/her/hers) has spent ten years as an Equity stage manager primarily working regional LORT contracts. Some theatres she has worked with include the Pittsburgh Cultural Trust, City Theatre, Texture Contemporary Ballet, The Dorset Theatre Festival, Carnegie Mellon University, Opera Theater of Pittsburgh, TriArts Sharon Playhouse, Prime Stage Theatre, Pittsburgh Irish and Classical Theatre, Attack Theatre, and the Kennedy Center American Theatre Festival. During her time stage managing, she also toured internationally to various destinations including France, Belgium, and Mexico. For several years Joanna spent time guiding young professionals in the ways of stage management when she spent time as a professor

Photo Courtesy of the author.

of stage management at both West Liberty University and Point Park University. Beginning in 2016, Joanna has moved into arts administration and now spends her time as the operations manager of the Benedum Center with the Pittsburgh Cultural Trust in Pittsburgh, PA. Joanna is a co-founder of Pittsburgh Arts Administrators of Color. She is a proud member of Actors' Equity.

Photo Courtesy of the author.

Kristi Ross-Clausen (she/her/hers) has been an IATSE stagehand for 25+ years working concerts, live theatre, expos, and film. She joined Actors' Equity Association as a stage manager in 2011. She's stage managed musicals, plays, operas, dinner theatre, Theatre for Young Audiences, industrials, and even an appearance by His Holiness, the Dahli Lama. She toured North America with *Mamma Mia*, *War Horse*, and *Priscilla, Queen of the Desert*; and worked as a local stagehand in every yellow card department. A former K-12 music/theatre teacher, she taught stage management and served as Production Stage Manager at the University of Wisconsin – Madison where she earned her Masters in 2010. Ross-Clausen has presented at numerous conferences including KCACTF, USITT, ATHE, AATE, SETC, Wisconsin School Safety Coordinators Association, and numerous school in-services/corporate staff development seminars. She serves on the Live Events council, Women's council, Live Events Advisory committee, and Membership committee for AVIXA. A contributor to the Event Safety Alliance Reopening Guide, she consults internationally as a theatre safety expert, and has appeared on numerous podcasts. She is currently a member-at-large of the Stage Managers' Association, past-president of the Alliance for Wisconsin Theatre Education, women's committee chair for IATSE Local 470, and Equity 2021–2022 convention Central Stage Management delegate. She resides in Appleton, WI.

Photo Courtesy of Photographer Enderlee Paris

Charlotte Sachetti (she/her/hers) is a production manager with Disney Cruise Line. Over the past nine years, she has stage managed at all four parks at Walt Disney World before moving to production in 2014. She has managed projects on all ships in DCL's expanding fleet including: *Beauty and the Beast*; *Aladdin*; and *Golden Mickeys*, *Very Merrytime Cruises*, *Star Wars Day at Sea* and countless shipwide shows. Before moving to Orlando, Charlotte got her sea legs as stage and production manager with Royal Caribbean Cruise Line. Stage management credits include: Blue Man Group, Cirque du Soleil, and multiple summer stocks. Charlotte hails from Bloomsburg, Pennsylvania with a Bachelor of Arts degree in Theatre-Stage Management, Business and English from Muhlenberg College.

Christopher Sadler (he/him/his) is an associate professor at the University of Oklahoma's Helmerich School of Drama, heading the stage management emphasis and teaching multiple courses in stage and theatre management and dramatic literature. He holds an MFA in stage management from the University of California San Diego and a BFA in theatre arts management from Ithaca College. A proud member of Actors' Equity Association since 1999, Chris has a successful freelancing career having been on stage management teams for over

Photo Courtesy of Photographer Jodi Asprey

100 productions at theatres nationwide, including La Jolla Playhouse, Capital Repertory Theatre, Great River Shakespeare Festival, 7 Devils Playwrights Conference, the National Playwrights Conference, PCPA Theaterfest, Shakespeare Santa Cruz, Theatre Rhinoceros, California Rep, Portland Stage Company, Great Lakes Theater, Berkshire Theatre Festival, the Hangar Theatre, and for seven seasons, PSM at the Idaho Shakespeare Festival. Additionally, Chris participates with the Kennedy Center American College Theatre Festival as a stage management respondent at regional festivals (since 2013) and was National Stage Management Coordinator from 2014–2018. He was a mentor for the USITT Stage Management Mentor Project in 2014 and 2019 and has contributed as a panelist on USITT webinars.

Dr. Jennifer Leigh Sears Scheier (she/her/hers) is a freelance AEA stage manager and a recent graduate from the University of Illinois Urbana-Champaign. Her dissertation, "The Quest for Professionalization: A 20th Century Cautionary Tale for American Stage Managers," focuses on reclaiming stage management history while investigating the field's current challenges through a historical lens. Several of her research articles have been published in *Stage Directions Magazine*. Her past stage management credits include: Illinois Shakespeare Festival, Knoxville Opera, La Jolla Playhouse,

Photo Courtesy of the author.

Lamb's Players Theatre, Long Beach Opera, San Diego Repertory Theatre, and Tennessee Repertory Theatre. She earned her MFA in Stage Management from the University of Iowa and is a proud member of Actors' Equity Association and the Stage Managers' Association.

Photo Courtesy of USITT's TD&T

Tina Shackleford (she/her/hers) has been an AEA stage manager for over 20 years, with credits across the United States with an emphasis on New Work, musicals, and a little bit of opera. For USITT, she serves as the management commissioner (2017–2022), on the board of directors (2017–2022), is a founding member of the Institute's EDI Gateway Mentor Program, and as a mentor for the Stage Management Mentor Project, serving as its coordinator from 2013–2016. She teaches in the Stage and Production Management Program at the Carnegie Mellon School of Drama.

Photo Courtesy of the author.

Jay Sheehan (he/him/his) is an Equity stage manager and Director of Production and Operations, having worked on over 50 shows during his career, including four years at the Old Globe Theatre, the San Diego Symphony, and the House of Blues overseeing the 20,000 seat Coors Amphitheatre in Chula Vista. He has been on the San Diego State University faculty for 20 years, running the production management and stage management areas for the School of Theatre, Television, and Film at SDSU. Additionally, Sheehan created and still leads the Entertainment Management Program Certificate. In addition to teaching, he oversees all production aspects for each season. A published author, Sheehan, wrote *The Production Manager's Toolkit* with co-author Cary Gillett; the first book on production management in the USA, Routledge Press published it in September of 2016. Sheehan also serves as the National Production Manager for Young Arts, dedicated to identifying and supporting the next generation of artists in the literary, performing, visual, and design arts. In this capacity, Jay oversees the annual Presidential Scholars program at the Kennedy Center in Washington D.C. Sheehan is the Cue One Productions owner. His event list includes the NFL Super Bowl and Major League Baseball's All-Star Games. He also produces non-profit charity events in and around the United States.

Amanda Spooner (she/her/hers) is an Equity stage manager and educator, based in New York. She has worked on and Off-Broadway, regionally, on tour, on events, and in television. She is the founder of Year of the Stage Manager, a grassroots campaign meant to increase visibility for stage managers, celebrate them, and educate people about what they do. With Year of the Stage Manager, Amanda curates free educational programming for both stage managers and their collaborators. She is the vice chair of the Stage Managers' Association, an ambassador for the Parent Artist Advocacy League, and serves on Council with Actors' Equity Association.

Photo Courtesy of Michael Kushner Photography

She has worked with Lincoln Center, New York Theatre Workshop, Center Theatre Group, Soho Rep, Playwrights Horizons, Signature Theatre, La Jolla Playhouse, Yale Rep, Center Stage, Westport, and Sundance. Amanda was named an American Theatre Magazine "Person to Watch" and was featured on the cover of Equity News with her very busy toddler named Jack, among countless other articles and interviews.

Matthew Stern (he/him/his) is the founder of the *Broadway Stage Management Symposium*. Stage manager credits on 20+ Broadway productions include: *Finding Neverland, On the Town, Doctor Zhivago, Side Show, Spider-Man: Turn Off The Dark, Death of a Salesman, An Evening with Patti LuPone & Mandy Patinkin, The Little Mermaid, Wicked, Fiddler on the Roof, The Phantom of the Opera, Enchanted April, The Full Monty, Grease*; Tours: *Mandy Patinkin: Dress Casual* and *Diaries, John Lithgow's Stories By Heart, Billy Crystal's 700 Sundays, Les Misérables*. Other: *Radio City Christmas Spectacular, Blue Man Group at the Hollywood Bowl*. Matthew has stage managed for numerous

Photo Courtesy of Photographer: Cherie B. Tay https://www.cheriebtay.com/

corporate events around the world for clients in tech, auto, pharma, and financial industries. Matthew is an alum of UC San Diego, part of the faculty at SUNY Purchase, and serves on the Board of Directors of the Stage Managers' Association. For more info about Matt his blog, or the Symposium visit www.broadwaysymposiuim.com

Photo Courtesy of USI Photography & Multimedia

Erin Joy Swank (she/her/hers) is a Denver-based freelancer who enjoys working in multiple genres, including plays, musicals, opera, dance, and cirque-style productions. Five Christmases were also spent touring with the *Radio City Christmas Spectacular*, featuring the Rockettes and three adorable camels. As an active member of the Stage Managers' Association, she hosts online discussions as well as social gatherings around the country. As a vice commissioner in Management with the United States Institute for Theatre Technology, Erin has coordinated the Portfolio Reviews & Interview Materials Prep sessions for the national conference, along with other special projects. She also enjoys guest lecturing and sharing her experience with student stage managers. Visit www.erinjoyswank.com for her blog, including an ongoing Opera SM 101 series. When not stage managing, Erin enjoys paddling any river possible, including as a professional guide. Member: Actors' Equity, AGMA, USITT, SMA.

Photo Courtesy of the author.

Ramón Valdez (he/him/his) was born and raised in Los Angeles, California as the eldest of two. He received his BA in Theatre with a focus on stage management from the University of Southern California School of Dramatic Arts, where he currently serves as the Assistant Director of Admissions. Since graduating he has been the Resident Stage Manager for Rogue Machine Theatre working on numerous west coast and world premieres. In 2019, Ramón joined L.A. Contemporary Dance Company's board.

Vale la pena.

Photo Courtesy Sylvia Hoke Photograph

Evangeline Rose Whitlock (she/her/hers) is a stage manager and the Head of Stage Management at the Conservatory of Theatre Arts at Webster University in St. Louis, MO. She has worked on and off Broadway, in regional theatres across the country, for professional dance companies, and on many large-scale corporate and industrial events. Select credits include *Farinelli and the King* (Broadway); *the way she spoke* (Audible Theater); *Pass Over* (LCT3/Lincoln Center); *Venus* (Signature Theatre); *Grounded, Father Comes Home from the Wars Parts 1, 2 & 3, Antony and Cleopatra* (The Public Theater); *Nice Fish* (co-production A.R.T./St. Anne's Warehouse); *Twelfth Night, The Tempest, The Odyssey, A Winter's Tale* (Public Works at The Public Theater).